H. H. McAshan

*Department of Educational Administration
and Supervision
University of North Florida*

THE
GOALS APPROACH
TO
PERFORMANCE
OBJECTIVES

1974
W. B. SAUNDERS COMPANY
Philadelphia, London, Toronto

W. B. Saunders Company: West Washington Square
Philadelphia, Pa. 19105

12 Dyott Street
London, WC1A 1DB

833 Oxford Street
Toronto, Ontario M8Z 5T9, Canada

The Goals Approach to Performance Objectives   ISBN 0-7216-5860-1

Last digit is the print number: 9   8   7   6   5   4   3   2   1

PREFACE

This book has been written as a result of the interest created by the publication of a previous text by this author entitled *Writing Behavioral Objectives: A New Approach.* Since publication of the first text the author has received approximately two hundred requests, by mail, phone, and in workshop sessions, for additional information and material concerning the rationale and uses of the "goals approach" writing technique.

Interest has been expressed by teachers; college and public school administrators; college professors; students; educational and business consultants; researchers; directors of reading clinics, medical-training programs, and curriculum development centers; and representatives from state departments of education. It is in response to and in appreciation of the work being done by these professional educators that this text has been written.

This text is designed to, first, benefit students through better planned, implemented and evaluated instructional programs. Second, the text will benefit educational administrators, and prospective teachers, who, acting in the capacity of decision makers, may be held accountable for both the amount and cost of student learning and in turn raise the level of student achievement. Finally, the text should help the educational community to better translate its goals and achievements to the lay community which it serves. These purposes are accomplished as follows:

1. Goals, rather than performance outcome evaluation statements, are established as desired program ends with intrinsic value.
2. Readers are thoroughly instructed in writing performance objectives by the goals approach technique.
3. Detailed information is presented on how to utilize the goals approach writing technique to write behavioral objectives at various classification levels of the affective and cognitive taxonomies.
4. The concepts of diagnostic teaching and goal identification are presented as ways to better individualize instruction.

5. The concept of performance based instruction is explored and illustrated through the development of competency modules.
6. The chapters of the text have been organized in a logical, sequential manner in order to eliminate needless repetition and to help the reader internalize, rather than just be aware of, their contents.
7. Comprehensive instruction is provided concerning the identification and use of performance objectives under the *Management By Objectives* concept for program and personnel accountability.

With reference to the writing and use of behavioral objectives in the affective domain, the author makes the following assumptions concerning the affective concepts developed in this text:

1. Understanding feelings and emotions should be simplified, making educational practitioners comfortable in setting affective goals, rather than attempting to contribute to psychological theory.
2. Problems of evaluating feelings and emotions should be identified and accepted in order to select evaluation alternatives more clearly.
3. Inability to be able to evaluate affective goal achievement with hard data is no excuse for failure to identify affective goals and implement strategies to achieve them.
4. Teachers should be comfortable writing affective goals and objectives both with and without the use of the affective behavior classification levels.
5. This text can provide help and encouragement for all educational practitioners who desire to write and achieve good behavioral objectives in the affective domain.

This book is in every respect both a "why" and "how to do it" text. The chapters have been carefully arranged in a logical and practical order as an aid to both learning and using the concepts presented. The text includes chapters devoted to the following topics:

1. Why we write performance objectives.
2. Why performance objectives are written by the "goals approach."
3. How to write both goal statements and performance objectives.
4. How to write both learning and non-learning oriented performance objectives.
5. How to use behavioral objectives in the development of competency modules.
6. How to use non-learning oriented objectives to establish both program and personnel accountability.
7. How to use learning oriented and non-learning oriented performance objectives for instructional and non-instructional purposes.

8. How to use the management by objectives approach to goal setting.
9. How to write both simple and complex objectives.
10. How to write cognitive objectives at all levels of the cognitive taxonomy.
11. How to write affective objectives both with and without the use of the affective taxonomy.

The reader and potential behavioral objective user should be aware that no educator can have sufficient expertise to envision all or even the best possible goals and evaluation performances in content areas in which he is untrained. In fact, educators probably will fall short in their own area of specialty. For that reason, it is recommended that teachers with common concerns develop objectives cooperatively. The same observation holds true for the authors of this text or for the authors of other texts. Everyone is limited according to his own background experiences. Each person should utilize available supporting expertise such as psychologists, counselors and social workers. The implication for readers of this text is that individuals must recognize their limitations. The intent of this text is to help meet the needs of more than 99 percent of the potential users of objectives in the affective domain. To accomplish this, the goal has been established as the desired end rather than the outcome performance statements used for purposes of evaluation. The concern here is with technique. It is hoped that each user of this text may apply the goals approach writing technique to behaviors developed in his area of interest more meaningfully than can anyone else without this motivation and subject matter content expertise.

Finally, the text can serve as either a complete course of study or as a course supplement. For example, if writing performance objectives is all that is required, a course supplement, the student can be assigned Chapters 3 and 4. These chapters are self-contained, dealing with the goals approach objective writing technique. Other chapters can be used in a similar manner. A glossary of terms has been placed at the end of each chapter for the reader's convenience.

Your ability to make functional use of the information and techniques presented in this text will be considered the only statisfactory evaluation of how well the author has achieved his specific intentions.

H. H. McAshan

CONTENTS

Chapter 1

INTRODUCTION

We think so because other people all think so; or because – or because – after all, we do think so; or because we were told so, and think we must think so; or because we once thought so and think we will still think so; or because, having thought so, we think we will think so.

Henry Sidgwick

CHAPTER GOALS

For the reader to:

1. conceptually understand the differences between the outcomes and goals approaches to writing behavioral objectives;

2. comprehend five assumptions a person must be willing to accept if they are going to use the outcomes approach objective writing technique.

3. comprehend five assumptions a person must be willing to accept if they are going to use the goals approach objective writing technique;

4. understand the effect both the outcomes approach technique and the goals approach technique have on instructional goal clarity, strategy development, evaluation performance and teacher-student motivation.

5. become knowledgeable of advantages attributed to the writing of both learning and non-learning oriented goals in performance terms.

6. comprehend the meaning and uses of criterion-referenced measurement.

7. understand how individualized instruction is enhanced through the use of behavioral objectives.

8. comprehend the term educational accountability.

Writing this text has been an attempt to alleviate some of the growing problems and concerns that are becoming associated with the behavioral objective movement. The use of behavioral objectives is not and never will be a panacea for solving major instructional problems.

1

At best, the use of behavioral objectives can be a valuable tool that aids and motivates teachers in their instructional preparation and provides additional guidance to students so that they may better achieve. At worst, behavioral objectives can be harmful in occupying too much teacher time and by confusing the real intents and values that should be achieved in learning situations.

There are two basic methods for stating behavioral objectives. One, the outcomes approach, implies that there is no difference between the *goals* of instruction and the desired *outcome behaviors* that can be used to evaluate success in achieving an instructional intent. A second method, the goals approach, draws a distinction between goals, defined as specific learning intents, and desired outcome behaviors that can be used to evaluate goal achievement.

Although there is much common agreement between the two approaches, each requires the listing of specific outcome evaluation behaviors that students should exhibit at the end of an instructional activity, the differences that do exist are conceptually incompatible. The future success or failure of the behavioral objective movement to make a significant contribution to education may depend upon the resolution of these differences.

No behavioral objective, affective, cognitive or psychomotor, is innately good because it specifies an outcome performance behavior. An objective's value must come from the contribution it makes to the total instructional process. Major factors to consider are: (1) clarification of instructional intent; (2) contribution to development of meaningful instructional processes or strategies; (3) improvement in evaluation of learning achievement; and (4) motivation of teachers and students. The purpose of this discussion is to consider the contributions of both the *outcomes* and *goals approach* to these four factors.

OUTCOMES APPROACH

CLARIFICATION OF INSTRUCTIONAL INTENT

Learning involves the acquisition of knowledge and understanding, the attainment of meaningful feelings or desired voluntary movements. Outcome approach advocates must operate under the following assumptions:

1. Goals are broad, global and generalized statements of intent.
2. *Specific goals* of instruction are best identified as *observable outcome performance behaviors* that can be evaluated.
3. Outcome behaviors used for evaluation purposes rather than

specific goal intents are the desired ends of instruction and have intrinsic value.

4. Miscellaneous outcome performance behaviors stated for evaluation of goals define the goal itself.

5. The outcomes approach implies that if it is unreasonable or impractical to state an outcome performance behavior that will adequately measure goal achievement, the goal should be changed to one that is reasonable and practical to evaluate.

For purposes of our explanations we shall refer only to the cognitive domain, but the same rationale will apply equally as well to both the affective and psychomotor domains. Instructional intents are goals which are designed to help impart knowledge or understanding. They can be broad global statements or very specific statements. The more specific a goal is stated the more specifically it can be evaluated and the more specifically instructional strategies can be developed to achieve the goal. *Assuming that goals must be defined as broad, global or generalized statements prohibits goal clarification or goal analysis that is required to determine more specific instructional intents.*

One must recognize that a goal designed to impart knowledge or understanding is a different thing entirely from a goal for changing behavior. Research has never been able to fully determine the relationship between knowledge and behavior. Teachers as well as other persons have accumulated knowledge from hundreds of hours of course work with sometimes very little change in behavior. *Behavior can imply knowledge, but knowledge on the other hand can imply many different types of behavior. Thus, defining instructional goals as outcome behaviors may confuse rather than clarify instructional intents.*

How can outcome behaviors used for evaluation be both their own intent and their own evaluation standard? They can't. This assumption implies that a statement made by someone can be proved to be true because the person making the statement says it is true. In other words, if an evaluation performance is its own intent then we perform evaluation for evaluation's sake and the means for determining truth becomes its own end.

General intents cannot be evaluated by any one set of outcome behaviors. In order to perform specific evaluation the instructional intent must be specific in order to match a specific evaluation behavior.

Finally, differences between imparting knowledge and specifying behavioral outcomes can be considerably different. *As long as the instructional intent is to impart knowledge, this becomes a desired end and cannot be replaced by the means of determining how well we achieve it.* This would be a case of placing the cart before the horse with no fixed purpose in mind.

CONTRIBUTION TO DEVELOPMENT OF MEANINGFUL INSTRUCTIONAL PROCESSES OR STRATEGIES

When specific learning *goals* or *intents* are identified instructional strategies are developed to achieve these intents. When only outcome behaviors are identified as both the intent and the evaluation, strategies may be developed primarily to achieve evaluation purposes. This can lead to teaching for a test or teaching for some relatively meaningless behavior.

EVALUATION OF LEARNING ACHIEVEMENT

Evaluation is not aided by specifying goals as behavioral intents. Traditionally we have measured learning by personal observation, rating scales, performance demonstrations, teacher made tests, subjective opinions, standardized tests and other devices. We still use the same devices and techniques for evaluating success in achieving goals stated in behavioral outcome terms. The problem with evaluation of outcome performance behaviors which are stated as their own intents is that evaluation may be, and frequently is, focused away from any really meaningful learning intent.

MOTIVATION OF TEACHERS AND STUDENTS

Teacher militancy and use of the expression "do you have B.O.?" is a direct result of attempts to make teachers conform to intents stated as outcome behaviors rather than goals which identify desired knowledge and understanding. Teachers are knowledge goal oriented and probably always will be. The same is true of students. Students want to know why they should exhibit defined behaviors. The true instructional "why" is omitted when intents are stated as outcome behaviors only.

In summing up the *outcomes approach*, one must admit its contribution to the behavioral objective movement. It was and is the catalyst that projected the writing and use of behavioral objectives to its prominent role in education today. *Owing to its severe limitations and the problems the outcomes approach creates, it is likely, unless behavioral objective users correct some of the stated assumptions and begin identifying true learning intents, that this approach will result in the eventual death of the behavioral objective movement.*

GOALS APPROACH

Goals approach advocates make the following assumptions:
1. Behavioral objectives should be developed from specific goal intents and defined as such.

2. Behavioral objectives should consist of two parts, a specifically identified learning intent in addition to the outcome performance behaviors specified for evaluation purposes.

3. Specific goals or learning intents are the desired ends to be achieved in an instructional program and outcome behaviors are means only to determining success in achieving goals.

4. Goals should be specific with reference to each instructional intent and the context in which it is used. There should be, insofar as practical, a congruence between each goal and its evaluation outcome behavior that approaches a one to one relationship.

5. Goals are the desired ends of instruction and are the only part of a behavioral objective that should be perceived as having intrinsic value. They should remain constant and strategies to achieve them ought to be carried out regardless of whether or not we are able to measure success in their attainment adequately. Failure to adequately evaluate a worthwhile instructional goal does not merit doing away with the goal.

A quick glance at these assumptions immediately informs the reader that, *conceptually speaking, a behavioral objective writer must make almost completely opposite assumptions to use the goals approach writing technique rather than the outcomes approach.* We will now look at how these assumptions affect the same four instructional process factors discussed above.

CLARIFICATION OF INSTRUCTIONAL INTENT

This is the primary purpose of goals approach users. General goals are acknowledged in their approach to be just what they are, broad global statements of intent. This approach, however, insists that general goals be broken down into more specific goal component statements in order to clarify the specific knowledge and understanding that is to be imparted to the students. The more specific the goal statements become, the better and more specifically they can be evaluated. In addition the development of instructional strategies to achieve these specific intents will be enhanced. Each of the goals approach assumptions not only enhances goal clarification, but insists upon it.

CONTRIBUTION TO DEVELOPMENT OF MEANINGFUL INSTRUCTIONAL PROCESSES OR STRATEGIES

The goals approach provides a proper focus for instructional strategy development. The systematic reduction of global intents to specific intents allows teachers to design instructional process strategies that achieve those specific intents.

EVALUATION OF LEARNING ACHIEVEMENT

Evaluation of knowledge achievement is indirectly improved by the goals approach. Evaluation remains limited to the traditional methods that were previously mentioned as limitations of the outcomes writing approach: we still use the same devices and techniques for evaluating knowledge acquisition. Evaluation is enhanced, though, because teachers identify specific intents to evaluate—requiring them to be more concerned with measurement. Thus, they plan evaluation procedures more carefully and attempt to be more objective. Specific goals encourage many teachers to work cooperatively in evaluation planning.

MOTIVATION OF TEACHERS AND STUDENTS

Hundreds of personal testimonies to the author and his colleagues have convinced him that teachers are far more motivated to use the goals approach. Typical teacher comments by teachers who study the goals approach for the first time after having been previously exposed to the outcomes writing technique only are as follows: (1) "now I understand for the first time"; (2) "this makes writing behavioral objectives much more meaningful"; (3) "how come we haven't been introduced to this technique before"; and (4) "last year we didn't make any progress in writing out curriculum objectives, now I'm going to try to get all of the curriculum writers to write their objectives by the goals approach technique."

No instructional program will be effective if the teacher involved is not at least minimally motivated. As with many other educational innovations, the writing and use of behavioral objectives has been too often regarded as a panacea for learning problems and has been implemented too fast by too many—and probably with the wrong assumptions.

In most instances of poor teacher morale the problem has originated with poor or overenthusiastic educational leadership. This problem, on the other hand, can be attributed to decision making authorities at several levels. State legislators have pushed for instructional accountability with almost immediate implementation requirements. Many legislators have been poorly informed and have employed consultants who are too far removed from the classroom to understand all of the problems involved.

State departments of education are understaffed and often have not had the expertise necessary to give sound guidance; in addition, they have sometimes moved too quickly without a formalized systems plan for obtaining the purposes of the program. Local system-wide administrators and school boards often have made decisions concerning behavioral objective programs without a single person's really understanding what the program was all about. Perhaps the most noticeable contributing factor to the staff morale problems has been the failure of local school administrators to provide the leadership, guidance, and planning necessary to satisfactorily implement curriculum development projects relating to statements of behavioral objectives.

Educator use of behavioral objectives is so recent that most teachers and administrators do not know that at least two writing techniques exist or the difference between the two techniques. Based upon theory, either technique can describe performance or behavioral objectives, but the term performance objective does not mean the same thing to all people and will not perform all of the same functions. With reference to teacher morale, teacher preference for the goals approach in situations where both techniques have been introduced is astounding if not conclusive.

This text uses "goal" to mean a target at which we aim that can represent broad global intents or very specific intents; the sum of the specific intents may equal the entire content of broad global goal statements. According to the *goals approach* writing technique it is the very specific intents which should be stated as goals and objectives of instructional situations. The rationale for the use of specific goal statements of intent in classroom situations is based upon the idea that the quality of the goal statement and/or objective must be based upon whether or not it serves the purpose for which it was created. *In other words, the specific goal must be functional within the situational context in which it is used if it is to have real value.*

Evaluation of goal achievement will provide information for decision makers. There are many levels and types of decision makers: each may need and utilize information in a different way. State departments of education need information on pupils—but not as individuals in the sense that they will take action to bring about changes in individual learners. They are interested in a more global outlook of the learners on a system-wide basis and will be more likely to compare systems than individuals. Thus, goals and behavioral objectives at the state department levels are more likely to be stated on a global basis, but may still be considered as specific within the context in which they are used.

School systems within a state, working within the constraints of statewide objectives, are likely to state goals and behavioral objectives based upon the comparison and improving of schools within the system. A school system's objectives will be less abstract or global than those of a state department, but they will still represent general intents. The school system is first of all concerned with upgrading schools or large groups of students rather than individual learners. Again, based upon the context in which they are used, these system-wide intents can be considered as specific for certain high level administrators.

The school principal is concerned with the development of goals and objectives that will improve the learning environment in each classroom and improve the achievement performances of all the learners in the school. He will share and utilize the information he obtains with his teachers, but not in a one-to-one relationship designed to increase the learning of individuals as such. His goals and performance objectives, which are within the constraints of both the school system and state department, are less abstract than either one, but still more general than those developed by a classroom teacher. They can, however, be specific intents for his level of decision making.

The behavioral changes that a teacher can bring about in a learner through the many instructional processes at his or her disposal is what education is all about. The teacher must identify very specific goals and objectives in order to bring about very specific behavioral changes in the learner. The key to the development of all specific performance objectives appropriate to the context in which they are used is systematic goal setting at each level of use.

It is important to understand that the pitfalls to be found in developing good behavioral objectives are not all related to the use of the outcomes approach technique, but that the problems are likely to occur more frequently with this approach due to the limitations of outcome definitions. The clarity and specificity with which an objective is stated is more likely to be adequate when teachers use the goals approach.

Behavioral objectives written by the goals approach decrease evaluation error by having the goal and evaluation behavior tied together so that each can be easily checked against the other at all times. The confidence produced by this cross referencing, the ease with which teachers produce goal statements, and the insights teachers obtain in deriving goals and program strategies cause considerably higher morale than does the outcomes approach.

Herzberg's[1] motivation theory states that there are at least five psychological growth or motivator factors intrinsic to a job that will bring about employee job satisfaction. These factors include:
1. Personal knowledge of achievement
2. Recognition of the achievement by others
3. The work itself
4. Responsibility
5. Advancement and growth

Each of these psychological growth factors have proved to be at least part of the reason why teachers prefer to use the goals approach after having been properly exposed to both techniques: they know they have achieved; their objectives are recognized by both students and peers, because of better communication; they enjoy doing what they can do well; they become willing to assume the responsibility for developing their own competency modules; and the total package leads to their further growth and advancement.

The primary purpose of writing the objectives of instructional programs in behavioral terms is to better evaluate student learning as evidenced by behavioral changes. In addition, other advantages to writing goals in performance terms include: (1) improved evaluation of the achievement of all goals with either short-range or long-range intents; (2) aiding teachers in individualization of instruction; (3) helping teachers learn more about their students in less time due to frequency of criterion evaluation; (4) remarkable benefits for teachers who develop their own behavioral objectives, particularly with reference to improved knowledge of their own subject areas and methods of evaluation; and (5) administration can establish educational accountability for the overall program or for individual projects more efficiently.

In order to establish educational accountability, whether for an administrator, a researcher or a classroom teacher, it appears that the first problem of concern is that of finding a commonly acceptable definition of quality. A principle generally attributed to Aristotle states "the excellence of anything can be determined only by reference to its proper function." His philosophy with reference to this principle was that all human activity was directed toward some end for which the activity was performed. Thus, all voluntary behavior or purposeful conduct is done for some end, and whatever is done to accomplish that end is the means. Practical application of this philosophy would indicate that the excellent military leader obtains victory, the excellent doctor heals the sick, or the excellence of a teacher must be judged in terms of how well his students learn. With only slight revision in terminology we find that Aristotle's principle is just as true today as it was in 350 B.C. In place of excellence we substitute quality and replace functions with goals or purposes. By restating the principle to make it applicable to education we submit that *quality education refers to the effectiveness of any educational program in meeting its own goals or purposes.*

As is probably the case with all school systems, individual schools within a single system may differ widely in the quality of their instructional programs. This same observation can be extended to include individual teachers, projects, and all planned activities. These differences may be due to such variables as number of educationally deprived students and the amount, extent, and cause of their deprivation; availability of instructional materials and equipment; peculiarities inherent among the local population; type of administrative leadership;

degree of experimentation and research carried out at the local level; as well as other factors. With these differences in mind and the realization that the same or related factors affect pupil progress in all schools, it seems imperative that detailed study of factors relating to quality program planning, development, and evaluation be undertaken by all persons involved in education.

Educational administrators and teachers need to accurately identify their specific objectives, within the context of their own philosophies and goals, before implementing a new program or attempting to evaluate its success. Once valid and meaningful objectives of a program have been properly identified, the quality of that program can best be judged only insofar as its own specific and locally defined objectives are accomplished or by the gains toward their accomplishment. This can be referred to as a type of criterion evaluation. Thus, the *quality of any school's instructional program must refer to the degree of its effectiveness in meeting its own specifically defined objectives.* The procedures for determining quality include the many processes of planning, research, development, experimentation, and evaluation.

CURRENT STATUS OF OBJECTIVES

National organizations such as the American Association of Colleges for Teacher Education, Teacher Corps, Leadership Training Institute, Performance Based Teacher Education Project, Multi-State Consortium, National Center on Competency Based Education, National Commission on Performance Based Teacher Education and numerous university professors, state departmental officials, and individual educators have contributed to recent educational literature with references depicting the advantages and disadvantages concerning the uses of performance objectives. In most instances the claims are not well supported with research specifics. Advocates of objectives are often users who ignore problems, and critics of objectives include many persons who have not yet had enough experience for their criticism to be justified. Advocates must yet await complete justification of their viewpoints; whereas, critics should remember that "if you haven't tried it, you shouldn't knock it."

It appears reasonable to state that there is some agreement by many educators concerning the value of using performance objectives for curriculum revision, improvement of evaluation strategies, development of systems programs for accountability, pupil benefits through individualization of instruction, and the conversion of education programs from the traditional experience-based (knowledge-oriented programs) to performance-based programs. The amount of agreement is not yet conclusive, but merits further research and development. This chapter will concern itself primarily with values relating to evaluation, individualization of instruction, and general educational accountability.

EVALUATION BY CRITERION-REFERENCED MEASUREMENT

Evaluation is a process designed to determine the excellence or worth of something. It usually provides information that will be useful to interested persons concerned with making future decisions. Evaluation in relationship to performance objectives is usually accomplished through some form of criterion-referenced measurement. *Measurement of this type is designed to determine the adequacy of any trait or factor that is under investigation by comparing it, either quantitatively or qualitatively, to an appropriate standard.*

One purpose of criterion-referenced measurement is to establish classroom accountability. In this instance the decision maker becomes the teacher and measurement may involve a test. Tests used to evaluate pupil achievement are both formal (standardized) and informal (teacher-made). Most tests used in classroom situations should, among other purposes, enable teachers to teach diagnostically. This involves continuous diagnosis by the teacher of the strengths and weaknesses of the learner and the development of goals, objectives and enabling strategies accordingly.

Teacher-made tests should, first of all, measure teacher objectives. They should reflect a state of affairs rather than a prediction. The differences which can be expected to be shown on tests are directly related to what goals are selected, what the curriculum teaches, the type of test employed—normed (designed to compare student achievement with group norms) or criterion-referenced (designed to compare student achievement with specific content coverage according to the criterion requirement of a specifically stated objective)—and the target group of students. Figures 1–1 and 1–2 illustrate conceptual differences between norm-referenced and criterion-referenced tests.

Figure 1–1 shows that norm-referenced tests are anchored in the middle and that pupils are evaluated according to their level of achievement in relation to the norm to other children, rather than to the specifics of what they actually know. This type of measurement violates principles of individualized instruction and is of little value in measuring individualized achievement.

The normed or standardized test is designed to show differences rather than individual strengths or weaknesses. In the construction of this type of test the items that are both too easy and too hard are eliminated and those showing closest to a fifty-fifty chance of success or failure are considered

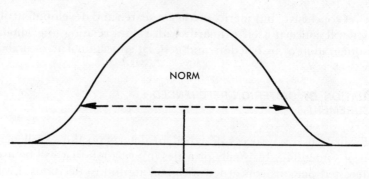

Figure 1-1 Norm-referenced test support.

to be the best. This type of test is designed to measure an area very broadly.

Criterion-referenced measurement is based upon specific content coverage. The goals of the content are usually stated by specific behavioral objectives that specify each skill to be attained and the *criterion-referenced test is designed to measure specific achievement of these well-defined skills.* Figure 1-2 reveals that criterion-referenced tests are anchored at each end and learners are evaluated according to the specifics of their own knowledge and undertakings rather than to the norm of other children.

In experimental situations the criterion-referenced test is often administered to a control group which has not had the benefit of exposure to the experimental variable. This, of course, may produce biased results unless a criterion-referenced test is also developed which is based upon the control group strategies and administered to both groups. Both criterion-referenced and standardized tests have an important role to play in evaluation and should be used in combinations dictated by content and strategies being tested. Performance objectives are, however, better adapted for use with criterion-referenced measures.

One advantage of criterion-referenced measurement is that it tells us what a student knows rather than how he compares with a norm. Thus, such measurement is better than norm measurement for individualization of

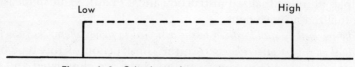

Figure 1-2 Criterion-referenced test continuum.

instruction. The term "criterion-referenced test" refers to a test that is deliberately constructed to define the behavior that the pupils who take the test can perform according to the test score they make. Simply stated, this process involves defining the skills to be taught and testing for attainment of these skills. Criterion-referenced tests normally have at least five characteristics:

1. Each behavior tested is representative of some specific and appropriate goal of the teacher and/or student.
2. The classes of behaviors are specified in advance.
3. Each item is individually important and unique.
4. Representative behavior must be used.
5. Necessary behaviors must be defined individually.

Criterion-referenced testing determines how much of a characteristic a pupil can demonstrate. Some testing experts say that the use of the term "criterion-referenced" should be applied to scores rather than tests. There is a dichotomy implied in criterion-referenced and norm-referenced tests. These tests should not, however, be considered to be mutually exclusive for there is a need in education for both the norm-referenced and criterion-referenced tests.

There are many problems that are inherent with the use of criterion-referenced tests and thus with the writing of behavioral objectives. Among these problems are the following:

1. These tests tell us what the standard is, but not what the standard should be.
2. Criterion standards are extremely hard to define in most areas of education. Criterions require much detail which may be unrealistic for practical use by some teachers. Many goals cannot have justice done to them if they must be stated as criterion-referenced objectives.
3. Some criterion tests encourage questionable conception of educational procedures. Teachers, in many instances, should guide rather than autocratically determine the standards and objectives of a student.
4. Many proponents of criterion-referenced tests have inadvertently led people to believe that accepted test construction procedures (validity, reliability, indices of discrimination, and variability) are not as necessary as in the development of standardized tests.

Criterion-referenced measurement is the principal evaluation technique for systems programs designed to establish accountability, due to the many types and uses of performance objectives in developing project activities. Mission, unit, interim, and other performance-stated objectives will be criterion-referenced in most instances. Criterion-referenced measurement refers to non-learning oriented objectives as well as to learning oriented or behavioral objectives. This evaluation process includes the selection of specific goals and stating them behaviorally as objectives prior to the implementation of program strategies. At the completion of the program strategies, planned data will be collected and used for determining the worth or excellence of the product investigated.

Basic goals in education will remain rather consistent; however, evaluation strategies designed to determine the degree of success achieved in obtaining these goals may vary widely. Individual teachers, with the same basic goals in mind, may differ widely in their selection of behavioral objectives, program strategies, and evaluation activities. Different evaluation activities will appear because of variables such as program philosophy and focus, differences in pupils, time allowed to produce change, abilities of professional staff members, availability of materials and equipment, as well as other factors. Thus, each teacher's accountability must be evaluated according to achievement concerning his or her own objectives rather than to common criteria which are applied to all classrooms, teachers or students. Common criteria automatically establish a norm; thus, they do not best tell what is accomplished by each teacher, but automatically place each teacher and class on a continuum that is designed to reveal differences rather than success or accomplishment.

INDIVIDUALIZED INSTRUCTION

Pupil differences and how to provide experiences to meet needs created by these differences through individualized instruction have long been among the greatest concerns of educators. Attempts to solve problems created by pupil differences include ability grouping, nongraded schools, the language experience approach in reading, and many other methods. None of these approaches have been sufficient within themselves to solve all of the problems.

Current research and innovation places strong emphasis upon individualized instruction as the primary method to meet pupil differences and interests. Two advantages of the individualized approach are (1) child-centered diagnostic teaching which breaks the lock-step or rigid use of curricula and materials, and (2) teachers who are free to use this approach within the framework of any school's organizational plan or grouping arrangement.

Individualized instruction means that each student has learning experiences suited to his unique characteristics as a learner. Individualization can be attained in large or small group lectures, small group discussion, and independent study, as well as in other arrangements. It is, however, only through the use of diagnostic teaching, the availability of adequate and flexible learning materials, and the selection of appropriate content that the benefits of individualized instruction can be effectively passed on to students. Educationally speaking, a strong need exists for a program development procedure that will assist in providing these essential characteristics.

Diagnostic Teaching. Flexibility is the fundamental idea behind the organization of any program based upon diagnostic teaching. *Diagnostic teaching requires continuous diagnosis of the strengths and weaknesses of the learner and the prescription of learning tasks accordingly.* This can be accomplished through diagnostic testing and teacher-pupil interaction in face-to-face contact. The testing procedures reveal a student's status with respect to learning skills such as listening and reading, and their ability to use organized knowledge such as library materials and reference books. The eye-to-eye interaction establishes rapport between student and teacher as well as revealing important student characteristics which cannot be determined through testing procedures. Thus, in individualized instruction, teachers should focus upon individuals and small groups, continually diagnose student needs and program intent, and maintain a broad view of the curriculum. In addition, the teacher must be able to record and transfer diagnostic data into specific goals, objectives and activities that will result in the desired behavioral change in pupils.

Methods for Individualizing Instruction. The first and basic step in developing a program of individualized instruction is to plan individualized objectives and evaluation strategies.

A child's educational goals and objectives should determine the learning experiences to be included and their arrangement in the curriculum. Objectives should relate to individual talents, needs, interests, and abilities. Such objectives should insure a meaningful goal or intent for each activity and a plan for assessing the level to which it is achieved.

Behavioral objectives are designed for just this purpose and should become a part of most directed learning activities. Individualizing the behavioral objectives for selected units of work should be especially beneficial for disadvantaged students who may have little chance to succeed in a program designed for large groups of learners. Behavioral objectives also aid the teacher in defining the content and behaviors that are to be developed and the strategies to bring about the desired behaviors.

Strategies for Individualizing Instruction. Teaching strategies for individualization based upon goals which are common to the group as well as unique for some pupils must include a wide variety of materials in each classroom, individual pupil-teacher interaction, self-selection of materials by pupils, self-pacing in the use of the materials, and both individual and group opportunities for skill development.

This type of program, as implemented by teachers who first determine the ability and interests of pupils, requires formulation of individual goals and behavioral objectives, and then securing a wide variety of materials for both teacher assignment and individual pupil selection. The key to the developmental strategies of the entire concept of individualization is the original goal selection and statement of objectives. Based upon currently available research data, even conventional classroom programs utilizing basal texts and rigid selection of materials achieve better results when behavioral objectives are first stated as guides for student study and evaluation.

SYSTEMS PROGRAMS FOR EDUCATIONAL ACCOUNTABILITY

Educational accountability is, in the strictest sense, program and personnel "management by objectives." This is a condition in which programs and people are evaluated to determine the quality of the results they obtain in achieving the objectives for which they have been given responsibility. Accountability is best accomplished through a systems approach to the planning, implementation and evaluation of educational programs.

A function of good management is to attempt to establish the best possible quality control of both educational services and products. The chief executive officer of any educational endeavor must be able to establish desirable goals and then delegate responsibility to his staff members. These staff members should not only share the responsibility for providing correct and efficient quality services or task performances, but should also help establish accountability at lower levels. Thus, accountability becomes not only management control, but functional control at all operational levels of an educational institution or system.

Adequate financing of educational programs in the future will depend upon the ability of educational administrators and teachers to be accountable for the quality of the programs they manage. This includes achieving their objectives and convincing the public that the program objectives are desirable. The determination of quality must be based on data which includes tangible evidence of program success. The point has already been established that program success refers to "a relative description of its effectiveness in meeting its own specifically defined objectives."

IMPORTANT ASSUMPTIONS

Some assumed teacher needs, which can be at least partially met through the use of performance objectives, include the following:
1. to promote increased pupil achievement

2. to increase their own subject matter competency
3. to plan long-range units of instruction and short-range individual skill development
4. to improve evaluation of instructional activities in order to:
   (a) aid students to progress in learning tasks
   (b) better understand individual student capabilities
   (c) aid students to develop self-understanding
   (d) help decision makers judge the effectiveness of the instructional and related programs
   (e) help implement curriculum revision programs
   (f) furnish evidence useful for the improvement of teacher-pupil learning strategies
5. to improve assessment strategies for determining needs and areas of the curriculum which need revision
6. to obtain hard data that will enable them to know their students better and more rapidly
7. to insure cognitive development in the learner at all levels of understanding rather than by memorization alone
8. to help the learner understand what is expected from him and even let the learner, in some instances, have a part in determining his own objectives
9. to aid in the individualization of instruction for all students
10. to aid teachers in planning and evaluating instructional strategies in the affective and psychomotor domains.

Another need of teachers is the ability to classify and categorize goals and objectives according to the behavioral taxonomies. Some educators who have utilized taxonomies for the cognitive, affective, and psychomotor domains to re-evaluate and restructure their curricular offerings through behavioral objectives have gained new insights concerning levels of learning and feeling and movement. These taxonomies provide a common foundation upon which teachers can organize learning experiences for children. They enable professionals to more accurately communicate and comprehend stated educational goals. In many instances awareness of the taxonomies stimulates thought concerning the learning process and the problems of education. Teachers have become more aware of cognitive, affective and psychomotor behaviors observable in children and therefore are now better prepared to develop curricula, instructional methods and measurement techniques in all three learning domains.

Future developmental programs will be based upon implications of present educational trends concerning: (1) the development and use of performance objectives; (2) individualization of instruction; (3) the use of systems processes and criterion-referenced measurements for developing programs of accountability; and (4) the development of performance-based curricula for providing both pre-service and in-service training for teachers and educational administrators.

Among the assumptions to be considered as these trends develop are:

1. The dynamic nature of educational program components requires constant change in program focus and goals. Thus, professional educators must be able to identify new goals and develop their own objectives.
2. Objectives that are self-developed will be better understood and used than will objectives furnished by external agencies.
3. Performance objectives, already extremely important in educational program development, will become even more important and necessary in the future.
4. Goal identification is a necessary prerequisite for the development of any performance objective. Objective statements which lose their goal identification fail to communicate valuable information.
5. Adequate financing of educational programs in the future is going to depend upon the ability of educational administrators to be accountable for the quality of the programs they manage. The determination of quality must include data that includes tangible evidence of program success.

GLOSSARY OF TERMS

Behaviorally Stated Objectives: a performance objective that states a specific goal, competency or intent and an evaluation outcome performance that will identify how successful a person must be in achieving the goal, competency or intent.

Criterion: a level of achievement or degree of success a person must meet or exceed in order to be considered successful in performing a required task.

Criterion Referenced Measurement: evaluative measurement designed to determine the adequacy of any trait or factor that is under investigation by comparing it either quantitatively or qualitatively with an appropriate criterion.

Educational Accountability: a condition in which educators and educational programs are evaluated to determine the quality of the results obtained in achieving the objectives for which they have been given responsibility.

Learning Oriented Goal: the statement of a goal, competency, or intent that is designed to identify a desired cognitive, affective or psychomotor change in some learner.

Non-Learning Oriented Goal: the statement of a goal, competency or intent that is designed to identify a desired end that is not primarily concerned with behavioral change in a learner.

Norm-Referenced Measurement: evaluative measurement designed to reveal differences in individuals by establishing a comparison of their level to achievement with an established norm.

Performance Objective: a specifically stated objective that includes a precise statement of a goal (the intent of the activity) and that, in addition, specifies some type of evaluation performance or outcome that can be utilized to determine the level of success obtained in achieving the stated goal.

Systems Programs: programs that are developed by use of the "systems approach" to problem solving. This involves the use of developmental processes involving systems analysis to achieve a desired mission or broad goal.

REFERENCE

1. Frederick Herzberg, "One More Time: How Do You Motivate Employees?" *Harvard Business Review* (January-February), 1968, pp. 53–62.

Chapter 2

GOALS APPROACH RATIONALE

To reason correctly, from a false principle, is the perfection of sophistry.

Emmons

Irrationally held truths may be more harmful than reasoned errors.

Thomas H. Huxley

Think wrongly, if you please; but in all cases think for yourself.

Lesserig

CHAPTER GOALS

For the reader to:

1. comprehend the rationale for establishing goals as ends and evaluation outcomes as means.

2. memorize a definition of performance objectives.

3. become knowledgeable concerning the two major classifications of performance objectives.

4. comprehend the difference between behavioral objectives written by the goals and outcomes approach techniques, according to the requirements of their definitions.

5. know the characteristics of both the goals and outcomes performance objective writing techniques.

6. memorize the difference between the two major classifications of performance objectives.

7. understand the problems created by naming objectives according to their use rather than by their essential characteristics.

8. comprehend the specific advantages to be gained by writing performance objectives by the goals approach technique.

Most historical accounts concerning the development of the behavioral objective movement start around the beginning of the second quarter of the 20th century with the contributions of Ralph W. Tyler and his associates. Tyler showed a great concern for goal development and was interested in improving the art of stating educational goals so that they would be more useful to educational practitioners, particularly in the area of evaluation. According to an American Educational Research Association report, Tyler outlined the processes of evaluation as: (1) identifying general objectives (goals); (2) specifying these goals in behavioral terms; (3) specifying situations in which the behavior can be observed; (4) devising and applying instruments for making observations; and (5) relating evidence obtained to the original objective. The current emphasis on writing both performance and behavioral objectives is partially a result of Tyler's viewpoints.

In simple terms, program development in any area involves a minimum of three components:

GOAL ⟶ STRATEGIES ⟶ EVALUATION

Strategies, sometimes referred to as procedures, are never stated in performance objectives. Thus, a specifically stated performance objective should have only two components, and can be defined by the following formula:

PERFORMANCE OBJECTIVE = GOAL + EVALUATION

Going back to Tyler's work, we find that he was interested in improving goals, not eliminating them. The definition of a goal according to a standard dictionary would be something like, "the end or final purpose which a person hopes to accomplish." In education the hoped for goals basically involve cognitive, affective, and psychomotor development. In the cognitive domain it is anticipated that a learner will have sufficient memory knowledge and skills training so that he can continually apply his knowledge and skills to new situations. *Thus, the real intent of a cognitive goal is for the learner to exhibit efficiently a knowledge or skill in recurring situations over his lifetime—not in a one-time testing situation.* The same is true with the development of healthy feelings and emotions in the affective domain and voluntary movement patterns in the psychomotor domain.

Since 1968, many school systems, state departments of education, and universities have been studying performance objective development and utilization programs. There is evidence that many of the frustrations experienced by teachers and administrators in the writing and use of behavioral objectives can be traced to writing techniques which are based upon performance objective definitions that omit specific goal references or merely imply goals rather than specifically stating them.

ENDS VERSUS MEANS

The ends of human action refer to the final goal(s) or intent for which an action is taken. The ends are valuable for their own sake or have intrinsic value. The means of human action are those things which are done for the sake of the ends and have extrinsic values only. In other words, means only have value as long as the ends to which they are applied have value, and then only to the extent to which the means actually accomplish the ends.

Referring to the three components representing the program development process we find that a goal is the only component in the process that has intrinsic value.

GOAL (end)   STRATEGY (means)   EVALUATION (means)

Intrinsic   Extrinsic   Extrinsic
Value   Value   Value

For example, the goals of instruction should represent specific intents or ends that a teacher believes to be desirable for the learner. The goal is expected to have both short-term and long-range usefulness that will continue to be valuable whether or not the instructional strategies bring about the desired behavioral changes as determined by evaluation processes. Thus, the goal can be said to have intrinsic value.

Strategies are not valuable for their own sake but receive their value only insofar as they aid the learner in achieving desirable goals. Evaluation also has only extrinsic value since its purposes are to determine the excellence or quality of the instructional strategies and to furnish an estimate of proof concerning the level of success that a learner has had in achieving his goal.

Viewed in this light we can now envision a performance objective formula as:

$$\text{Performance Objective} = \text{GOALS (Intrinsic Value)} + \text{EVALUATION (Extrinsic Value)}$$

According to this formula, any definition or writing of a behavioral objective, which is one type of performance objective, should include both a goal and evaluation component and of the two components the goal must be considered the most important. This can be illustrated by the following behavioral objective statement.

A. To improve the agility of seventh grade girls as determined by each girl's ability to increase by at least three the number of squat-thrusts performed during one minute.

Critique:

1. *Goal Component*—To improve the agility of seventh grade girls.

2. Evaluation Component — Determined by each girl's ability to increase by at least three the number of squat-thrusts performed during one minute.

In this example it is obvious that agility is the intent or primary competency aimed at in the objective and that it can have continuous long-range intrinsic value; whereas squat-thrusts, which are performed for the sake of determining agility, are short-range measurements with only extrinsic value. In other words, squat-thrusts are not performed for their own value, but only to measure agility — which is considered to be valuable.

PROBLEMS OF DEFINITION

As previously stated, current problems in performance objective development and use appear to have their beginnings with the ways in which objectives and other key terms relating to objectives are defined. Objectives are based upon diagnosed goals. *The first problem occurs with the definition of a goal as being "a statement of broad general purpose that is rather global in nature" or some other definition that is equivalent. Such a definition can serve operationally for a general goal only.* Examples of general goals are as follow:

1. General mathematics students must acquire the knowledge and skill necessary to use instruments of measurement.
2. Students in American Ethnic and Regional Literature should become sufficiently knowledgeable of the concepts, definition and characteristics of the American short story, that they can discuss them intelligently.

Both of these goals, representing the General Mathematics and Language Arts curriculum, have been globally stated to include a large portion of the content to be included in the respective courses. Each goal could be divided into many sub-concepts and stated as more specific intents.

A goal can be general or it can be specific. A specific goal should have a very specific intent and it is this type of goal that should be used in the development of objectives which require specific performances in evaluation. *Specific evaluation for general goals and general evaluation for specific goals are not very meaningful. Specific evaluation for specific goals is, however, a better and more appropriate way to establish program success.* This is the only type of evaluation that can approach a one-to-one relationship between the goal and its evaluation component. The following goals are sub-concepts taken from the two previously stated general goals which have been stated as more specific intents that can be more readily evaluated.

1. General Mathematics students are expected to develop skill in measuring with a meter stick.
2. Students should develop an in-depth comprehension of Edgar Allan Poe's theory of the short story.

Each of these goals represents a much more refined and specific intent than did the general goals from which they were derived. Evaluation to determine success in achieving these more specific goals will be easier to prescribe, more specific and will represent a closer one-to-one relationship with the goal than is likely to occur in the evaluation of the general goals.

In the past, performance objective users have attempted to write objectives from very general and even abstract goals. Thus, in many instances the evaluation for success has either been meaningless or, at best, controversial. When a goal is too general or abstract, it should be broken down into very distinct goal components before any attempt is made to restate it as an objective.

It should be clearly understood that all measurable objectives can be considered as being performance objectives. A performance objective can be defined as any *specifically stated objective that includes a precise statement of a goal (which is the intent of the activity) and which, in addition, specifies some type of evaluation performance which can be utilized to determine the level of success in achieving the stated goal.*

A second problem is that the user of performance objectives must realize there are two types of performance objectives that fit the performance objective definition. The two types are: objectives that are learning oriented and objectives which are non-learning oriented. The distinction between these two types of performance objectives is easy to see.

Learning oriented behavioral objectives should specify in their goal statements a learning task that is designed to bring about a learning change (cognitive, effective, or psychomotor) in some learner. The evaluation component of this type of objective is based upon some performance, behavioral activity, or instrumentation that will determine the level of success in achieving this learning change.

Examples of this type of objective follow:

For first year accounting students to acquire a knowledge of bookkeeping terminology, so that when given a list of twenty words, 90% of the students will be able to match them to their correct definition with 80% accuracy.

For tenth grade math students to acquire the knowledge of changing common fractions to their decimal equivalent, so that when given ten common fractions on a test 95% of the students will be able to correctly list their decimal equivalent with 100% accuracy.

For twelfth grade advanced Film Literature students to acquire a
knowledge of specific facts concerning the early film pioneers, so
that when given a written exam, they will correctly match the
names of ten pioneers with a list of twenty film history items (film
titles, "inventions," etc.) with at least 80% accuracy.

Each of these examples identifies a goal for a learning group that is
tied to a specific learning task designed to show achievement or behavioral change at the knowledge level of the cognitive domain. In each
instance an evaluation component has been added to the goal statement
that is consistent with the intent of the goal. Similar objectives can be
written to indicate learning achievement or behavioral change in the
psychomotor or affective domains.

Non-learning oriented performance objectives specify no learner
or learning task as the specific intent of its goal, but identifies who is
accountable and what program task needs to be accomplished. The
evaluation component of non-learning oriented objectives specifies an
activity or performance that will determine the success in achieving the
goal based upon criteria that are efficient for the program task that has
been identified in the goal statement.

Examples of the non-learning oriented type of objectives might
include the following:

For the English Department of Florida Junior College to develop
performance objectives for all English courses by January 1,
1975. Success will be determined by a written document containing performance objectives for each course, by course number,
that is approved for use by the Director of Academic Affairs.

For the Sandalwood Senior High English Department to develop
and provide plans for a student resource center in the English
pod by the end of the next school year. Proof this goal is achieved
will be evidenced by the principal and the county supervisor of
English approving a written master plan submitted by the English
teachers prior to the specified date.

For the guidance counselor at Fletcher Junior High to administer
by May 1974, the Stanford Achievement Test to all eighth grade
students. Success will be evidenced by the names of each student
being recorded on a master check list indicating they have taken
the test within the prescribed time period.

Each of these examples indicate a goal for which someone other
than a learning group will be accountable. The goals are not designed
to reveal learning achievement upon the part of the teacher or
counselor, but to establish that they are accountable for some administrative task to which they have been assigned. The evaluation is designed to realistically determine success in achieving the goals, not to
measure cognitive, affective or psychomotor growth.

Figure 2–1 illustrates the two different types of performance objectives.

There are currently two major techniques or approaches to writing performance objectives: the outcomes and goal approaches. A serious definition problem occurs with the definitions being coined for the "outcomes approach" to performance objective development. Most performance objectives developed in the United States have used this approach, thus there are many outcome definition statements. In essence, "outcomes approach" users define behavioral objectives as *objectives which identify anticipated learning outcomes, performances, or activities that a learner will be able to accomplish as proof that he has successfully completed the objective.* This type of objective is stated as *a performance or behavioral activity expected from the learner, a criterion standard by which it can be judged and some writers include any special conditions that will be necessary in order for the performance to occur satisfactorily.*

In reality, an objective written in this manner becomes a one-component evaluation statement which as three parts. It is a simple statement of how the objective will be evaluated upon completion of the implementation of program strategies. *It is important to note that the outcomes approach definition does not specify that objectives should identify goals.*

In contrast to this definition, the "goal approach" definition refers to performance objectives as being *two-component objectives which include*

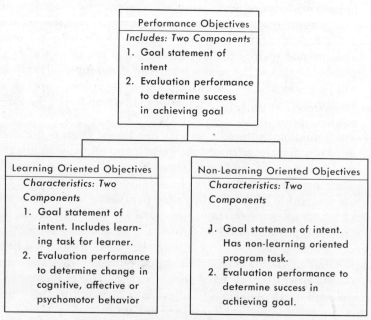

Figure 2–1 Types of performance objectives.

a goal and the anticipated outcome or evaluation of the goal, The key character-istics of this type of objective are: (1) The goal component identifies the specific intent of the learning oriented objective by indicating the learning task, learner, and behavioral domain. (2) In addition, the evaluation component identifies the performance activity, instrumentation, or behavior the learner will exhibit as a means of determining his or her success in achieving the goal and the level of success the learner is expected to achieve.

The outcome approach definition actually could be considered as a definition for the evaluation component of the goals approach. In other words, the outcomes approach definition and the evaluation component of the goals approach both represent how success or achievement will be determined. *The real difference is found in the addition of the goal component to the goals approach definition which tells why the evaluation outcomes are desirable or what the intent is for which we are attempting to determine success.* The chart below depicts the requirements of both the outcomes and goal approach techniques.

It is obvious after a casual reading of this chart that *the "goals approach" covers everything that is included in the outcomes approach and more.* This additional information and the response given to the goals approach by hundreds of teachers and administrators have convinced many educators that the goal statement components are a needed part of any behavioral objective.

An illustration of the differences that may develop in objectives written according to each of the two definitions can be obtained from the following example:

    I. Objective Written According to Outcomes Approach Definition:
        Given ten building blocks, each child will be able to place by shape eighty per cent of the blocks into their correct categories. *Critique:*
        1. Goal Component—None, but the statement implies that the

OUTCOMES APPROACH	GOALS APPROACH

A. Specific Goal
   (none stated)
	A. Specific Goal
	   1. Basic statement
	   2. Communication checks
	     a. learner
	     b. specific learning task including identification of content and behavioral domain.

B. Evaluation
   1. Performance, activity, or behavior
   2. Criterion standards
   3. Important conditions
	B. Evaluation
	   1. Performance, activity, behavior or instrumentation
	   2. Expected success level standards
	   3. Optional statements

goal is to correctly place eighty per cent of the blocks into their categories.

2. Evaluation Component — Includes the entire statement.

II. Objective Written According to Goals Approach Definition: To develop in preschool children the abilities of visual acuity and prehension movement so that when given ten building blocks each child will be able to place by shape eighty per cent of the blocks in their correct categories.

Critique:

1. Goal Component — To develop in preschool children the abilities of visual acuity and prehension movement.
2. Evaluation Component — so that when given ten building blocks, each child will be able to place by shape eighty per cent of the blocks in their correct categories.

In this example, the specific intent of the objective is identified by the goal statement which is required by the definition in the goals approach. The specific intent of the objective is not identified in the objective written according to the outcomes approach definition.

The goal competency, or long-range intent, omitted from the outcomes-defined statement is included in the objective written by the goals approach definition. The goal of this objective was to develop visual acuity and prehension movement — an entirely different thing from the outcome behavior that was stated to determine successful achievement of the goal. The goal was the only component of the objective that had long-range intrinsic value. Thus, its omission from the objective statement written by the outcomes definition detracted from the real value of the objective and creates several functionally important problems.

The outcomes definition requires only that an objective specify an outcome performance and some criterion to determine the standard acceptable for the performance. The performance and criterion included in the previous outcome illustration was as follows:

A. *Performance* — to place blocks by shape into categories
B. *Criterion* — eighty per cent of the blocks will be in correct categories

This objective met all of the major requirements of writing a behavioral objective by the outcomes approach definition; however, there was no reference to the goal or real intent of the objective. The statement contained an evaluation component which has no intrinsic but only extrinsic value. The assumption need not be made that the writer of the outcomes objective had no goal in mind; he obviously did, and the goal might be the same one. It would be impractical to think that anyone would write outcome performance statements without first having some previous understanding of the purpose for which the outcome of performance statements were written. The point is that the outcomes approach objective is unable to stand by itself as having value other than that of producing evaluation data. This point becomes significant when teachers attempt to develop strategies from objectives prescribed to them by someone else.

Another problem of definition is the misuse of the terms "performance objective" and "behavioral objective." This misuse most often refers to statements which indicate that the two terms are synonymous. As stated earlier in this chapter, a performance objective refers to any specifically stated objective that identifies a goal and specifies some type of evaluation activity or performance; and it can be either learning or non-learning oriented. Thus, all behavioral objectives can be classified as performance objectives, but not all performance objectives are behavioral objectives.

The diagram below illustrates the two different classifications of performance objectives. Again, casual observation tells immediately why behavioral objectives and performance objectives cannot be used interchangeably. In some instances performance objectives may not concern cognitive, affective, or psychomotor development at all; thus, they should never, in this sense, be referred to as behavioral objectives. Evaluation of non-learning oriented performance objectives becomes extremely difficult if they are treated as behavioral objectives and the evaluation can be no better than some form of transmitted relationship. The problem of transmitted relationships will be further discussed in a later chapter.

A fourth definition problem concerns the use of conflicting terms to name and define different behavioral objective classifications. In

PERFORMANCE OBJECTIVES

Non-Learning Oriented Objectives	Learning Oriented Objectives *(Behavioral Objectives)*
A. Any performance objective with non-learning oriented goal statement.	A. Any performance objective with learning oriented goal statement designed to change cognitive, affective, or psychomotor behavior.
B. Applications 1. structures or facilitates 2. processes 3. non-learning oriented products such as materials, equipment, guidelines.	B. Applications 1. teachers 2. students 3. other rational beings
C. Includes both goal and evaluation components	C. Includes both goal and evaluation components

addition the lack of distinction between naming and defining a term is seldom apparent. To name something means to give it a distinctive designation. To define something refers to making its meaning distinct by setting its limits or determining its essential qualities.

George Washington was the name given to distinctively designate a specific human being. He was, however, a human being due to other essential qualities that placed him into the human classification. Objectives can be named for many things including, most frequently, the uses they are designed to serve. They should, however, be defined based upon their own specific qualities.

The basic reason for the discrepancy in terms is that, both in the attempt to be original and to explain an objective by how it is being used, various contributors to the behavioral objectives movement have already coined names and partially defined objectives as follows:

1. program objectives
2. program level objectives
3. learner objectives
4. informational objectives
5. minimum level objectives
6. instructional objectives
7. planning objectives
8. desired level objectives
9. organizational objectives
10. specific noninstructional objectives
11. grade level objectives
12. content area objectives
13. measurable objectives
14. curriculum level objectives
15. division level objectives
16. curriculum objectives
17. terminal performance objectives
18. intermediate performance objectives
19. specific objectives
20. procedural objectives
21. criterion objectives
22. strategy objectives
23. teacher objectives
24. direct objectives
25. representational objectives
26. criterion-referenced objectives
27. performance objectives
28. mission objectives
29. behavioral objectives
30. nonbehavioral objectives
31. instructional level objectives
32. staff level objectives
33. unit level objectives
34. indirect objectives
35. means objectives
36. enabling objectives

This list represents only a brief summary of the long list of names available. The point is that we can name, although the practice is not desirable, an objective anything we wish based upon its use. In reality it would be better to name objectives by their intent and classification levels.

This means that performance objectives should be referred to as learning oriented (behavioral) or non-learning oriented and called a criterion-referenced performance objective if it includes a criterion as well as an outcome performance. A behavioral objective is a behavioral objective not because of any use that may be made of it, but because it identifies an intended goal and behavioral outcome. Both the goal and evaluation outcome should be clear and specific. The minimum level or performance objective classification (as stated in the goals approach) merely states that a particular objective has met the minimum requirement for being called a behavioral objective; that is, it has a stated goal and a behavioral outcome, but does not have a criterion specified.

The desired level or criterion-referenced performance objective classification (advocated in the goals approach) indicates that the objective has gone beyond the minimum requirement of stating a goal and a behavioral activity by specifying a criterion standard that indicates the success level required for the learner. Defining objectives in this manner gives objective development a taxonomic effect in which both the objective classifications and their names are based upon a hierarchical arrangement or sequential order.

This concept of naming objectives by a hierarchical type of classification according to the content of the evaluation component is in support of the current thinking by many testing experts that the term criterion-referenced should be applied to success level scores rather than to tests or other measurement instrumentation. In other words, criterion-referenced testing is best applied to *how much* of a specified characteristic a pupil can demonstrate, rather than to the *method* used to obtain the score.

We have established that all behavioral objectives are performance objectives and that the difference between performance and criterion-referenced performance objectives is the presence or absence of the criterion standard. It appears that since there are only two types of performance objectives and since both of these types can be classified according to their hierarchy level of development, it is more appropriate to define and refer to objectives by these classification levels. This would help eliminate much of the confusion that is already being expressed by classroom teachers who have been exposed to the expertise of more than one consultant.

This critique does not intend to imply that the classifications of: (1) goal, (2) learning oriented objective, and (3) non-learning oriented objectives and the learning and non-learning oriented subcategories based upon minimum and desired level characteristics will be sufficient to handle all coding problems. They will, however, be sufficient to form the basis of a coding or classification system which could eliminate many of the problems caused by naming objectives based upon use.

GOALS VERSUS OUTCOMES

The current popularity accorded the development and use of performance objectives can be attributed to the increased emphasis upon accountability. Accountability in turn is primarily concerned with goal setting and attainment. Success in the attainment of goals is determined through various methods of evaluation. In the final analysis, however, it is the achievement of goals which are the ends for which people are accountable, not the evaluation or *means* by which success is determined.

An established goal can be considered as a target at which to shoot or toward which actions are directed. Developing performance or evaluation outcomes without first very specifically defining goals is like shooting an arrow without first deciding upon the specific target. In programs involving educational accountability there are many pitfalls which may occur from preoccupation with outcomes rather than goals.

A few examples taken from contemporary curriculum projects, utilizing the outcomes approach writing technique, may serve well in defining some obvious problems and also help to evaluate the merits of the *goals* and outcomes approach writing techniques. The first example involves objectives developed for a university physical education program. These objectives were written and published as follows:

PSYCHOMOTOR DOMAIN

I. OBJECTIVES
    A. *General Objective*
        It is the mission of this module to develop overall body strength in the student and to provide potential physical education instructors with an exercise foundation upon which to base their instructional activities.
    B. *Specific Objectives*
        1. Given a 60 pound bar, the student will correctly perform 10 bent rowing exercises.
        2. Given a 50 pound bar, the student will correctly perform 10 arm extensions.
        3. Given a 60 pound bar, the student will correctly do 5 dead lift, stiff-leg exercises.
        4. Given a 50 pound bar, the student will correctly perform 10 trunk bend-extensions.
        5. Given a 40 pound bar, the student will correctly perform 6 side bender exercises.
        6. Given an exercise board slanted at a 10 degree angle, the student will do 35 sit-ups with his legs straight.
        7. Given a 70 pound bar, the student will correctly perform 10 dead lifts with his knees bent.
        8. Given a 65 pound bar, the student will correctly perform 15 Jefferson straddle lifts.
        9. Given a universal exercise weight lifting machine, the

student will correctly perform 20 toe lifts with 100 pounds of weight.
10. Given a 70 pound bar, the student will correctly perform 15 two arm curls.

The average user of performance objectives would probably find little fault with this program. *Indeed, only those persons who are knowledgeable in the area of physical education and persons trained by the goals approach writing technique to recognize specific intents as the desired learning ends would be expected to question the program.* This competency module, representing a better than average attempt at developing program accountability, does, however, have several unforseen problems. These problems may be best focused upon by comparing this module with another module developed for the same course. To illustrate the differences we will now develop the same program using the goals approach technique.

Harrow's[1] *Taxonomy of the Psychomotor Domain* defines strength as a person's ability to exert tension against resistance. Strength is measured by the maximum amount of force exerted by a muscle or muscle group. Thus, the overall body strength referred to in the general objective really means to strengthen muscles in various body regions. Using the goals approach to develop a system of goals the writer would begin as follows:

Subsystems (By Body Regions)

	1. Shoulder Girdle (Posterior)
	2. Trunk (Posterior)
	3. Hips, Lower trunk (Anterior and Posterior)
	4. Trunk (Lateral)
	5. Trunk, Hip (Anterior)
SYSTEM	6. Trunk, Legs (Posterior, Anterior)
	7. Legs (Anterior, Posterior)
	8. Lower Leg, Foot (Posterior, Inferior)
	9. Neck (Posterior)
OVERALL BODY STRENGTH	10. Neck (Anterior)
	11. Neck (lateral)
	12. Shoulder (Superior)
	13. Shoulder Upper Arm (Anterior, Superior, Posterior)
	14. Upper Arm (Anterior)
	15. Upper Arm, Lower Arm (Anterior, Posterior)
	16. Chest (Anterior, Posterior)
	17. Chest, Upper Arm (Anterior, Posterior)

This illustration converts the general goal of overall body strength into a system composed of seventeen subsystems. Each subsystem is identified as a body region which will be expected to be strengthened under the concept of overall body strength. Each of these body regions is characterized by a group of muscles which were identified as follows:

Body Region	*Muscles*
1. Shoulder Girdle (Posterior)	1. Rhomboids, Posterior Deltoid, Trapezius (all three), Elbow Flexors, Latissimus Dorsi, Teres Major
2. Trunk (Posterior)	2. Erector Spinae, Gluteus Maximus, Hamstrings
3. Hip, Lower Trunk (Anterior, Posterior)	3. Gluteus Maximus, Hamstrings, Erector Spinae, Abdominal and Hip Flexors
4. Trunk (Lateral)	4. Lateral Abdominals, Lateral Erector Spinae
5. Trunk, Hip (Anterior)	5. Abdominals (Upper and Lower), Flexor of Hip (Psoas Major)
6. Trunk, Legs (Anterior, Posterior)	6. Erector Spinae, Gluteus Maximus, Hamstrings, Quadriceps, Soleus, Gastrocnemius, Levator, Trapezius
7. Legs (Anterior, Posterior)	7. Gastrocnemius, Soleus, Quadriceps, Hip Extensors (Gluteus Maximus), Erector Soleus
8. Lower Leg, Foot	8. Gastrocnemius, Spinae Plantar Flexors of Foot
9. Neck (Posterior)	9. Sacrospinalis, Deep Cervical Muscles, Trapezius
10. Neck (Anterior)	10. Prevertebral Muscles, Sternocleidomastoid

11. Neck (Lateral)	11. Sacrospinalis, Deep Cervical Muscles, Trapezius, Prevertebral Muscles, Sternocleidomastoid
12. Shoulder (Superior)	12. Trapezius (upper) Levator, Biceps Middle Deltoid
13. Shoulder, upper arm (Anterior, Superior, Posterior)	13. Deltoids (all three) Upper Pectoralis Major Triceps
14. Upper Arm	14. Biceps, Brachialis
15. Upper and Lower Arm (Anterior, Posterior)	15. Biceps, Brachiovadialis Finger Extensor (lona) Wrist Extensors
16. Chest (Anterior, Posterior)	16. Pectoralis Major and Minor, Triceps, Latissimus Dorsi, Servatus Anterior, Upper Pectoralis Major, Triceps
17. Chest, Upper Arm (Anterior)	17. Upper Pectoralis Major, Anterior Deltoid, Triceps

Now that the goals and their muscle components have been identified it is possible to restate the specific psychomotor objectives under the umbrella of the same general objective, but this time utilizing the goals approach.

I. OBJECTIVES

A. It is the mission of this module to develop overall body strength in the student and to provide potential future physical education instructors with an exercise foundation upon which to base their own instructional activities.

B. *Specific Objectives*

For P.E. 100 students to strengthen:

1. *their shoulder girdle* so that when given a 60 pound bar, they will correctly perform 10 bent rowing exercises and 10 arm extensions.
2. *their trunk muscles* so that when given a 60 pound bar, they will correctly do 5 dead lift, stiff-leg exercises.
3. *the muscles in their hips and lower trunk* so that when given a 50 pound bar, they will correctly perform 10 trunk bend-extensions.

4. *their trunk muscles* so that when given a universal exercise weight lifting machine, they will correctly perform 6 side bender exercises with 40 points of weight.

5. *their trunk and hip muscles* so that when given an exercise board slanted at a 10 degree angle, they will correctly perform 35 sit-ups with their legs straight.

6. *the muscles in their trunk and legs* so that when given a 70 pound bar, they will correctly perform 10 dead lifts with their knees bent, and 6 "hack" lifts.

7. *their leg muscles* as determined by their correctly doing 15 full squats and 15 Jefferson straddle lifts with a 65 pound bar.

8. *the muscles in their lower leg and foot* so that when given a universal exercise weight lifting machine, they can correctly perform 20 toe lifts with 100 pounds of weight.

9. *their posterior neck muscles* so that when given a neck sling weighted with 25 pounds, they can correctly do 5 neck extension exercises.

10. *their anterior neck muscles* as evidenced by their correctly doing 5 neck curls.

11. *their lateral neck muscles* as measured by their correctly performing 5 lateral neck lifts with 10 pounds of weight.

12. *their shoulder muscles* so that when given a universal exercise weight lifting machine and 110 pounds of weight, they can correctly do 10 shoulder shrugs and 10 abductor lifts.

13. *the muscles in their upper arms and shoulders* as determined by their correctly performing 10 military presses and 10 shoulder presses with an 80 pound bar.

14. *their upper arm muscles* so that when given a 70 pound bar, the student will correctly perform 15 two arm curls.

15. *their upper and lower arm muscles* as determined by their correctly doing 20 two arm reverse curls with a 55 pound bar.

16. *their chest muscles* so that when given a 50 pound weight and a bench, they can do 10 straight arm and 10 bent arm pullovers.

17. *their chest and upper arm* so that when given a universal weight lifting machine and 120 pounds of weight they can correctly perform 8 bench presses.

These specific objectives could have been stated in two ways: (1) by referring to the body regions as the goals; or (2) by referring to the individual muscle groups. In this instance the program results would have been essentially the same since the body regions could not have received the prescribed exercises without exercising the muscles which were in each region.

In the goals approach there were thirty-seven muscles identified as being important in the development of overall body strength. Thus, it was possible to plan exercises and evaluation activities to determine success in strengthening all thirty-seven muscles. In the shot-gun approach used in the outcomes performance statements, the muscles were not identified nor were the body regions. They could have been, but the outcomes approach definition does not require this; therefore, more frequently than not, there are no real specific targets at which to aim.

A comparison of the two different approaches in developing objectives for the psychomotor module is shown by the following check list.

| | ACCOUNTED FOR | | | ACCOUNTED FOR | |
MUSCLES	Out-comes	Goals	MUSCLES	Out-comes	Goals
Abdominal (2)	XX	XX	Prevertebral		X
Biceps	X	X	Psoas Major	X	X
Brachialis	X	X	Quadriceps	X	X
Brachioradialis		X	Rhomboids	X	X
Deep Cervical		X	Sacrospinalis		X
Deltoids (Anterior)		X	Servatus Anterior		X
Elbow Flexors	X	X	Soleus	X	X
Erector Spinae	XX	XX	Sternocleidomastoid		X
Finger Extensors		X	Teres Major	X	X
Gastrocnemius	X	X	Trapezius (Upper)		X
Gluteus Maximus	X	X	Triceps	X	X
Hamstring	X	X	Upper Pectoralis		X
Hip Flexors	X	X	Major		X
Hip Extensors	X	X	Wrist Extensors		X
Latissimus Dorsi	X	X	Foot Flexors	X	X
Levator		X			
Pectoralis (2)		X			
Foot Plantar Flexors		X			
Middle Deltoid		X			
Posterior Deltoid	X	X			

The specific objectives stated by the outcomes performance approach accounted for the exercise and evaluation of 21 of the 37 important muscles. Thus, only fifty seven per cent (57%) of the specific goals which could have been identified within the constraints of the general objectives were included. Another value of the exercises that will be required in order to achieve the seven additional objectives is that in addition to the strengthening of 16 additional muscles, additional strengthening of the other muscles is experienced since there is great overlap in muscle development with these types of activities.

The contrast between a general goal and a specific goal may best be shown by the following illustration:

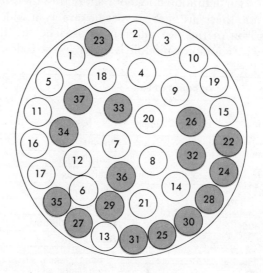

In this example the large outer circle, containing all of the smaller circles, represents a general goal statement. The smaller inner circles represent specific goals or specific intents which are included within the constraints of the general goal. It can be assumed that general goals may contain anywhere from a very few to several hundred smaller and more specific, goals and/or intents. This will depend upon factors such as how global the general goal is stated, the content area, the context within which it is used and the type and number of constraints that are applicable.

The point is that evaluation performances should match the specificity of the goal which they are to evaluate. General goals require a more general evaluation. Specific goals should have specific evaluation components. When specific evaluation performance statements, designed to evaluate small but specific goals, are used to evaluate general goals it creates a condition similar to the archer shooting at random and not caring what target he hits as long as it is within the constraints of the general target goal. In other words, he doesn't care what he hits because, as far as he is concerned, any target will be accepted for determining success in achieving the general objective.

Such is the case with the specific objectives written under the general objective in the sample Physical Education program. In this instance, outcomes evaluation or performance statements were attached to a general goal and as a result the program has far less value than might have been the case. Graphically, we find one difference in the two approaches used to develop the psychomotor module to be as follows:

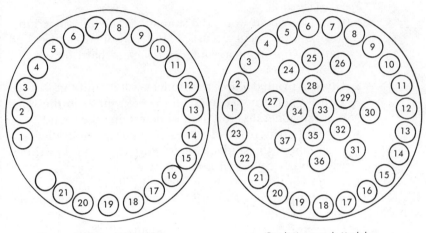

Outcomes Approach Module   Goals Approach Module

This illustration emphasizes that specific evaluation outcomes stated for general goals will not give as accurate or thorough an evaluation or provide as much useful data as will specific objectives which are developed from specific goals. In the goals approach many more targets are identified and success in achieving the desired ends is much more reliable than in the outcomes approach.

A second example can further enlighten objective writers concerning problems which may occur if specific goals are not identified for all evaluation performances designed to show learning achievement or change. This example has been included with the permission of the project director of a teacher training project designed to train elementary teachers. This project, as is the case with many others utilizing outcomes approach writing techniques, has proved to be very valuable to the teachers trained under its auspices. The project, as was the case with the first example, will not be named since only its negative rather than positive characteristics will be noted.

WORD ANALYSIS SKILLS (Outcomes Approach)

I. OBJECTIVES
  A. *General Objective*
  It is the pioneer task of this module to discern the prospective teacher's awareness of and skill in phonic analysis, structural analysis and syllabication. It is also an attempt to provide the prospective teacher with a background in word analysis skills as a crucial foundation for effective instruction in reading and the language arts.
  B. *Specific Objectives*
  1. Given a printed word, the student will identify in writing, with 90 per cent accuracy, the consonant letters and specific consonant irregularities such as hard or soft "c," silent "b," etc.
  2. Given a printed word, the student will identify in writing, with 90 per cent accuracy, the vowel sounds in the word and the generalization used to determine the sounds.
  3. Given a written list of words containing vowel digraphs diphthongs, the student will identify the forms in writing, with 90 per cent accuracy.
  4. Given a group of words, the student will identify in writing, with 90 per cent accuracy, consonant digraphs and consonant blends.
  5. Given two lists of words, the student will
     a. identify in writing the prefixes and suffixes in those words which contain them.
     b. identify in writing the root word in those words which contain affixes (prefixes and/or suffixes), and
     c. form new words by adding in writing prefixes and/or suffixes to root words.
     A criterion of 90 per cent accuracy will be acceptable.
  6. Given a list of words, the student will be able to do the following tasks, with 90 per cent accuracy:
     a. write the number of vowel sounds in each word.
     b. write the number of syllables in each word.
     c. write a generalization concerning the relationship of the number of vowel sounds to the number of syllables in a word.
  7. Given a list of words, the student will be able to perform the following tasks, with 90 per cent accuracy:
     a. divide the words into syllables by rewriting them.
     b. write five syllabication generalizations and state in writing to which words each applies.

8. Given two lists of words the student will be able to:
   a. re-write compound words to indicate each component word.
   b. divide compound words into syllables by rewriting them.
   c. derive compound words by combining in writing two words.
9. Given a list of words, the student will be able to:
   a. write the plurals with 100 per cent accuracy.
   b. write three generalizations concerning the formation of plurals.
   c. identify in writing those words for which plurals are formed by a change in the word form.

Again, objectives have been stated as part of a learning module. The global goal of the module has been stated as a general objective. Specific evaluation performance statements have been listed as specific objectives under the general objective. Note that none of the objective statements specify the smaller specific goals which are evaluated by the specific performance statements. Instead, all are used as evaluation components for the general objective or imply that their performance requirements are the same as the goal statements would be if they were stated.

If, however, a performance requirement for evaluation purposes is the same thing as a goal, then there is no difference between stated intents and the evaluation of how well an intent is achieved. This cannot be the case or else the *means* would become their own *ends* which is not good logic. Several questions may be asked at this point which may help emphasize areas of concern with this type of objective statement. Pertinent questions related to this example are as follows:

1. Do we know the specific goal or intent for each of the specific objectives as stated? — No
2. Do we know that the specific objective (performance statements) are adequate or specific enough to properly evaluate the un-stated specific goals? — No
3. Does the information provided in the specific objectives (performance statements) provide enough information for the user to develop additional ways to evaluate the same specific goal that it represents? — No
4. Can a teacher choose program strategies, procedures, materials, and plan other activities efficiently if she has nothing but evaluation statements to work from? — No
5. Is the coverage of the content that is encompassed by the gen-

eral objective likely to be as thorough and complete when the specific goal components are not specified? — No

In order to understand why a "no" answer was given to each of these questions, the work of another group of teachers who developed objectives for word analysis skills utilizing the goals approach will be helpful. These objectives were adapted from Paulson's reading program materials in Hillsborough County, Florida.

WORD ANALYSIS SKILLS (Goals Approach)

I. Objectives

A. *General Objective*

To develop and improve in elementary children the skills essential for *word analysis.*

B. *Specific Objectives*

For elementary students to develop their ability

1. *to recognize initial consonants* as evidence by _____% of the class orally naming and sounding 19 consonant letters written on cards with _____% accuracy.

2. *to name the letter representing the final consonant sound* as evidenced by _____% of the pupils making _____% correct responses from a list of 10 words pronounced by the teacher.

3. *to name the sound of single consonants* in the medial position as evidenced by _____% of the class responding orally with _____% accuracy to a list of 10 words pronounced by the teacher.

4. to make the sounds represented by initial blends in one syllable words as evidenced by _____% of the class being able to attack new words containing blends with a _____% degree of accuracy.

5. to *name the vowel letters* as evidenced by _____% of the class orally responding to the teacher with _____% accuracy.

6. to pronounce *endings s, ing,* and *ed* when added to known words as evidenced by _____% of the children being able to pronounce a list of 10 words with _____% accuracy.

7. to *make new words* with common two and three letter word families as evidenced by _____% of the class orally responding to teacher and circling or underlining written words with _____% degree of accuracy.

8. to *recognize compound words* as evidenced by _____% of the class drawing a line around 10 words with _____% accuracy.

9. to *notice word form* clues as evidenced by _____% of the children identifying likenesses and differences, such as capital and small letters, numbers of letters, and double letter words orally and on written teacher-made worksheets with _____% degree of accuracy.

10. to pronounce words with *ed* endings, as evidenced by _____% of the class being able to pronounce 4 out of 5 known words after *ed* has been added.

11. to *see little words in big words* as evidenced by _____% of the class correctly underlining the little word in a big word with a _____% degree of accuracy.

12. to *recognize similarities in rhyming words* as measured by the child's ability to hear and orally state rhyming words when listening to poems or selections in which _____% of the students can score _____% on a test for rhyming words.

13. to make new words by adding *possessives and word endings* (ing, er, est, ly, etc.) as evidenced by _____% of the pupils being able to form new words from a list of 20 with _____% degree of accuracy.

14. to understand how *contractions* are formed as evidenced by _____% of the children being able to match the correct two words with the appropriate contraction with a _____% degree of accuracy.

15. to *hear consonant and consonant blend sounds* as evidenced by _____% of the children scoring _____% or above on an Informal Phonics Survey.

16. to increase *word recognition* as evidenced by their ability to read word families, whereby _____% of the pupils can pronounce all word families studied with a _____% degree of accuracy.

17. for *auditory discrimination* as evidenced by _____% correctly marking the long or short vowel sound in one syllable words with a _____% degree of accuracy.

18. to understand the *function of y* as a consonant at the beginning of a word and as a vowel anywhere else as evidenced by _____% of the pupils correctly marking the use of Y with a _____% degree of accuracy from a list of 20 words.

19. to *recognize compound words* as determined by a written test on which pupils will draw a line between the two words forming the compound word so that _____% of the pupils display a _____% degree of accuracy.

20. to hear the 2 sounds represented by *C and G* so that

_____% of the children can correctly write the initial letter of 10 dictated words representing the various sounds of c and g with _____% accuracy.

21. to extend *word recognition skills* as evidenced by the ability of _____% of the pupils orally attaching new words having a 3 letter initial blend with a _____% degree of accuracy.

22. to hear the *number of syllables* in words and be able to distinguish the accented syllable as evidenced by _____% of the children being able to clap out the syllables in 8 out of 10 words, clapping heaviest on accented syllables.

23. to know that *vowels are influenced* when followed by *r, w and l,* (star, saw, all) so that when given sound recognition activities using phonics charts, chalkboard drill, reading materials, and written exercises, _____% of the pupils will score _____% correct answers.

24. to apply the rule that when *2 vowels* come together in a word, the first is long and the second silent, so that when given sound recognition activities such as the chalkboard drill, or written exercises, _____% of children will score _____% correct answers.

25. to identify all *initial consonant* sounds and blends so that _____% of the pupils will write the initial consonant and blends on an Informal Phonics Survey with a _____% degree of accuracy.

26. to increase their word attack skills as evidenced by _____% of the children being able to apply the *vowel rules* taught by marking the vowel sound and pronouncing these words with a _____% degree of accuracy.

27. to *analyze possessive forms* as evidenced by _____% of the students scoring _____% or above on a 20 item test of the following type: matching possessive form with meaning; changing non-possessive to possessive by adding 's; changing non-possessive to possessive by adding an apostrophe.

28. to *recognize prefixes and suffixes* as evidenced by _____% of the pupils being able to circle prefixes, suffixes and roots from a list of 15 words with a _____% degree of accuracy.

29. to identify *root words* as evidenced by _____% correctly circling with a _____% of accuracy the root words from a list of 25 words containing prefixes or suffixes.

30. to maintain *recognition of contractions* as evidenced by _____% correctly reading 20 *contractions* in a given reading with a _____% degree of accuracy.

31. to apply the rules for changing words by adding *ing, s, es, d, ed, er, est,* as evidenced by the ability of _____% of the students to correctly add these endings to a list of root words with a _____% degree of accuracy.

32. to *change words* by doubling the consonants before adding *ing* as evidenced by performance on a teacher-made test whereby _____% of the pupils will score _____% or higher on the test.

33. to apply the *syllabication* rules — V/cv, VC/cv — as evidenced by _____% of the children correctly dividing a list of 15 words into syllables with a _____% degree of accuracy.

34. to understand the use of the *primary accent mark* so that _____% of the students can correctly place the accent mark in a list of words with _____% degree of accuracy.

35. to learn the rules concerning plurals and applying them as evidenced by _____% being able to correctly form plurals from a list of 10 singular words with a _____% degree of accuracy.

36. to become familiar with the similarity of *sounds of cks and x,* as evidenced by their ability to spell words having these sounds with a _____% degree of accuracy.

37. to *syllabicate* simple words by using the vowel rule of 1 vowel sound per syllable, as evidenced by _____% of the class being able to syllabicate a list of words with a _____% degree of accuracy.

38. to increase their *word attack skill* as evidenced by _____% of the children being able to attack words having the various *vowel teams* such as ai, aw, oy, ow, our, etc. with a _____% degree of accuracy.

39. to *recognize silent letters* in specific combinations, such as *wr, kn,* and *gn,* as evidenced by _____% of the class being able to cross out the silent letters in a list with a _____% degree of success.

40. to apply the *rules of syllabication* as evidenced by the circling of syllables from a list of 25 words, exemplifying the rules, so that _____% of the children will score a _____% degree of accuracy.

41. to *make and use* new words by adding appropriate *prefixes and suffixes* to 10 root words and using these words in a sentence with a _____% degree of accuracy.

42. to understand how *a change in accent* can affect the pronunciation and meaning of words as determined by oral
reading of a list of 5 pairs of words from a teacher-made
test and using these words in sentences, so that _____%
of the class shall get _____% of the words and sentences correctly.

The five questions posed earlier to which a "no" answer was then
given in each case now elicit a "yes." The specific goal or intent for each
of these forty-two specific objectives is known. A competent person can
check each evaluation performance statement to see if it is appropriate
to evaluate its goal. *Yes,* the inclusion of the specific goal or intent does
provide enough information to develop additional ways to evaluate the
same specific goal. A teacher can better choose her program strategies
because she now knows her specific goal and is not limited to the selection of strategies to achieve a particular outcome. *Yes,* the content coverage is much greater (42 objectives to 9) because time was taken to first
identify as many specific intents as possible.

A goal must communicate to many more people than just the person
who states it. It may need to communicate to another teacher, an
administrator, a student, a parent, a state department official, a person
from the United States Office of Education, or lay citizens. The completion and evaluation of each objective will provide information which
is, or should be, of use to some decision-maker. The information provided is much more useful if it includes the intent as well as the outcome.

One method for determining the magnitude of the problems that
can be caused by failure to identify specific intents is to attempt to
cross reference the word analysis objectives written by the two different
writing techniques. For example, by starting with the *goals approach*
objectives it can be seen that, based upon the communication presented
in the *outcomes approach* objectives, the outcomes objectives have no
coverage of specific objectives 6, 10, 13, 18, 20, 23, 31, 36. These objectives have specific intents which cannot be readily discerned in the
outcomes approach statements.

The same observation is true of most of the other objectives.
If, however, a specific goal were stated for each of the outcome statements, cross referencing the two different approaches to stating specific
objectives would become a simple task. In the outcomes statements a
learner is expected to perform a specific behavior without knowing why
he is performing it. In addition, there appears to be no *goals approach*
objective to match outcome objective number one.

Taken as a total program, the word analysis objectives written by
the goals approach must be considered to be more complete and to
provide more information than do the objectives written by the outcomes approach. This is because the outcomes objectives represent one
level of abstraction beyond those stated by the goals approach. This

level of abstraction can be seen in the systems example shown in Chapter 5. The outcome objectives were stated from the subsystem component general goal of word analysis. The goals approach, however, broke this general goal into its interim component skills before deciding upon the outcome performances to be used for evaluation. This critique does not intend to imply the correctness or incorrectness of the goal and evaluation component selection of the *goals approach* objectives or the rightness or wrongness of the outcome performance statements in the specific objectives developed by the outcomes approach technique. The intent of the critique is to say that, given the same expertise in goal and evaluation performance identification, the use of the goals approach technique for writing performance objectives will tend to solve the following problems.

CLARITY AND SPECIFICITY

Clarity in behavioral objective writing is essential due to factors such as use, communicating objectives to other interesting parties, insuring appropriate evaluation, developing useful strategies and procedures for implementing change activities. *Objectives can be written by the outcomes definitions, meeting all requirements, and still not identify the specific intent of the objective. In addition, they do not specify anything with intrinsic value that could stand alone without a supporting reference.*

Objectives not only should be clear but also should be specific; objectives should be accurate, precise, and well adapted to goal and content. Specific parts of any problem area should be studied and stated as such. Conclusions drawn from the results of an objective's evaluation should be specific in their generalizations. Each statement of an objectives goal should be clear and the method by which success in achieving the goal will be evaluated should be both clear and specific.

EVALUATION ERRORS

Lack of clarity and specificity in the writing of behavioral objectives is damaging, but not nearly so damaging as some of the problems which are appearing in many objectives that are being written without first formalizing a goal statement. These errors must be considered crucial since accountability through better evaluation is essentially what behavioral objectives are all about.

The first problem is basically one of philosophy. One text employing the outcomes approach states that "the first task in preparing instructional objectives is to list all of the specific behaviors that can be utilized to show objective attainment." Another text states "the first requirement for the teacher is to specify all activities that can be considered adequate evaluation outcomes."

The question involved here is one of priority. Literal interpretation of the quotes just cited would be that the authors feel that some intrinsic value is to be found in evaluation, that it is an end in itself, and we have already established that this is not so. As indicated earlier, evaluation has only extrinsic value and should serve as a means for determining the effectiveness of instructional strategies in helping students obtain the program goals. In other words, the evaluation processes or outcomes specified are used for the sake of goal evaluation and not the other way around. It is easy to lose sight of this relationship if specific goals are not first stated as the basis for developing evaluation outcomes.

The second evaluation problem concerns the possibility that, due to human fallacies, evaluation statements may not be appropriate for the goal when behavioral objectives are written as simple outcome or performance statements. This problem can be illustrated by examples taken from objectives written for the process standards stated for accreditation in one state department of education. A typical example of this problem which occurred in an objective written by the outcomes approach definition and later changed by the goals approach definition follows:

A. Outcomes approach:
    Given the opportunities to participate in assembly programs, testing programs, carreer days, and to read the student handbook and daily bulletin, the student can identify the procedure for obtaining counseling services by his reaction on a written multiple choice student survey instrument administered to a sample of homeroom groups representing one homeroom for each grade level.
B. Goals approach:
    For each student to have the opportunity to obtain counseling services as measured by a teacher log which specifies the dates the opportunities were provided and whether or not the student counseling services were completed.

It is immediately apparent that these two objectives specify entirely different outcome statements or measures of evaluation, thus a check of the original need and intent is necessary. Going back to the state accreditation standards, we find that they require that an objective should be written specifying that each student be given the *opportunity* to obtain counseling services. The important variable or program task, according to the way the state standards are written, is not that the students receive some behavioral change or even that they take advantage of obtaining counseling services, but they must have the opportunity.

This clear intent is seen in the objective stated by the goals approach and appropriate evaluation is provided which specifies whether or not the students actually do receive the opportunity. The outcomes approach not only missed the key variable, "opportunity," but based the evaluation upon student reaction to a chain of events rather than to the specific intent of the standard as stated.

A third evaluation problem can also be illustrated by the same example. This error involves the attempt to evaluate non-learning oriented performance objectives as though they were behavioral objectives through the use of transmitted relationships. To be a behavioral objective, the goal of the objective must include a learning task that is intended to produce a cognitive, affective, or psychomotor behavioral change in the learner.

No such intent was included in the specific statement from the state accreditation standards. The program variable in this standard or goal was to *provide an opportunity*, not measure the cognitive ability of students to give back information based upon learning experiences. A second standard or objective might well be written as a follow-up to the opportunity statement which would have as its intent a change in student behavior. This was not the case, however, with the stated standard.

Evaluation by transmitted relationship can never be direct and should be used only when there are no other alternatives available. Transmitted relationship can be seen in the following example:

a is done for the sake of b

b is done for the sake of c

thus

a is done for the sake of c

In this example, let (a) be the standard, (b) stand for opportunity, and (c) stand for behavioral change. We can now state that the standard is written for the sake of providing an opportunity. The opportunity is provided so that students will have a change in behavior. Thus the standard is also written in order to change student behavior. This indirect transfer of intent can be referred to as a transmitted relationship. It is not, however, good evaluation practice and does not represent the true goal of the objective. Not only did the outcomes approach fail in regard to clarity and specificity, and produce an evaluation error, but it also failed to distinguish between a behavioral or learning oriented objective and a non-learning oriented performance objective.

STRATEGY DEVELOPMENT

Need reduction, whether learning or non-learning oriented, is accomplished through a series of process steps such as: (1) needs assessment; (2) problem identification; (3) goal selection; (4) objective specification; (5) strategy development; and (6) evaluation.

Objectives are used to aid in the development of program strategies and evaluation. If strategies are developed from evaluation performance statements only, they are apt to represent activities designed to achieve test results rather than to promote goal achievement. Another problem is that frequently not enough information is given in evaluation components, written by the outcomes approach, to enable a teacher or program director to develop suitable strategies.

Specifically speaking, under the goals approach writing technique there are two "givens" which can be used to aid in strategy development: (1) a goal, and (2) an evaluation performance. In the outcome approach there is only one "given," an evaluation performance. *It stands to reason that the more information provided a program planner, the better he will be able to perform his function.* This is particularly true with objectives which are not written by the program implementor, but are provided from an outside source.

TEACHER MORALE

Teacher morale is perhaps the greatest problem and concern of any program based upon the development and use of performance objectives in instructional or classroom situations. This "fringe" benefit is becoming increasingly important each year as a general militancy has developed among teacher groups due to a national trend to decrease educational expenditures and a desire to have a greater voice in determining their own objectives and professional responsibilities.

A few of the problems associated with writing behavioral objectives which affect teacher morale have already been mentioned. Another problem for teachers concerns the *use* of behavioral objectives after they have been written. This problem is created by the failure of existing texts and consultant materials to explore this problem in any depth. In one state, teacher morale was affected to the point that a moratorium was called by some of the state school systems against continuing program development based upon behavioral objectives written for state accreditation standards.

Teachers and other educators are, and always have been, goals oriented. Developing formal goal statements concerning program purposes is not a new practice for most teachers, but implying goals, rather than specifically writing them, can create a vacuum in behavioral objective writing that is reflected over and over again in inappropriate educational strategies, evaluation, and in teacher frustration resulting in morale problems.

Teachers who are not trained in developing specific goal statements for each objective are easily upset when they try to write objectives as outcomes. This causes lack of clarity and specificity, and evaluation errors. It also deprives them of the satisfaction they receive through development of good goal statements which clearly identify their intent. People usually like what they do well. Teachers can write good goal statements that communicate their specific intent and give them a much firmer basis for attacking the evaluation components. The writing of behavioral objectives thus becomes more pleasant, easier to accomplish through better understanding, more accurate through clarification, specificity, and better evaluation, and much easier to check for total adequacy.

MISCELLANEOUS

Definition errors, as referred to in Chapter 2, the development of objectives utilizing taxonomies, referred to in Chapters 6 and 7, teaching for a test and problems of diagnosing student strengths and weaknesses for individualized instruction are additional problems which may be reduced or eliminated by use of the goals approach writing technique.

Historically, it has been estimated that it sometimes takes worthwhile innovative programs and materials forty to fifty years to really become known or recognized. Based upon the first inception of the idea by Ralph Tyler this period of time has already elapsed. It is important that we further examine the contributions of the outcomes and goals approaches to writing objectives in order to reduce any further time lag in identifying needed improvements in this field. Reducing the time lag is particularly important in the event that our thesis is correct in assuming that specific goal statements are necessary in behavioral objective writing.

Evaluation problems are likely to be more frequent when educators use the outcomes approach. This is due to the lack of a specific goal or stated intent, which increases the likelihood of problems occurring that are caused by the evaluation activity not truly representing an appropriate outcome of the objectives intent. The outcomes approach also increases the opportunity for evaluation problems through lack of discrimination between direct evaluation and evaluation through transmitted relationships due to the lack of flexibility in stating objectives both with and without criterion standards.

Behavioral objectives written by the goals approach decrease evaluation error by having the goal and evaluation behavior tied together so that each can be easily checked against the other at all times. The confidence produced by this cross referencing, the ease with which teachers produce goal statements, and the insights teachers obtain in deriving goals and program strategies causes considerably higher morale than does the outcomes approach.

Individual expertise by behavioral objective writers using either the goal or outcomes approach technique can either eliminate or reduce many of the current problems. The major premise in this text is, however, that everything else being equal, behavioral objectives written by the goals approach will be more functional, clearer, more specific, more appropriate, better evaluated, and will produce higher teacher morale on the average than will behavioral objectives written by the outcomes approach.

GLOSSARY OF TERMS

Competency: the statement of a goal or specific intent that identifies a desired end to be achieved through a program's activities.

Criterion-referenced Performance Objective: a performance objective that includes a criterion standard in its evaluation component in addition to a precise goal statement and an evaluation performance.

Desired Level Performance Objective: a term that is synonymous with the meaning of criterion-referenced performance objective.

Ends: the final intents for which actions or activities are undertaken. Ends have intrinsic value.

Evaluation Error: any type of philosophical, theoretical or practical error or breakdown in the quality of an evaluation performance designed to determine success in goal achievement. Errors of this type make evaluation measures less appropriate and/or needlessly establish evaluation by indirect rather than direct means.

Extrinsic Value: an instrumental goal or value that is extraneous or non-essential within itself and is sought as the means to some other goal or value. Examples are: (1) surgical operation; (2) diligent study; and (3) program strategies and evaluation.

General Goal: a global type of intent or purpose that can be broken down into multiple subgoals of a more specific nature.

General Objective: a non-specific goal or intent. An objective that does not state an evaluative performance outcome which can be used to determine the level of success in achieving the stated intent.

Goals Approach: an approach to writing performance objectives that requires a specific statement of a goal in addition to an evaluation performance outcome.

Goals Approach Module: a competency module in which the specific performance objectives have been stated by the "goals approach" objective writing technique.

Intrinsic Value: a type of good or value that is perceived to be essential and is judged worthy of being sought for its own sake or that is considered an end in itself. Examples are: (1) happiness; (2) the solution to a problem that eliminates a defined need or deficiency in something.

Learning Oriented Objective: a term that is synonymous with the meaning of behavioral objective.

Means: activities which are performed for the sake of achieving an end which gives purpose to an undertaking. Means have extrinsic value.

Minimum Level Performance Objective: a term applied to a performance objective that contains a goal and an evaluative outcome, but no success level criterion.

Non-Learning Oriented Objective: a performance objective that states a specific non-learning oriented goal and an evaluation component that is designed to measure achievement of the goals. Neither the goal nor the evaluation component are primarily concerned with changing a learner's cognitive, affective, or psychomotor behavior.

Outcomes Approach: an approach to writing performance objectives that requires only the statement of an evaluative outcome performance, criterion and condition. Does not require inclusion of a specific goal as part of the objective.

Outcomes Approach Module: a competency module in which the specific performance objectives have been stated by the "outcomes approach" objective writing technique.

Specific Goal: a specifically stated competency, intent or end that is capable of being evaluated by some form of measurement that approaches the establishment of a one-to-one relationship between the goal and its evaluation measure.

REFERENCES

1. Anita J. Harrow, *A Taxonomy of the Psychomotor Domain: A Guide for Developing Behavior Objectives.* New York: McKay, 1972.
2. Marcia M. Paulson, "Ideal Elementary Reading Program," Hillsborough County Public Schools, Tampa, Florida, 1970.

Chapter 3

WRITING LEARNING ORIENTED BEHAVIORAL GOAL STATEMENTS

> As you go through life, brother
> Whatever be your goal,
> Keep your eye upon the doughnut
> And not upon the hole.
>
> *Anonymous*

CHAPTER GOAL

For the reader to:

1. develop skill in writing unique behavioral goals.

IMPORTANCE OF GOAL SELECTION

There is no problem in documenting the importance of goal selection as a basis for the development of performance objectives. There has, however, been very little written concerning the writing of goal statements or the inclusion of specific goal intents in performance objective development.

Preparing Instructional Objectives by Robert F. Mager[1] has, in the past, been by far the most popular written material which defines and trains educators to write behavioral objectives by the outcomes approach. Mager states:

> When clearly defined *goals* are lacking, it is impossible to evaluate a course or program efficiently, and there is no sound basis for selecting appropriate materials, content, or instructional methods. . . . Too often, however, one hears teachers arguing the

accountability

relative merits of textbooks or other aids of the classroom versus the laboratory, without ever specifying just what *goal* the aid or method is to assist in achieving. . . . Unless *goals* are clearly and firmly fixed in the minds of both parties, tests are at best misleading; at worst they are irrelevant, unfair, or useless. To be useful they must measure performance in terms of *goals.* Unless the programmer himself has a clear picture of his instructional intent, he will be unable to select test items that clearly reflect the student's ability to perform the desired skills. . . . A meaningfully stated objective is one that succeeds in communicating to the reader the writer's instructional *intent.* . . . The best statement is the one that excludes the greatest number of possible alternatives to your *goal.*

Despite this goal emphasis, the book does not require goal specification as part of a stated behavioral objective and does not distinguish between the two types of performance objectives: learning and non-learning oriented.

Anderson[2] brought out the relationship between the objectives of an instructional program and the program's *goals* when he wrote, "Without well-stated objectives there is no basis for making any judgment as to whether or not the program has achieved the desired *goals.*" Riles[3] explained accountability as a process of setting *goals,* making resources available for meeting the specified *goals* and conducting regular evaluations to determine if the *goals* had been attained. He further emphasized that *goals* have intrinsic value and need to be stated in order to design a relevant evaluation of and be accountable for the program being conducted.

Individualization and evaluation are basically what performance objectives are all about when applied to classroom instruction. Evaluation is closely tied to the current emphasis upon educational accountability. The term accountability refers to assuming certain responsibilities, being evaluated for the successful achievement of these responsibilities, and being accountable to some individual or group for those responsibilities. Thus, accountability can refer to both learner oriented and non-learner oriented goals.

The importance of *goal* identification in programs of accountability has been brought out by many writers. Bano[4] says "accountability can be defined very broadly to include not only responsibility for performance in achieving *goals,* but also for selecting appropriate or relevant *goals* in the first place." Grayboff[5] pointed out that, with reference to performance contracts, "the educator sets both the *goals* and the specific objectives that are to be met through the employment of contracted services. . .the district should first state what immediate and long-range *goals* it expects to reach through execution of the performance contract. . . ."

Grayboff further indicates that in bidding for performance contracts the bidder should include a Request for a Design Solution (RFDS): "In the RFDS the performance objective, the ultimate goal each student is to reach via the contracted program, should be stated."

Lopez[6] writes on the concept of *goal setting:*

> The underlying concept of the *goal-setting* approach is simple: the clearer the idea you have of what you want to accomplish, the greater your chance of accomplishing it. *Goal-setting,* therefore, represents an effort on the part of the management to inhibit the natural tendency of organizational procedures to obscure organizational purposes in the utilization of resources. The central idea is to establish a set of *goals* for the organization, to integrate individual performance with them, and to relate the rewards system to their accomplishment. . . . *Goals* and objectives are the tangible expression of the organization's purposes. Goals are long-range, concrete end results specified in measurable terms. . . . Each major subunit — school district, division or department meets to define its *goals* and objectives and to prepare its charter of accountability. Since these *goals* and objectives can differ substantially according to the needs of specific localities, the criteria of accountability will also differ. This is the important, even crucial point that constitutes the major advantage of the *goal-setting* process. It provides for multiplicity of measures of accountability that are tailored to the needs and hence the goals of specific operation units.

Nottingham and Zeyen[7] state that the first ingredient in an action plan is the development of *goals* and that the first component of a change model is the identification of *goals.* They further state that "the indicators for the *goals* selected for emphasis must be translated into behavioral or performance objectives."

Weaver[8] indicated that something desirable for the future should be referred to as a goal. Spencer[9] was concerned with goal ambiguity. He stated:

> Virtually all educational organizations exhibit goal ambiguity. . . . The administrator, and particularly the chief administrator, of an institution or a unit of an institution can profitably place his efforts toward clarification of goals. . . . It is impossible to establish measures of accountability without first understanding not only the broad institutional goals but also specifying the objectives which are seen as contributing to the goals.

It is not the purpose of this chapter to present a detailed review of literature and research concerning goals. The persons cited represent only a minute sample from the total population of professional people who are concerned with the intrinsic values of goals and their selection and development. The references are used to support the emphasis upon the importance of goal statements in the development of worthwhile objectives.

WRITING LEARNING ORIENTED GOALS

Operationally speaking, in the context of the goals approach to writing performance objectives, the term "goals" is used to identify a competency or the exact intent or end that is desired from any course of action. Thus, a goal, competency or specific intent is used as a point of departure in the statement of complete and meaningful performance objectives. (Goal selection will be discussed later in this text.) The purposes of this chapter will be partially achieved if the reader can conceptualize goals as being the chief concern or target of any program. Goals are, more than anything else, the intrinsic ends which a program is designed to achieve, despite misconceptions created through over-statement of the value of evaluation performances.

Goal statements for learning oriented behavioral objectives are basic statements of intent which consist of several components. Each component can be checked to determine the goals communication value. Each component must be considered essential if the goal is going to succeed in communicating satisfactorily.

THE BASIC STATEMENT OF INTENT

The goal identified by the basic statement of intent is usually determined by study of information provided in written material, pre-scription by authority, or through personal observation. In each case the basic statement of intent is a written statement that represents the identification of the exact intent of a course of action that is to be followed by evaluation performances. Some examples of basic compe-tency statements are:

1. For Jane Smith to acquire a knowledge of terminology useful in solving problems in geometry.
2. For eighth-grade students to become familiar with specific facts concerning some of the world's greatest musical composers.
3. For first-year college students to know how to properly footnote library research reports.
4. For ninth-grade students to develop a knowledge of the effects of air pollution on the future economy of the United States.
5. For fifth-grade students to acquire a knowledge of the classifi-cations of the four basic food groups — milk, meat, breads, and fruits and vegetables.
6. For English teachers at Jones Junior High School to memorize the components utilized as the basic criteria for judging the quality of a behavioral objective written by the goals approach technique.
7. For ninth-grade science students to acquire a knowledge of

methodology for determining the harmful effects of smoking on one's health.

8. For twelfth-grade American History students to know why it is probably best for the national government to be democratic.

9. For Johnny Jones to be able to recall information concerning the Malthusian theory on population and subsistence.

None of these goal statements would be difficult for a teacher to identify for a particular course of study, provided they are teaching a subject in which they have expertise. In fact, some of these statements could represent the first thoughts that came to them in their lesson preparation. Grammarians will prefer to state each goal as a complete sentence. This will not, however, effect the writing technique.

THE COMMUNICATION CHECK OF BASIC GOAL STATEMENTS

The communication check of a goal's basic statement of intent serves the purpose of building the confidence of the behavioral objective developer. Also the check helps to insure that the target audience for each objective will understand the goal on, at least, a minimum level of communication. It is difficult to achieve perfection in stating goals. It is mandatory, however, that the specific intent of each goal be communicated to all persons who will eventually make use of the objective.

The communication check is made up of two components: first, the identification of the learner or learner group for which the objective is intended; second, specification of a learning task. These components may be defined this way:

LEARNER OR LEARNER GROUP

Learner or learner group means the person or persons who are expected to have a change in behavior as a result of the strategies that are used to attain the ends spelled out in the goal statement. The term "learner" can refer to any recipient of a program's instructional activities—students, staff members, lay citizens or other rational beings.

LEARNING TASK

The learning task component is made up of two parts: (1) the content area (skill); and (2) the behavioral domain classification. The content area (skill) specifies the actual content that is to be learned and later evaluated. The behavioral domain refers to use of cognitive, affective, and/or psychomotor domains of behavior:

1. Cognitive Domain: All behaviors which deal with the recall or recognition of knowledge and development of intellec-

tual abilities and skills. The best explanation of this domain presently available is probably Bloom's[10] taxonomy which divides the cognitive domain into six hierarchical levels of understanding.

2. Affective Domain: All behaviors which describe changes in interests, attitudes, values and the development of appreciations and adequate adjustment. The best interpretation of this domain is probably Krathwohl's[11] taxonomy dividing the affective domain into five behavioral levels.

3. Psychomotor Domain: All behaviors which are primarily concerned with the performance of voluntary movement activities. The best presentation of this domain is Harrow's[12] taxonomy which divides the psychomotor domain into six hierarchical behavioral levels.

This text will cover the cognitive and affective domains, in depth, in later chapters.

This chapter is primarily concerned with developing the techniques for writing goal statements. It is not important, at this point, that the learner understand or be familiar with any of the taxonomies; however, it is desirable that the learner is aware that the domains exist for purposes of communication in writing basic statements of intent. Evaluation components which will later be joined to goal statements will be, at least partly, dependent upon the behavioral domain communication that is provided in the basic goal statement.

GOAL STATEMENT CRITIQUE

Every goal statement should be given a communication check critique by its developer. Keep in mind that the only person, in all probability, who will ever critique the goal statement component of a behavioral objective is the person writing the objective. The critique is intended to increase the writer's proficiency in the specification of intents. The previously stated goals will serve as examples to illustrate a technique for critiquing goal statements.

1. For Jane Smith to acquire a knowledge of terminology useful in solving problems in geometry.
   Critique:
   A. Basic Statement
      (1) Learner—Jane Smith
      (2) Learning tasks—acquire a knowledge of terminology useful in solving problems in geometry
         (a) Content area skill—knowledge of geometry terminology
         (b) Behavioral domain—cognitive (knowledge)
      (3) Communication check—complete—basic statement of intent communicates at least at the minimum level since all of the communication checks are met

2. For eighth-grade students to become familiar with specific facts concerning some of the world's greatest musical composers. composers.
   Critique:
   A. Basic Statement
      (1) Learner group—eighth-grade students
      (2) Learning task—to become familiar with specific facts concerning some of the world's greatest musical composers
         (a) Content area skill—knowledge concerning some of the world's greatest musical composers
         (b) Behavioral domain—cognitive (knowledge)
      (3) Communication check—complete with all communication checks met
3. For first-year college students to know how to properly footnote library research reports.
   Critique:
   A. Basic Statement
      (1) Learner group—first year college students
      (2) Learning task—develop an understanding of how to properly footnote library research reports
         (a) Content area skill—how to properly footnote library research reports
         (b) Behavioral domain—cognitive (understanding)
      (3) Communication check—complete with all communication checks met
4. For ninth-grade students to develop a knowledge of the effects of air pollution on the future economy of the United States.
   Critique:
   A. Basic Statement
      (1) Learner group—ninth-grade students
      (2) Learning task—develop a knowledge of the effects of air pollution on the future economy of the United States
         (a) Content area skill—effects of air pollution on the future economy of the United States
         (b) Behavioral domain—cognitive (knowledge)
      (3) Communication check—complete with all communication checks met
5. For fifth-grade students to acquire knowledge of the classifications of the four basic food groups—milk, meat, breads, and fruits and vegetables.
   Critique:
   A. Basic Statement
      (1) Learner group—fifth-grade students
      (2) Learning task—knowledge of the classifications of the

four basic food groups—milk, meats, breads, and fruits and vegetables

    (a) Content area skill—classifications of the four basic food groups—milk, meat, breads, and fruits and vegetables

    (b) Behavioral domain—cognitive (knowledge)

  (3) Communication check—complete with all communication checks met

6. For English teachers at Jones Junior High School to memorize the components utilized as the basic criteria for judging the quality of a behavioral objective written by the goals approach technique.

Critique:

A. Basic Statement

  (1) Learner group—English teachers at Jones Junior High School

  (2) Learning task—to memorize the components utilized as the basic criteria for judging the quality of a behavioral objective written by the goals approach technique

    (a) Content area skill—components utilized for judging the quality of a behavioral objective written by the goals approach technique

    (b) Behavioral domain—cognitive (memorize).

  (3) Communication check—complete with all communication checks met

7. For ninth-grade science students to acquire a knowledge of methodology for determining the harmful effects of smoking on one's health.

Critique:

A. Basic Statement

  (1) Learner group—ninth-grade science students

  (2) Learning task—to acquire a knowledge of methodology for determining the harmful effects of smoking to one's health

    (a) Content area skill—the harmful effects of smoking to one's health

    (b) Behavioral domain—cognitive (knowledge)

  (3) Communication check—complete with all communication checks met

8. For twelfth-grade American History students to know why it is probably best for the national government to be democratic.

Critique:

A. Basic Statement

  (1) Learner group—twelfth-grade American History students

(2) Learning task—to understand why it is probably best for the national government to be democratic.
   (a) Content area skill—why it is probably best for the national government to be democratic.
   (b) Behavioral domain—cognitive (to understand)
(3) Communication check—complete with all communication checks met.
9. For Johnny Jones to be able to recall information concerning the Malthusian theory on population and subsistence.
Critique:
A. Basic Statement
  (1) Learner—Johnny Jones
  (2) Learning task—to be able to recall information concerning the Malthusian theory on population and subsistence
    (a) Content area skill—Malthusian theory on population and subsistence
    (b) Behavioral domain—cognitive (recall)
  (3) Communication check—complete with all communication checks met

It takes at least three things to write good goals and objectives: (1) A knowledge of technique; (2) subject area expertise; and (3) the ability to structure sentences. In this instance, the goals are primarily concerned with presenting the goals approach writing technique.

Another point is that the choice of verbs and/or terms such as "to understand," "to appreciate," and "to know," are not of great concern in the goal statement. Such words are of more concern when used as part of the evaluation component which converts the goal into a behavioral objective. These words and others are critical when used in objectives written by the outcomes approach. However, the specificity and support that the goals and evaluation components give to each other when they are both included in an objective automatically makes their usage clear if the objective is correctly stated.

SUGGESTED PRACTICE EXERCISES

A. Develop and critique five learning oriented (behavioral) goal statements utilizing the following format.
  1. GOAL _____

  Critique
  (A) Basic statement of intent
    (1) Learner or group _____

(2) Learning task
    (a) Content area skill _____

_____

    (b) Behavioral domain _____

_____

(3) Communication check _____

_____

GLOSSARY OF TERMS

Communication Check: a mental exercise performed by someone developing performance objectives. The check helps the performance objective writer to develop greater proficiency in stating their specific intents in goal statements. In addition the communication check aids in clarifying and making evaluation outcome performance statements more specific.

REFERENCES

1. Robert F. Mager, *Preparing Instructional Objectives,* Palo Alto, California: Fearon, 1968, pp. 3–10, Passim.
2. Ronald D. Anderson, "Formulating Objectives for Elementary Science (Part 1)," *Science and Children,* Vol. 5, No. 1, September 1967, pp. 20–23.
3. Wilson C. Riles, Public Expectations, "Proceedings of the Conferences on Educational Accountability," Princeton, New Jersey: Educational Testing Service, March 1971, pp. G1–G5.
4. Steven M. Bano, "An Approach to Developing Accountability Measures for the Public Schools," *Emerging Patterns of Administrative Accountability: A Reader,* ed. L. H. Browder, Jr. (Berkeley, Calif.: McCutchan Publishing Co., 1971), p. 364.
5. Marilyn N. Grayboff, "Tools for Building Accountability: The Performance Contract," *Emerging Patterns of Administrative Accountability: A Reader.* ed. L. H. Browder, Jr. (Berkeley, Calif.: McCutchan Publishing Co., 1971), pp. 418, 420, 423.
6. Felix M. Lopez, "Accountability in Education," *Emerging Patterns of Administrative Accountability: A Reader,* ed. L. H. Browder, Jr. (Berkeley, Calif.: McCutchan Publishing Co., 1971), pp. 387–390, Passim.
7. Marvin A. Nottingham and Louis D. Zeyen, "A Commitment to Accountability," *Emerging Patterns of Administrative Accountability: A Reader,* ed. L. H. Browder, Jr. (Berkeley, Calif.: McCutchan Publishing Co., 1971), pp. 503, 504, 505.
8. W. Timothy Weaver, "The Delphi Forecasting Method," *Emerging Patterns of Administrative Accountability: A Reader,* ed. L. H. Browder, Jr. (Berkeley, Calif.: McCutchan Publishing Co., 1971), p. 178.
9. Ralph L. Spencer, "Accountability a Classical Organization Theory," *Emerging Patterns of Administrative Accountability: A Reader,* ed. L. H. Browder, Jr. (Berkeley, Calif.: McCutchan Publishing Co., 1971), pp. 90–91, Passim.
10. Benjamin Bloom, et al. *Taxonomy of Educational Objectives.* Handbook I: Cognitive Domain, New York: McKay, 1956.
11. David R. Krathwohl, *et al. Taxonomy of Educational Objectives.* Handbook II: Affective Domain, New York: McKay, 1956.
12. Anita J. Harrow, *A Taxonomy of the Psychomotor Domain: A Guide for Developing Behavioral Objectives.* New York: McKay, 1972.

Chapter 4

CONVERTING GOALS TO BEHAVIORAL OBJECTIVES

> Evaluation is purposeful only if it furnishes an estimate of the amount of success attained in achieving something more valuable than itself.
>
> *Anonymous*

CHAPTER GOAL

For the reader to:

1. develop competency in writing behavioral objectives.

In a previous chapter it was stated that a performance objective should have two components, a *goal* plus *evaluation*. Once the goal statement is established, the addition of an evaluation statement, indicating what performance will be acceptable for determining whether or not the goal is achieved, is all that remains to convert the goal into a performance objective.

Evaluation is the process of providing information through both formal and informal means that will be useful in determining goal achievement and quality. Evaluation, as used in this text, will refer to the performance (activity, behavior, or instrumentation) that will demonstrate the level of success obtained as an outcome of the activities undertaken to achieve a goal.

Learning oriented evaluation performances or activities normally fall into one of three categories: (1) oral response that requires listening to what someone will say; (2) written response, involving tests or reading what a person is able to write; and (3) voluntary movement response revealing how a person can perform. Examination and comparison of content, listening to sounds, looking at pictures and other derivations of oral, written or movement response represent evaluation possibilities for learning oriented objectives.

Once a goal has been stated, the behavioral objective developer turns his attention to identifying the type of performance — oral, written or movement — that is appropriate for use in evaluation to determine success in achieving the goal of that particular objective. Techniques include case study, interviews, normative comparison, rating scales, subjective analysis, objective testing, surveys and check lists, free response essays, personal observation of behavior, and observation of movement responses.

Evaluation statements, as in the case with goal statements, may be written in various forms. Length should not be the crucial factor but rather specificity, appropriateness and communication.

The primary concerns of evaluation are: (1) identification of the correct type of performance; (2) identification of appropriate situations in which to observe measurable performances; (3) determining proper success level criterion standards; and (4) deciding upon how to collect the desired data without contaminating the results. Each of these concerns becomes increasingly difficult to accomplish as the higher levels of cognitive and psychomotor behaviors are approached, and especially for any classification level of the affective domain.

Normal conditions for observation of overt learning behavior are frequently not available, particularly in the affective domain. Thus, information may have to be secured from student verbal behaviors, personal involvement, writing, or close association with the learning or program task under consideration. In the affective areas, the learner should not know what response is desired, or he may supply it for that reason alone.

Most evaluation of behavioral objectives will take the form of tests which attempt to determine how successful the students and/or teachers have been in achieving the intended goal of the objective. These tests may be standardized or specially constructed by the teacher or staff. In some instances, however, objective measurement may be unavailable and evaluation may have to be carried out using subjective measures, such as clinical observation or teacher judgment. In either event it must be kept in mind that the evaluation processes utilized are means to an end and have no intrinsic values of their own. In other words, tests are used for the sake of evaluation of goal achievement, and not the other way around. The evaluation of goal achievement will in some instances merely involve observation of voluntary motor movement activities. In fact, evaluation can involve the observation or measurement of any activity which indicates a change in a phenomenon that is specified by the goal statement.

Objectives can be stated for either short-term or long-range results; they can be concerned with either individual skills or large units of instruction. In either case, the statement of evaluation should reflect the type of data that will be appropriate for evaluation of the specific goal of each objective. For evaluating some instructional projects, it may be necessary to use control groups along with experimental groups to establish comparisons between the participants. If standardized tests are used, they may be best employed in long-range longitudinal or cross-sectional time studies. In this event, system norms may serve as better indicators of progress and comparisons than will the national norms. As stated in Chapter I, criterion reference measurement such as that established by the use of performance objectives should be based upon specific content. Thus, norm referenced measurement is not generally the most appropriate type, particularly if individualization of instruction is the intent for which objectives are used.

PROCESS LEVELS FOR WRITING PERFORMANCE OBJECTIVES

The development of all performance objectives including all component parts of goal and evaluation statements, may be best understood by the writing of all objectives as a three step or level process. These levels can be viewed as being taxonomic or hierarchical in their arrangement. Here are the levels outlined in sequential order.

Goal Statement. Level one consists of the basic statement of intent and check for communication. Goal statements are sometimes confused with general objectives. The difference is that goals in the context of the "goals approach" writing technique represent specific rather than general intents. The absence of an evaluation performance statement is all that prevents the goal from being considered a performance objective.

Minimum Level Performance Objectives. Level two consists of the goal statement plus a basic statement of the performance to be used in evaluation. At this level, the goal first becomes a performance objective. The objective is called a "minimum level or performance objective" because it now has the minimum performance statement to remove it from the goal level category. This level is differentiated from the higher "desired level" or criterion-reference performance objective classification by the absence of a success level criterion standard from the evaluation component.

Desired Level or Criterion-referenced Performance Objectives. Level three consists of the goal statement, a basic statement of evaluation performance, plus the inclusion of a success level criterion standard. The objective is called a "desired level objective" because it is desirable to state all performance objectives at this level if the goal is amenable to evaluation which includes an appropriate and meaningful standard of success. Desired level or criterion-referenced performance objectives may or may not include optional statements as part of the statement of evaluation performance or as part of the statement of the success level standard. Optional statements specify givens, conditions, or any other information that may be desirable to improve communication. These are not necessary or essential in many objectives.

MINIMUM LEVEL BEHAVIORAL OBJECTIVES

In Chapter 3, goal statements, the first process level, were developed for nine learning oriented objectives. From these goals minimum level behavioral objectives can be developed by adding a behavioral evaluation performance statement to each goal as follows:

1. For Jane Smith to acquire a knowledge of terminology useful in solving problems in geometry *so that when given the names of six geometric figures, she will be able to write the formulas for determining their areas.*
   Evaluation Critique:
   A. Basic statement of performance
      (1) Performance—she will be able to write the formulas for determining their areas.
      (2) Optional statement—so that when given the names of six geometric figures.

2. For eighth-grade students to become familiar with specific facts concerning some of the world's greatest musical composers *so that when given three lists including the names of ten composers, the titles of ten musical compositions, and a list of ten time periods, the students will be able to orally match name, titles, and periods of time.*
   Evaluation Critique:
   A. Basic statement of performance
      (1) Performance—the students will be able to orally match names, titles, and periods of time.
      (2) Optional statement—so that when given three lists including the names of ten composers, the titles of ten musical compositions and ten time periods.

3. For first-year college students to know how to properly footnote

library research reports. *Success will be determined by the students writing the ten basic rules established for typing, numbering, referencing, and styling books of a non-technical nature.*

Evaluation Critique:

A. Basic statement of performance

    (1) Performance—students writing the ten basic rules established for typing, numbering, referencing and styling books of a non-technical nature.

    (2) Optional statement—none

4. For ninth-grade students to develop a knowledge of the effects of air pollution on the future economy of the United States *so that when given the opportunity to view two one-hour sound films which introduce economic side effects of air pollution students will be able to recall and prepare a written list of the economic effects shown on the film.*

  Evaluation Critique:

  A. Basic statement of performance

    (1) Performance—students will be able to recall and prepare written list of the economic effects shown on the film.

    (2) Optional statement—so that when given the opportunity to view two one-hour sound films which introduce twenty-five economic side effects of air pollution.

5. For fifth-grade students to acquire knowledge of the classifications of the four basic food groups—milk, meat, breads, and fruits and vegetables, *as evidenced by their orally distinguishing between types of food by placing them under their proper food group classification categories.*

  Evaluation Critique:

  A. Basic statement of performance

    (1) Performance—the entire evaluation statement

    (2) Optional statement—none

6. For English teachers at Jones Junior High School to memorize the components utilized as the basic criteria for judging the quality of a behavioral objective written by the goals approach technique. *Success to be determined by their ability to correctly prepare written definitions for the criteria components.*

  Evaluation Critique:

  A. Basic statement of performance

    (1) Performance—the entire evaluation statement

    (2) Optional statement—none

7. For ninth-grade science students to acquire a knowledge of methodology for determining the harmful effects of smoking on one's health *as determined by their orally identifying a logical approach to the problem.*

Evaluation Critique:
A. Basic statement of performance
    (1) Performance—the entire evaluation statement
    (2) Optional statement—none

8. For twelfth-grade American History students to know why it is probably best for the national government to be democratic *as measured by the students writing their reasons for this conclusion.*
Evaluation Critique:
A. Basic statement of performance
    (1) Performance—the entire evaluation statement
    (2) Optional statement—none

9. For Johnny Jones to be able to recall information concerning the Malthusian theory on population and subsistence *as determined by his ability to prepare a written outline of the three major points of the theory.*
Evaluation Critique:
A. Basic statement of performance
    (1) Performance—the entire evaluation statement
    (2) Optional statement—none

Figure 4–1 illustrates the requirements of a behavioral objective stated at the minimum level.

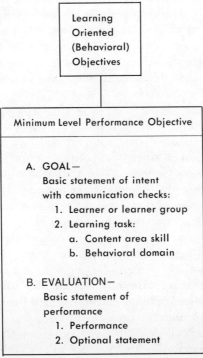

Figure 4–1 Characteristics of minimum level behavioral objectives.

DESIRED LEVEL OR CRITERION-REFERENCED
BEHAVIORAL OBJECTIVES

A desired level behavioral objective is merely an extension of a minimum level objective to include success level criterion standards. The objectives previously stated at the minimum level can be converted to desired level objectives in this way:

1. For Jane Smith to acquire a knowledge of terminology useful in solving problems in Geometry so that when given the names of six geometric figures she will be able to *correctly* write the formulas for determining the area of *each one*.
   Evaluation Critique:
   A. Basic statement of performance
      (1) Performance—she will be able to write the formula for determining the area of each figure
      (2) Optional statement—so that when given the names of six geometric figures.
   B. Success level criterion standard
      (1) Learner requirement—to correctly write each one of the six or to have 100% correct answers.
      (2) Optional statement—none.

2. For eighth-grade students to become knowledgeable about specific facts concerning some of the world's greatest musical composers so that when given three lists including the names of ten composers, the titles of ten musical compositions, and ten time periods, *seventy-five per cent of the students* will be able to orally match the names, titles, and periods of time with *at least eighty per cent accuracy*.
   Evaluation Critique:
   A. Basic statement of performance
      (1) Performance—the students will be able orally to match the names, titles, and periods of time.
      (2) Optional statement—so that when given three lists including the names of ten composers, the titles of ten musical compositions, and ten time periods.
   B. Success level criterion standard
      (1) Learner requirement—correctly match with at least eight per cent accuracy.
      (2) Optional statement—seventy-five per cent. (This is called the teacher expectancy. It enables a teacher, consultant, or other leader to establish a goal for himself in addition to the student requirement.)

3. For first-year college students to know how to properly footnote library research reports. Success will be determined *by ninety per cent* of the students writing the ten basic rules established for

typing, numbering, referencing and styling books of a non-technical nature *with at least eighty per cent accuracy.*

Evaluation Critique:

A. Basic statement of performance

    (1) Performance—students writing the ten basic rules established for typing, numbering, referencing and styling books of a non-technical nature.

    (2) Optional statement—none

B. Success level criterion standard

    (1) Learner requirement—with at least eighty per cent accuracy

    (2) Optional statement—ninety per cent representing teacher expectancy

4. For ninth-grade students to develop a knowledge of the effects of air pollution on the future economy of the United States so that when given the opportunity to view two one-hour sound films which introduce economic side effects of air pollution students will be able to recall and prepare a written list of *at least twenty of the twenty-five* economic effects which may affect the United States.

Evaluation Critique:

A. Basic statement of performance

    (1) Performance—students will be able to recall and prepare a written list of economic effects shown on the film.

    (2) Optional statement—so that when given the opportunity to view two one-hour sound films which introduce economic side effects of air pollution.

B. Success level criterion standard

    (1) Learner requirement—at least twenty of the twenty-five (or 80% correct answers).

    (2) Optional statement—none

5. For fifth-grade students to acquire knowledge of the classifications of the four basic food groups—milk, meat, breads, and fruits and vegetables, as evidenced by *ninety per cent* of the students being able to orally distinguish between *twenty* types of food and *correctly* place *each type* under the proper food group classification category.

Evaluation Critique:

A. Basic statement of performance

    (1) Performance—as evidenced by the students being able to orally distinguish between twenty types of food and place each type under the proper food group classification.

    (2) Optional statement—none

B. Success level criterion standard
  (1) Learner requirement—correctly place each of twenty types (infers 100%)
  (2) Optional statement—ninety per cent is teacher expectancy.

6. For English teachers at Jones Junior High School to memorize the components utilized as the basic criteria for judging the quality of a behavioral objective written by the goals approach technique. Success to be determined by their ability to correctly prepare written definitions for *each one* of the criteria components.
Evaluation Critique:
A. Basic statement of performance
  (1) Performance—success to be determined by their ability to prepare written definitions.
  (2) Optional statement—none
B. Success level criterion standard
  (1) Learner requirement—each one (100%) of the criteria components.
  (2) Optional statement— none

7. For ninth-grade science students to acquire knowledge of methodology for determining the harmful effects of smoking on one's health *so that when given four written statements representing possible scientific approaches to producing the needed evidence* the students will orally identify the *correct statement* that will most logically be the best approach to the problem.
Evaluation Critique:
A. Basic statement of performance
  (1) Performance—the students will orally identify the most logical approach to the problem.
  (2) Optional statement—so that when given four written statements representing possible scientific approaches to producing the needed evidence.
B. Success level criterion standard
  (1) Learner requirement—identify correct statement from four he is given
  (2) Optional statement—none

8. For twelfth-grade American History students to know why it is probably best for the national government to be democratic *so that when given a list of ten reasons for the democratic form of government, five of which are correct, ninety-five per cent* of the students will be able *to identify* in writing *four of the five correct reasons.*

Evaluation Critique:
A. Basic statement of performance
  (1) Performance — students will be able to identify in writing.
  (2) Optional statement — so that when given a list of ten reasons for the democratic form of government, five of which are correct.
B. Success level criterion standard
  (1) Learner requirement — four out of five correct from a list of ten
  (2) Optional statement — ninety-five per cent is teacher expectancy

9. For Johnny Jones to be able to recall information concerning the Malthusian theory on population and subsistence as determined by his ability to correctly prepare a written outline on *each* of the three major points of the theory *according to the subjective judgment of the instructor.*

Evaluation Critique:
A. Basic statement of performance
  (1) Performance — to prepare a written outline of the three major points of the theory.
  (2) Optional statement — none
B. Success level criterion standard
  (1) Learner requirement — correctly prepare each of three major points (100%) according to subjective judgment of the instructor
  (2) Optional statement — none

Again we have illustrated a mental critiquing exercise that each behavioral objective writer can use when developing desired level behavioral objectives by the goals approach. Note that the phrasing of the evaluation component is sometimes changed slightly when success level criterion standards are inserted into an objective previously written at the minimum level. Note, also, that there is an overlapping in word use when one critiques both the performance and the success level criterion standard. This is unimportant to the objective itself. The important thing is that the objective should communicate how successful attainment of the goal will be evaluated and should do this so well that someone who is unfamiliar with the course content could administer the test, and evaluate the learners with no help except the evaluation statement and the necessary testing materials. Goals approach objectives are a little longer than objectives which are written as outcome statements only; they should be longer since they accomplish much more. This will be explained in greater detail in the chapters devoted to writing objectives at all levels of the cognitive taxonomy.

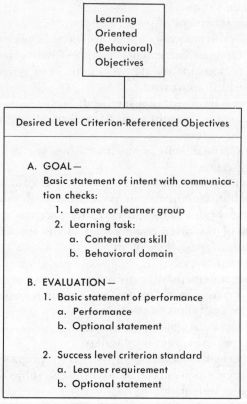

Figure 4-2 Characteristics of desired level behavioral objectives.

Figure 4–2 illustrates the requirements of a behavioral objective stated at the desired level.

USE OF VERBS IN EVALUATION

In the statement of evaluation, many words are too general or open to too many interpretations to be considered as the best alternatives for communicating the real intent of the measurement prescribed. The verb choice is not so important in the statement of the goal, since the basic requirement is that the goal statement convey meaningful information in a reasonably well-stated manner. *An entirely different situation arises when words are selected for the evaluation component.*

A performance objective writer must be concerned with the way certain words communicate better than others do. Many verbs that can be used in evaluation components are full of descriptive meaning and action while others describe inadequately, or are almost devoid of action commitment. Thus, a behavioral verb should be used that will give the best description of the performance action expected from a learner in any given situation.

Any verb that describes an action which is observable can be used. The verb should be chosen with at least three characteristics in mind: first, it should provide good descriptive and observable action commitment; second, it should aid in interpreting the behavioral level of application for which it is being used; and finally, it should be appropriate for the content or subject matter to which it will be applied.

Examples of verbs used at different cognitive behavior levels include: (1) to translate, interpret, extrapolate, rephrase and to illustrate to show comprehension; (2) to solve, apply, and demonstrate to imply the application level of understanding; and (3) to analyze, deduce, differentiate and discriminate to indicate the analysis level of understanding. There are, of course, other action words that can be used at these three levels of understanding as well as verbs that are appropriate for the knowledge, synthesis and evaluation levels of the cognitive domain. The same types of characteristics should be looked for when objectives are written in the Affective and Psychomotor domains. Chapters 6 and 7 will give a much more complete coverage of verbs used with the classification categories of a taxonomy for the Cognitive Domain.

Examples from content or subject matter are: (1) to blend, to baste, to alter and to cut (from the area of Home Economics) or, more specifically, from the subject matter of cooking and sewing; (2) to construct or design (from the areas of Mechanical Drawing or shop); (3) to write, compose or create (from the areas of English, Music, or Art); and (4) to argue, prove, compare and validate (from areas such as Law, Math, Physics, and the Natural Sciences).

Verbs employed by users of the writing technique found in this text seldom stand alone; that is, they are not used in isolation in the development of basic statements of evaluation. For example, we might indicate in one instance that a student will take a "written examination." In this case the reading audience knows that the student will be involved in a writing activity and from the goal statement of the objective they know exactly what the writing activity will be concerned with. Another person might have stated, in the same example, that the student will take a "standardized examination." Again the reading audience knows that the student will take a "written standardized examination." This statement might also specify the particular name and battery of the standardized test. In any event, the statement will not need to stand alone regardless of its sophistication or specificity because the specific goal is always included as part of the objective. This gives the "goals" approach writing technique a decided advantage over the "outcomes" writing approach.

The idea is that teachers should communicate the intent of their evaluation so well that someone who is unfamiliar with that particular subject area or class could come in, during the teacher's absence, and evaluate the class by merely reading the information stated in the behavioral objective. This assumes that the necessary evaluation given, conditions, and materials are available. If the choice of the right verb is the only way this communication can be attained, then the right verb should be used. If the mere identification of instrumentation will accomplish the same task, then the instrumentation can be used. If, however, the evaluator is totally unfamiliar with the evaluation requirements, he or she can easily develop their own evaluation instrument since the goal or specific intent of the objective is stated.

Emphasis should be placed upon verb usage, but it should not be overemphasized. Probably all that is necessary is for the teachers to use behavioral verbs that appear to be commonly acceptable by most persons without definition. If there is a choice of more than one such verb, the one that seems to best communicate the desired behavior should be used. Then by clearly relating the verb to the other component parts of the evaluation statement, little doubt will remain concerning the appropriateness of the message.

SUGGESTED PRACTICE EXERCISES

    A. Construct and make written evaluation critiques of three behavioral objectives written at the minimum level. Use the format outlined below.
      1. Objective: _____

      Evaluation Critique:
      a. Basic statement of performance
        (1) Performance _____

      b. Optional statement _____

    B. Construct and make written evaluation critiques of three behavioral objectives written at the desired level. Use the following format.
      1. Objective _____

      Evaluation Critique:
      a. Basic statement of performance
        (1) Performance _____

(2) Optional statement _____

_____

_____

b. Success level criterion standard
(1) Learner requirement _____

_____

_____

(2) Optional statement _____

_____

_____

GLOSSARY OF TERMS

Desired Level Objective: a criterion-referenced performance objective consisting of a specific goal statement of intent, an evaluative performance outcome, and a success level criterion.

Evauation Critique: a mental act that involves making a critical estimate of a stated evaluation component, including both the performance outcome and criterion, to determine whether or not the component will properly communicate to its intended audience.

Goal: a specific statement of an intent, competency or desired end to be obtained from a planned course of action.

Learner Requirement: the criterion or success level standard that determines how well a learner must achieve his evaluative performance outcome.

Minimum Level Objective: a performance objective consisting of a specific goal statement of intent and an evaluative performance outcome, without a success level criterion.

Optional Statement: any statement of information in the evaluation component of a performance objective that is included at the option of the objective writer as a means of better communicating the outcome performance requirements. This includes givens, conditions or other information that are not essential to all performance objectives.

Process Levels for Writing Performance Objectives: a logical, sequential and hierarchical order of developing performance objectives in a step by step process. The steps include: (1) statement of a goal; (2) conversion to a minimum level performance objective; and (3) adding a criterion to bring the objective up to the desired level or criterion-referenced objective classification.

Teacher Expectancy: an optional statement, representing a goal a teacher sets for himself, that may be inserted into the evaluation component of a behavioral objective.

Chapter 5

THE IDENTIFICATION
OF GOALS
(COMPETENCIES):
A SYSTEMATIC
PROCESS

Common sense is the knack of seeing things as
they are, and doing things as they ought to be done.

C. E. Stowe

One pound of learning requires ten pounds of
common sense to apply it.

Persian Proverb

CHAPTER GOALS

For the reader to:

1. become knowledgeable concerning specific terms useful in the development of a systems approach to goal identification.

2. demonstrate ability to apply systems processes in the identification of goals.

A goal represents a specific intent, competency or end, designed to eliminate a need or to solve a problem. A goal is considered to be a desired end, to have long range purpose, and to be valued for its own sake. The problem of goal specificity has prevented many programs from obtaining adequate measures of accountability and is the greatest hindrance to the development of adequate performance objectives.

State departments of education, public school systems, and local schools have frequently been hampered in developing accreditation standards, curriculum projects and general programs of accountability due to the statement of goals that are too general. A goal can be general or specific, but only specific goals can be properly evaluated. Thus, it is again evident that goal identification rather than evaluation of performance is the first and most important function in the development of performance objectives. The best method for converting general goals to specific goals is through a process of systems analysis.

In this text the area of Language Arts has been chosen to illustrate goal selection for the writing of performance objectives. The same processes used in this illustration can apply equally well to other learning and non-learning oriented problem areas. Appropriate modification will need to be made based upon the program variables that are present in each new application.

Since new applications of systems analysis will require modification and since space requirements for a complete detailed explanation of all components involved in strategy analysis procedures would go beyond the intent and purposes of this text, only a brief description of systems and the use of systems processes to develop goals and objectives for a developmental language arts program will be given in this chapter. Sufficient detail will be stated, however, to aid the reader in using this approach to make his own objectives more specific and meaningful.

INTRODUCTION TO SYSTEM CONCEPTS

A system is an organized set of compatible elements or activities representing a whole unit. Each element has its own purpose, as well as the purpose of the system, and all are related sequentially, in logical fashion. A subsystem is a set of interrelated elements or activities within a system which has the same characterstics as the system, is part of the system, and also has a purpose of its own. Subsystem components (major elements of a subsystem) have the same relationship to subsystems that subsystems have to systems. Interim components represent a further breakdown of subsystem components into smaller units. Finally, a systems analysis is a procedure for choosing from alternative approaches to a problem a procedure for presenting a problem in a reasonable, logical and understandable pattern so that it can be executed or controlled efficiently. Graphically speaking, the parts of a system could be broken down as shown in Figure 5–1.

A system may be broken down into any size, shape or number of levels. Systems can have an indefinite number of subsystems, subsystem components or interim components. The size of a system and breakdown of its components will depend upon the purpose for which it is being developed and the complexity of its content. The illustration presented in Figure 5–1 will serve adequately for the goal identification purposes of this chapter.

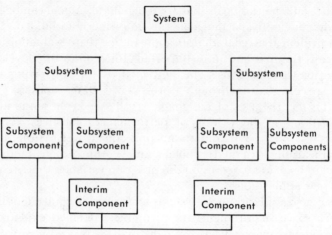

Figure 5-1 Elements of a system.

GOAL IDENTIFICATION

The process of identifying goals, hence objectives, through systems processes, is equivalent to determining specifics from various levels of abstraction through a process of division. The first goal that is established is the most general or abstract goal and it may sometimes be referred to as a mission statement.

The mission statement is the first phase in the identification of the goals. Mission goals are established to identify the overall intent or function of the program being developed. They are usually rather general in nature, a mission statement globally defines the system that is to be developed. For purposes of illustration in the area of Language Arts a goal might be stated as follows:

> For the Language Arts Curriculum Committee to develop, by September, 1974 a comprehensive program in all Communication Skill areas.

Systematic analysis assumes that the approach is based upon some systems model. The mission goal will thus represent a goal for the system. Systems are broken down into subsystems, therefore, the second goal level can be referred to as subsystem goals. The same breakdown can also be assumed for smaller system divisions. In this illustration we can break the system down into goals based upon the communication skill content areas of instruction identified under Language Arts.

Each of the content skill areas can represent a subsystem of the total system as well as be considered as a further breakdown of the project's goals. In addition, each level of goal breakdown can be converted, if necessary, to a performance objective to aid in process evaluation of the project. The breakdown of the mission goal into subsystems can be graphically shown as follows:

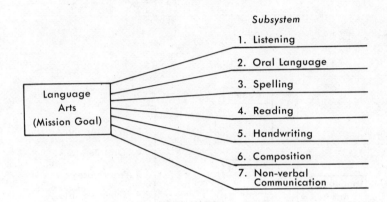

Subsystem
1. Listening
2. Oral Language
3. Spelling
4. Reading
5. Handwriting
6. Composition
7. Non-verbal Communication

Language Arts (Mission Goal)

As was the case with the mission goal, each subsystem goal could be stated like the following goal that has been stated for Reading:

> To develop, by September 1974, an improved continuous progress reading program for all students from grades one through six.

The use of systems processes may require the specification of both learning oriented and non-learning oriented performance objectives based upon the context in which they are used and the functions they will serve. The type of performance objective to be developed will depend upon whether or not the goal identified is intended to be evaluated for successful achievement by a cognitive, affective or psychomotor change in a learner or by some other performance.

In this instance we have chosen to illustrate reading as the program task or subsystem goal. Thus, this goal as stated would eventually become a non-learning oriented objective with success being determined by the document produced and criteria specified for the document rather than anyone taking a test to see if behavioral change has occurred. Similar goal statements also would be appropriate and could be written for the other six subsystems identified. Non-learning oriented goals and objectives will be handled in more detail later in the text.

Reading will continue to be the subsystem chosen to illustrate the present systematic model for goal selection and performance objective development. Goals identified under this subsystem component might include: (1) word analysis; (2) oral reading; (3) vocabulary; (4) comprehension; (5) dictionary reference; (6) attitudes; and (7) visual and auditory readiness. These subsystem goals components are shown in the following chart.

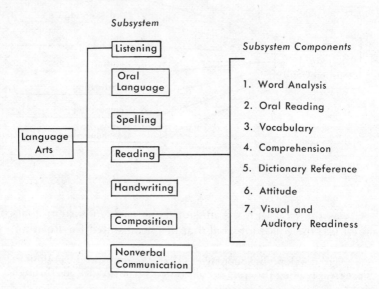

Stated more specifically, we might convert them into statements like the following two examples:

    (1) To develop and improve the skills of elementary children which are essential for word analysis.
    (2) To develop positively the attitude of elementary children toward reading as a means of expanding reading interests and literary appreciation.

Interim component reading goals represent a further division of the subsystem components to include specific skills related to each subsystem component. It is at this level that the classroom teacher becomes most interested as he plans his daily strategies. Goals identifying individual skills are plentiful and require a lot more expertise in their selection than do the broader goals previously stated.

Skill goals, referred to as interim components, under the word analysis subsystem component could include:

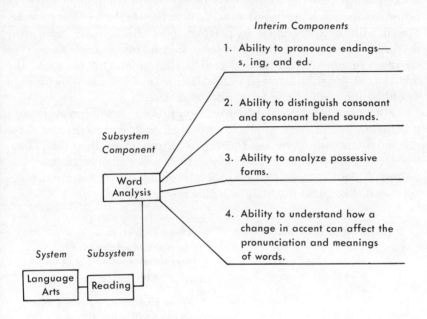

Interim Components

1. Ability to pronounce endings— s, ing, and ed.

2. Ability to distinguish consonant and consonant blend sounds.

3. Ability to analyze possessive forms.

4. Ability to understand how a change in accent can affect the pronunciation and meanings of words.

Subsystem Component

Word Analysis

System   Subsystem

Language Arts   Reading

These new goals can be stated as follow:

1. To develop in level 1 pupils the ability to pronounce *endings—s, ing,* and *ed,* when added to known words.
2. To increase in level 2 children the ability to *hear consonant and consonant blend sounds.*
3. To review and refine the ability of primary 3 students to analyze possessive forms.
4. To develop in 4th level children the ability to understand how a change in accent can effect the pronunciation and meaning of words.

In addition to these examples there are innumerable other goal statements possible for the word analysis subsystem component alone. The division of subsystem components into interim components has finally broken the system down into individual skills. The number of skill goals developed may be optional and will depend upon the contents being broken down and the use to be made of the goal statements. The goal breakdown in our present illustration would end with the identification of skill level goals. Once these goal statements have been completed, it is time to select the teaching units, state behavioral objectives and plan program activities.

One of the prevailing problems with the utilization of "outcomes approach" writing techniques is that curriculum goals are seldom broken down past the second level or subsystem component stage. In other words, goals are rarely identified at the skill level. They are replaced with simple evaluation performances which, more frequently than not, can never be traced to their specific intent, but can only be classified under a broad general goal classification. This can make the selection of program strategies and activities much more difficult than would be the case if goals are known and stated.

For example, under the "outcomes approach" definition evaluation statements would have replaced the skill goal statement and these specific intents would be lost forever to anyone other than the person who wrote the outcome statements. In some instances he too may eventually lose contact with the specific intents. Under the outcomes approach the system might appear this way:

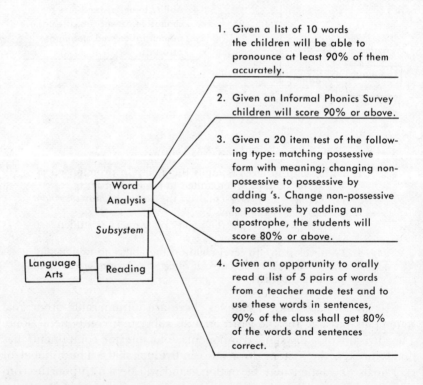

1. Given a list of 10 words the children will be able to pronounce at least 90% of them accurately.

2. Given an Informal Phonics Survey children will score 90% or above.

3. Given a 20 item test of the following type: matching possessive form with meaning; changing non-possessive to possessive by adding 's. Change non-possessive to possessive by adding an apostrophe, the students will score 80% or above.

4. Given an opportunity to orally read a list of 5 pairs of words from a teacher made test and to use these words in sentences, 90% of the class shall get 80% of the words and sentences correct.

Word Analysis

Subsystem

Language Arts

Reading

In this illustration it can be seen that it may be possible to interpret the specific intent occasionally, such as number three (ability to analyze possessive forms), but experiences have proven that in most instances these goals are lost and that the outcomes evaluation statements are not easily worked into a teacher's instructional program.

The evaluation tasks shown in the outcomes statements are not the only ones which can be used to measure success in achieving the stated goals; they may not be the best ones. There is a constant challenge to improve the selection of appropriate evaluation tasks and then to state them both clearly and specifically. Yet, they serve only the purpose of identifying an evaluation activity. In order to complete the behavioral objective statements, these evaluation performances must be combined in a meaningful manner with the corresponding goal statements. This is easily accomplished by using the previously stated behavioral objective formula: Behavioral Objective = Goal + Evaluation

By this definition, behavioral objectives for curriculum development projects involve, first of all, a systematic approach to the establishment of goals as the basis for the statement of teaching unit behavioral objectives. Thus, behavioral objectives are first concerned with goal identification, as already presented in this chapter. Once this has been accomplished, the objective statements are accomplished by simply adding evaluation components to each goal statement.

In converting goals to objectives it is beneficial to identify several evaluation performances, if possible, so that alternative approaches to evaluation may be selected by the teacher according to her teaching strategies, background experiences and contextual situation. The guideline for this task is to be sure that each outcome or evaluation task identified is appropriate for each skill goal to be evaluated and that each evaluation task selected includes the necessary specifics. Assuming the evaluation performance statements identified by the "outcomes approach" are appropriate for the previously identified interim component or skill goals, they can be used as the evaluation component under the "goals approach" behavioral objective formula. *The following examples complete the behavioral objective writing process and represent the types of objectives that should be developed for all of the subsystems of the language arts program.*

Word Analysis

1. To develop in level 1 pupils the ability to pronounce *endings — s, ing,* and *ed,* when added to known words as evidenced by the children being able to pronounce a list of 10 words with *90%* degree of accuracy.
2. To increase in level 2 children the ability to hear *consonant* and *consonant blend sounds* as evidenced by the children scoring 90% or above on an Informal Phonics Survey.
3. To review and refine the ability of primary 3 students to *analyze possessive forms* as evidenced by the students scoring 80% or above on a 20 item test of the following type: matching posses-

sive form with meaning; changing non-possessive to possessive by adding an apostrophe.

4. To develop in 4th level children the ability to understand how a *change in accent* can affect the pronunciation and meaning of words from a teacher-made test and using these words in sentences so that 90% of the class shall get 80% of the words and sentences correctly.

SUGGESTED PRACTICE EXERCISE

1. Using the systems approach outlined, develop a system which takes a broad general, global type, learning oriented goal and breaks it down into interim component or skill goals. State a minimum of three desired level behavioral objectives from the skill goals identified.

Develop this system under the following format:

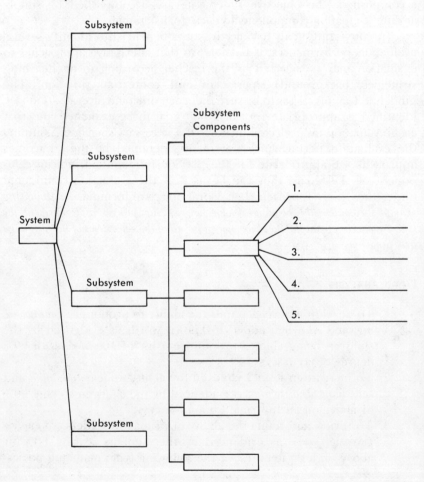

GLOSSARY OF TERMS

Interim Component: an identifiable interrelated or independent element within a subsystem component which has its own purpose as well as being a functioning part of the subsystem component, a subsystem and a system.

Mission Goal: Synonymous with mission statement.

Mission Objective: A global type of performance objective composed of a mission statement (goal) plus an evaluation component specifying what outcome will be acceptable for determining success in achieving the mission.

Mission Statement: A precise statement that represents the overall intent of a total program or system.

Subsystem: An identifiable network of interrelated or independent elements within a system which is a functional part of that system and also has a purpose within itself.

Subsystem Component: An identifiable network of interrelated or independent elements within a subsystem which has its own purpose and is also a functioning part of the subsystem and system.

System: A master plan composed of an organized set of compatible elements, representing a whole unit, each element having its own purpose as well as a purpose for the system and all elements being related sequentially in logical order.

Systematic Analysis: A process for analyzing and presenting a problem in a reasonably logical and understandable pattern.

Chapter 6

INTRODUCTION TO WRITING BEHAVIORAL OBJECTIVES AT DIFFERENT COGNITIVE CLASSIFICATION LEVELS

> To know by rote is not knowledge; it is only a retention of what is entrusted to the memory.
>
> *Montaigne*

CHAPTER GOALS

For the reader to:

1. acquire an understanding of the technique for writing behavioral objectives at the knowledge level.
2. develop an understanding of the knowledge classification level of Bloom's[1] Taxonomy of Educational Objectives: Cognitive Domain.
3. develop skill in writing behavioral objectives at the knowledge level of the cognitive taxonomy.

The principal concern of Chapter 6 will be to present a method for using the "goals approach" writing technique to enable educational practitioners to write better objectives for different classification levels of *The Taxonomy of Educational Objectives: Cognitive Domain.* This taxonomy identifies and defines six levels and twenty-one sub-categories of cognitive understanding. None of the classification levels are defined behaviorally, but sufficient information is provided to enable a behavioral objective writer to determine the behavior required at each level. In addition, sample verb lists that can be used in developing evaluation components for behavioral objectives are provided.

The cognitive domain taxonomy is divided into two parts. The first part deals with simple memory knowledge and the second part shows a concern for complex behaviors, abilities or skills. It is anticipated that most students or teachers who are learning to write behavioral objectives will apply their first efforts to the memory knowledge category and then later move into the more complex behaviors as they become more proficient in writing. This text was prepared with that thought in mind. The idea of learning the writing technique using, initially, simple memory knowledge objectives, is probably good, and to be expected, but it is equally important that writers of objectives for curriculum development programs gradually learn to define and measure the more complex abilities and skills.

The cognitive taxonomy is based upon the premise that there are several types or levels of cognitive thinking or understanding. Writers of behavioral objectives must, therefore, plan learning strategies upon the various levels if learning is to be properly focused and implemented.

Two basic problems are encountered in writing behavioral objectives using a taxonomy as a guideline. First, it is virtually impossible to write behavioral objectives in the complex behavior categories which can be legitimately classified into one category which is mutually exclusive of all other categories. This difficulty arises because each of the higher levels of understanding requires the learner to be able to understand or think at each of the lower levels. This problem gives the "goals approach" writing technique a distinct advantage over the "outcome approach" technique. "Outcomes approach" users have only an evaluation component to communicate the manner of response and type of thinking to be required of the learner. "Goals approach" users can specify the taxonomic category first in the goal statement and then reinforce the communication in the evaluation component. An example is:

> *Outcomes Approach:*
> Given a choice of the proper comparison criteria, students will be able to orally describe correctly, based upon teacher judgment, the relative advantages and disadvantages of the Spanish and American systems of government.

The intent of this outcomes objective could range from the application to the evaluation level of the taxonomy. If the students had previously learned how to properly select comparison criteria and the emphasis of the objective is interpreted as applying this knowledge to the comparison of the two systems, the objective could be classified as application. If the objective is primarily intended to show the ability to break down the two systems into their component parts in order to compare them, the objective could be classified as analysis. If, however, the intent of the objective, according to the teacher's judgment, is to organize the component parts into a total system or to place judgments upon the qualities of the two systems, then the correct classification of the objective would be synthesis or evaluation, respectively.

> *Goals Approach:*
> For twelfth-grade American History students to be able to *compare* and *evaluate* the Spanish and American systems of government so that, given the proper evaluative criteria, students will be able to orally describe correctly, based upon teacher judgment, the relative advantages and disadvantages of each of the two systems and *judge* their effectiveness.

The use of the goal statement as part of the objective has now taken away all doubt concerning the intent of this objective. The specific intent is now known to be "to compare or evaluate." This information allowed the writer to replace "comparison criteria" in the evaluation component with "evaluative criteria" which reinforces the taxonomic level. In addition, the statement "judge their effectiveness" was added to fulfill the evaluation requirement of the goal statement.

A comparison of one objective written by the two techniques emphasizes the fact that the goals approach objectives can be more effective in respect to clarity, specificity, reduction of evaluation component errors, and, generally speaking, represent more meaningful or worthwhile statements. This, in turn, aids the student and complements the instructor causing a reduction in teacher morale problems resulting from the obfuscation produced by the use of evaluation components alone. This example points out the fact that the intent of the objective must not only be clearly defined to the learner, but the learner must have received prior training in how to think and communicate his thoughts at the level the objective is stated.

Although this first problem of clarity or communication is real and must be of some concern to the teacher it should not pose any real threat to the writing of the objective. There is no intrinsic learning value in placing any objective into one of the taxonomy categories or into another. Regardless of its taxonomic classification, it is the learning or understanding that take place that are important. The teacher should remain primarily concerned with the thinking requirements placed upon the students, his or her strategies for accomplishing the goal of the objectives through instructional experiences, and planning evaluative activities which will be appropriate in determining student successes or failures.

A second problem to consider in the development of cognitive objectives both with and without use of the taxonomy is that of the objectives' importance or appropriateness. In other words, objectives must be appropriate for both individuals and groups, and be meaningful rather than trite. For example, students have many differences which teachers must keep in mind if they are to teach diagnostically. Some objectives may be stated for all students in a group; other objectives should be designed with an eye to individual student differences as well as competencies.

Figure 6–1 emphasizes possible relationships between taxonomic

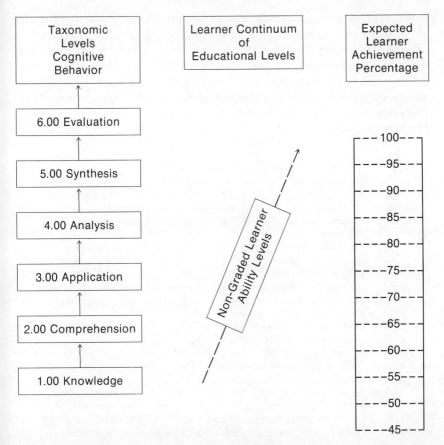

Figure 6–1 Flexible relationships between levels of cognitive behavior, educational ability levels, and achievement percentage.

cognitive behaviors, learner educational levels, and the use of percentages in establishing success level standards.

This figure reveals that students, regardless of age or grade, represent many educational ability levels. Thus, behavioral objective writers should take these individual characteristics and abilities into account in the development of learning oriented objectives. The cognitive behavior levels are shown beginning with simple memory understandings and moving progressively to more complex understandings. The choice of the behavioral level is one way to individualize instruction. The achievement level chosen for student success requirements is also optional so that a teacher's group expectancy and the individual student requirements may be adapted to fit each individual or group that is concerned.

The flexibility created by the potential for interplay between the six cognitive classification levels, student differences, and achievement percentage requirements can be a significant factor in determining the appropriateness of any objective for its target audience or for purposes of individualization. It can also be a creative challenge for the teacher. The basic importance of the objective will be established primarily by the selection of the specific intent of the goal statement and the adequacy of the evaluation component to determine success. The following examples illustrate two applications of this flexible approach to statement of objectives.

(1–a) To help twelfth-grade English students *acquire knowledge useful in the analysis and evaluation* of TV programs so that when given a list of twenty criteria, ten of which have been previously taught in class, students can correctly select for use 90 per cent of the criteria to which they have already been exposed.

(1–b) To help twelfth-grade English students *acquire skill in the analysis and evaluation* of TV programs so that when given the proper evaluation criteria, 75 per cent of the students can, in a written essay, break a given program down into its component parts and correctly *evaluate* the program as a whole, utilizing all of the evaluation criteria.

(2–a) To develop the basic skills and concepts of seventh grade students in solving problems dealing with operations in rational numbers as determined by a test of 25 problems devised by the teacher on which *85% of the students* will *achieve scores of 90%* or better.

(2–b) To develop the basic skills and concepts of seventh-grade students in solving problems dealing with operations in rational numbers as determined by a test of 25 problems devised by the teacher on which *80% of the students* will *achieve scores of 75%* or better.

In example (1–a) the student has been given an objective that is in the knowledge category since the goal only requires him to remember or recall information that he has previously learned. Example (1–b), which restates the goal, has been written at a much higher level, evaluation. Both the goal and evaluation component require students to break down something new into its component parts and then to make judgments concerning them. These two examples illustrate how objectives can be changed to accommodate learners at different educational levels.

Examples (2–a) and (2–b) illustrate another method for adapting behavioral objectives to learners with different educational levels. This time the change is through the manipulation of percentage figures used to indicate both the teacher expectancy and student requirement. In the first example the teacher expectancy was eighty-five percent and the student requirement was ninety percent. The second example lowered the teacher expectancy to eighty percent and the student requirement to seventy-five percent. Again it may be assumed that the differences in the two objectives, which could have been written and utilized by the same teacher, were intended to compensate for differences in learner educational levels.

In summary, we find that Figure 6–1 represents three basic methods for accounting for individual or group differences by using the taxonomy approach to the development of behavioral objectives in the cognitive domain. *First, change the level of cognitive behavior. Second, change either the teacher expectancy or learner requirement or both. And third, change any combination of cognitive behavior and expected achievement percentages.* This is accomplished by changing the specific intents in the goal statements and by changing the performance and criteria standards in the corresponding evaluation components.

Another relationship that can be ascertained from Figure 6–1 is that students with lower educational ability levels are likely to be unable to cope with many of the higher levels of cognitive behavior. Thus, it is likely that, with certain of these students, more emphasis will need to be placed upon the acquisition of knowledge level objectives than on the more complex skills. This is because the knowledge understandings are needed as tools to be utilized in the more complex skill thinking situations. Students at all educational levels are capable of handling some of the more complex types of objectives and should be given the opportunity to cope with them. It must be assumed, however, that the higher the learner's educational level, the more potential he has for problem solving and other complex skill assignments. Thus, a teacher should write all of this behavioral objectives to fit his group of students and each individual student in so far as possible.

This does not mean that lower ability level students have only knowledge level objectives. They, too, need objectives to develop skills and abilities, but the number of higher level behavioral objectives must, in part, depend upon a student's ability and readiness to cope with a particular level of understanding in relationship to a particular content area.

A teacher's primary commitment to the use of the classification levels of a taxonomy is that of doing justice to himself and his students. Textbook materials appear to be most frequently utilized in preparing behavioral objectives at the simple knowledge or memory level. *Almost any concept can, however, be presented at other levels than memory or knowledge provided the teacher will take the time to plan the activity.* Cognitive objectives can be very difficult or very easy to achieve at any of the six levels. This will depend upon how they are stated, what activities are involved, and how well the students have been prepared for the evaluation experience they will encounter. The behavioral change expected of the student definitely will be dependent upon the level at which the objective is written.

OBJECTIVES BASED UPON KNOWLEDGE, RECALL OR MEMORY

Objectives based upon knowledge, recall, or memory may be considered to be concerned with understanding in its simplest form. "Knowing," in this sense, has often been referred to as rote memory. Information obtained through memory is useful in its own right, but it is even more important for its usefulness in serving as the necessary tool for development of higher levels of understanding.

Memory knowledge does not involve the use of the higher thought processes. As previously indicated, however, it is necessary as a storage bank for learners to call on in the development of intellectual abilities and skills. Naturally, learners may be able to cope more easily with objectives stated at the knowledge level since they are by definition less complex. This does not mean that all objectives at the higher levels are more difficult to attain than objectives stated in the simple recall category. There can be both difficult and easy objectives written at any level of knowledge.

Slow students, as stated previously, generally do not memorize information as easily as do average or advanced students; therefore, the slow student's storage bank of recall information will be substantially less than that of the more academically talented students, and he will not be as well prepared to succeed in accomplishing the goals of the objectives stated at the higher level of knowledge. He will nevertheless need the opportunity to develop some competency at reasoning within the limits of the upper levels of understanding. There is probably no known method for determining what percent of a student's objectives should be at the simple knowledge level, and what percent should encompass more complex behaviors. Any percentage established would also be relative to the subject area and other variables. Probably the greatest weakness of too much concentration on the knowledge category is that memory learning is the most easily forgotten and may cause a teacher to neglect the development of the student's other intellectual processes.

Some psychologists and educators have had a tendency to downgrade cognitive understanding or knowledge at the memory level. Statements have been made which insinuate that all knowledge may be useless which cannot be used in some way. In other words, unless knowledge is used in demonstrated thinking activities requiring understanding at the comprehension through the evaluation levels, it has no meaning. Persons who hold to that theory too rigidly may eventually come into conflict with some constituents of the affective domain. Knowing without using knowledge in a demonstrated or literal sense could be important in the development of interests, appreciations and self-concept.

Bloom's taxonomy continuum at the knowledge level may be viewed in Figure 6–2.

CLASSIFICATION SUB-CATEGORIES	GENERAL DEFINITION	ACTION WORDS FOR EVALUATION
1.10 – *Specifics*	The ability to recall by	To outline,
1.11 – Terminology	memory. To bring into mind	distinguish,
1.12 – Specific facts	appropriate materials,	memorize,
1.20 – *Ways and means of dealing*	knowledge of specifics	recognize,
with specifics	and universals, to recall	relate, tabu-
1.21 – Conventions	methods processes, struc-	late, identify,
1.22 – Trends and sequences	tures, setting and patterns.	name, order,
1.23 – Classifications and categories	Is primarily concerned with	define, recall,
1.24 – Criteria	the psychological process	list, write,
1.25 – Methodology	of remembering and being	acquire
1.30 – *Universals and Abstractions*	able to furnish the stored	
in a field	up knowledge in orderly	
1.31 – Principals and generalizations	fashion when needed.	
1.32 – Theories and structures		

Figure 6–2 Sub-category knowledge behavior levels identification. (Adapted from information presented in Bloom's *Taxonomy of Educational Objectives: Cognitive Domain.*)

In Chapter 4, the minimum and desired level behavioral objectives were developed as being representative of sub-category objectives of the knowledge classification level. They will be reviewed again at this point to help the reader further conceptualize the development of objectives by a taxonomy.

1.10 – SPECIFICS

1.11 – TERMINOLOGY:

For Jane Smith to acquire a knowledge of terminology useful in solving problems in geometry, so that when given the names of six geometric figures she will be able to correctly write the formulas for determining the area of each one.
Critique:
A. Goal
  1. Learning task
      (a) Content area skill – knowledge of geometry terminology
      (b) Behavioral domain – cognitive at 1.11 knowledge level (knowledge of terminology)
B. Evaluation
   Performance must be representative of how success can be determined for the specific learning task specified in the goal with reference to both content and level of cognitive behavior. This is true for all of the objectives; therefore, the evaluation components at the knowledge level will not be critiqued again.

1.12 – SPECIFIC FACTS:

For eighth-grade students to become familiar with specific facts concerning some of the world's greatest musical composers so that when given three lists including the names of ten composers, the titles of ten musical compositions, and ten time periods, seventy-five percent of the students will be able to orally match the names, titles, and periods of time with at least eighty percent accuracy.
Critique:
A. Goal
  1. Learning task
      (a) Content area skill – familiarity with some of the world's greatest musical composers
      (b) Behavioral domain – cognitive at 1.12 knowledge level (knowledge of specific facts)

1.20—WAYS AND MEANS OF DEALING WITH SPECIFICS

1.21—CONVENTIONS:

For first-year college students to know how to properly footnote library research reports. Success will be determined by ninety percent of the students writing the ten basic rules established for typing, numbering, referencing and styling books of a non-technical nature with at least eighty percent accuracy.
Critique:
A. Goal
   1. Learning task
      (a) Content area skill—how to footnote library reports.
      (b) Behavioral domain—cognitive at 1.21 knowledge level (this skill can be considered a convention although the word convention was omitted)

1.22—TRENDS AND SEQUENCES:

For ninth-grade students to develop a knowledge of the effects of air pollution on the future economy of the United States so that when given the opportunity to view two one-hour sound films which introduce economic side effects of air pollution, students will be able to recall and prepare a written list of at least twenty of the twenty-five economic effects which may affect the United States.
Critique:
A. Goal
   1. Learning task
      (a) Content area skill—effects of air pollution on the future economy of the United States
      (b) Behavioral domain—cognitive at 1.22 knowledge level (knowledge of effects of—future implies a trend, but evaluation component helps this one out although it still may remain in a "gray" or unclear area concerning its sub-category classification)

1.23—CLASSIFICATION AND CATEGORIES:

For fifth-grade students to acquire knowledge of the classification of the four basic food groups—milk, meat, breads, and fruits and vegetables, as evidenced by ninety percent of the students being able to orally distinguish between twenty types of food and correctly place each type under its proper food group classification category.

Critique:
A. Goal
   1. Learning task
      (a) Content area skill—knowledge of four basic food groups
         —milk, meat, bread, and fruits and vegetables
      (b) Behavioral domain—cognitive at 1.23 knowledge level
         (knowledge of classifications)

1.24—CRITERIA:

For English teachers at Jones Junior High School to memorize
the components utilized as the basic criteria for judging the quality
of a behavioral objective written by the goals approach technique.
Success to be determined by their ability to correctly prepare written definitions for each one of the criteria components.
Critique:
A. Goal
   1. Learning task
      (a) Content area skill—components utilized for judging the
         quality of a behavioral objective written by the goals
         approach technique
      (b) Behavioral domain—cognitive at 1.24 knowledge level
         (memorize components used as basic criteria)

1.25—METHODOLOGY:

For ninth-grade science students to acquire a knowledge of methodology for determining the harmful effects of smoking for one's
health so that when given four written statements representing
possible scientific approaches to producing the needed evidence,
the students will orally identify the correct statement that will
most logically be the best approach to the problem.
Critique:
A. Goal
   1. Learning task
      (a) Content area skill—harmful effects of smoking on one's
         health
      (b) Behavioral domain—cognitive at the 1.25 knowledge
         level (knowledge of methodology)

1.30—UNIVERSALS AND ABSTRACTIONS IN A FIELD

1.31—PRINCIPLES AND GENERALIZATIONS:

For twelfth-grade American History students to know why it is
probably best for the national government to be democratic so

that when given a list of ten reasons for the democratic form of government, five of which are correct, ninety-five percent of the students will be able to identify in writing four of the five correct reasons.

Critique:

A. Goal
  1. Learning task
     (a) Content skill — why it is probably best for the national government to be democratic
     (b) Behavioral domain — cognitive at 1.31 knowledge level (knowledge or understanding of principles and generalizations)

1.32 — THEORIES AND STRUCTURES:

For Johnny Jones to be able to recall information concerning the Malthusian theory on population and subsistence as determined by his ability to correctly prepare a written outline on each of the three major points of the theory, according to the subjective judgment of the instructor.

Critique:

A. Goal
  1. Learning task
     (a) Content area skill — Malthusian theory on population and subsistence
     (b) Behavioral domain — cognitive at the 1.32 knowledge level (understanding a theory)

It is not necessary for an instructor to intentionally develop behavioral objectives for each sub-category of a cognitive classification level. *The important ingredients are that he focus on an appropriate goal and state it so that the student's evaluation response will indicate competency at the level of understanding that is desired.* For example, the sub-category knowledge level identifications were not as important as was the fact that all evaluation performances required that the student respond with only recall or memory type of information.

The identification of the specific intent of the behavioral domain classification level does, however, become significant when the learner is to change his response from one level to another. An illustration of this might be seen by retaining the same content area identification in the learning task while at the same time raising the cognitive domain level to a higher classification. This, in turn, would require a restatement of the evaluation component so that the required learner response will remain appropriate.

Communication always remains important. There was no problem in identifying the sub-category classification intent at the 1.11, 1.12, 1.23, 1.24, 1.25, 1.31, and 1.32 levels in the example objectives because key words were used in the basic statement of intent in the goal. The 1.21 and 1.22 sub-categories, however, do not communicate as easily since there was no effort made to incorporate key words, but the goal and evaluation were stated to imply these sub-categories. It is not difficult to imagine the difficulty of providing adequate communication if the evaluation component had to do the entire job alone. The next chapter on writing objectives for higher level skills and abilities will further emphasize and clarify the problems of communicating goals and evaluation performances.

SUGGESTED PRACTICE EXERCISES

Develop and make written critiques of six knowledge level behavioral objectives with not more than two of the objectives being stated for any one sub-category classification level. Use the following format:

I. Objective: _____

_____

_____

_____

_____

    A. *Goal Critique:*
      1. Basic statement
        a. Learner _____

        b. Learning task _____

_____

_____

          (1) Content area skill_____

_____

_____

          (2) Behavioral domain and classification level_____

_____

    B. *Evaluation critique:*
      1. Basic statement of performance
        a. Performance_____

_____

        b. Optional statement _____

_____

      2. Success level criterion standard

        a. Learner requirement _____

        b. Optional statement _____

GLOSSARY OF TERMS

Cognitive Classification Levels: the six hierarchical classification levels of thinking and understanding presented in the book entitled *The Taxonomy of Educational Objectives: Cognitive Domain.*

Cognitive Taxonomy: Bloom's *Taxonomy of Educational Objectives: Cognitive Domain* published by David McKay Company, Inc.

Intellectual Abilities and Skills: refers to the top five hierarchical classification levels of the cognitive taxonomy. These levels require understanding that involve comprehension, application, analysis, synthesis, and evaluation.

Learner Continuum: a colloquialism generally referring to students as having a continuous and uninterrupted range of skills, abilities, readiness and other traits.

Taxonomic Classification: an expression that refers to the hierarchical classification level as defined by the cognitive taxonomy. In writing behavioral objectives, a person may also refer to taxonomic classification with reference to taxonomies for the affective and psychomotor domains.

REFERENCES

1. Bloom, Benjamin, et al. (ed.) *Taxonomy of Educational Objectives: Cognitive Domain,* New York: David McKay Company, Inc., 1956.

Chapter 7

WRITING BEHAVIORAL OBJECTIVES FOR SKILL AND ABILITY LEVELS OF THE COGNITIVE TAXONOMY

> The essence of knowledge is, having it, to apply it; not having it. . . .
>
> *Confucius*

> What is not fully understood is not possessed.
>
> *Goethe*

CHAPTER GOALS

For the reader to:

1. develop a comprehension of the skill and ability classification levels of Blooms's taxonomy of educational objectives: cognitive domain.

2. develop skill in writing behavioral objectives at the complex behavior and skill levels of the cognitive taxonomy.

Educators must eventually make decisions concerning the problem of just what is the purpose of formalized education. Is the purpose of instructional efforts to teach a few basic skills, overt behaviors, and test item performances, or to develop more fully a child's cognitive, affective and psychomotor resources? Developing and evaluating individual knowledge and skills is relatively simple. However, the development and evaluation of a child's total resources is quite different.

The present conceptualization of performance contracting is an excellent example. It is easy to contract for the improvement of a clearly defined goal, but it is another matter entirely to contract for all of the purposes that are generally considered to be important if a learner is to become a whole, complete, well-adjusted, productive member of society.

Another key question which must be answered is: should educational goals be primarily concerned with content coverage or designed to teach behaviors such as problem solving or critical, creative, and reflective thinking? The rationale and philosophy upon which the "goals approach" to writing performance objectives is based were partly developed due to a belief in the dual purposes of educational goals: instruction in content and the cognitive process levels of understanding.

The *Taxonomy of Educational Objectives* refers to these behaviors as "intellectual abilities and skills." Other authorities have referred to these behaviors as "critical thinking," "creative thinking," "reflective thinking," and "problem solving."

Good's (1959) *Dictionary of Education* defines these terms as follows:

Critical thinking: Thinking that proceeds on the basis of careful evaluation of premises and evidence and comes to conclusions as objectively as possible through the consideration of all pertinent factors and the use of valid procedures from logic.

Creative thinking: Thinking that is inventive, that explores novel situations or reaches new solutions to all problems, or that results in thoughts original with the thinker.

Reflective thinking: Active, persistent, and careful inquiry into any belief or knowledge claim in the light of the grounds and evidence that support it and the further considerations to which it leads.

Problem solving: A process employed by all people at all levels of maturity of discovering or educing new relationships among things observed or sensed.

The five levels of cognitive understanding referred to as intellectual abilities and skills (comprehension, application, analysis, synthesis, and evaluation) are not nearly as distinct as they appear in written or graphic form. Many objectives will be hard to identify within one distinct category, but will often appear to overlap one or more categories. Usually they can be correctly defined into one or more of the five classification levels. This process can be greatly enhanced through specific identification in the goal statements. A general rule for classifying objectives is to refer to a behavioral objective's classification level according to its highest level of use.

COMMUNICATION PROBLEMS:

No objective communicates enough specific information to insure that there will be no error made in the performance required for evaluation. This is particularly true in writing objectives for the more complex behaviors. Behavioral objectives written in the cognitive domain usually result in an evaluation performance involving some form of test. It is difficult to communicate in one short statement exactly what type of thinking will need to occur in order to correctly answer the prescribed test questions. The only sure method would be to build a sample test question into the objective itself.

For example, an evaluation component might state that *students will be able to derive or analyze orally each of two correct conclusions from a list of five statements.* It is obvious that the performance will be oral, that the success level criterion is one hundred percent accuracy and that the two correct answers must come from a list of five possible alternatives. The performance statement implies that the learners will need to be able to think at the analysis level. We cannot be sure of this, however, unless we see the test question that will be used. In fact, the two correct answers might be selected through memory.

Any person is naive who thinks behavior will be changed just because a teacher or behavioral objective writer knows the vocabulary associated with a taxonomy. In fact, in many instances, persons using terms such as analysis, synthesis or application have been found not to have the slightest conception of the types of behavioral responses necessary to fulfill the requirements of these words. Anyone can verbalize a behavioral term, but at this date few people understand their true meanings and they often are used by coincidence.

In order to be sure that the evaluation performance which will be required is appropriate or at the analysis level as implied, the complete objective would need to be written so that the entire problem will be identified. This could be accomplished, and sometimes is, by objective statements such as the following example.

Problem Identification Communication Style:

For twelfth-grade students to be able to think analytically in order to discover essential parts of a communication so that when given the following question they will orally derive each of the two correct conclusions:

Two basketball coaches were comparing the advantages and desirability of using the ball control versus the fast break type of basketball system for their college team. Coach number two stated he thought that: "(1) basketball fans would not want to see the ball control style of play; (2) he personally did not object to ball control; (3) most of his players had very quick movements; and (4) recruitment of player talent would be more difficult if the scores of the games were low. Therefore, the answer to which system we use is obvious."

Which two of the following statements are the logical conclusions to be drawn from the coaches' discussion based upon the comments of coach number two?

(a) Ball control basketball is unsatisfactory for use with college level teams.

(b) Spectators will not attend ball control games regularly even if the team wins most of its games.

(c) The team would probably be successful using the fast break system.

(d) The future success of the basketball program of that college might be jeopardized if the team played ball control.

(e) The fast break system of play is more successful than the ball control style.

Critique:

A. Goal

   1. Basic statement of intent—

      For twelfth-grade students to be able to think analytically in order to discover essential parts of a communication

   2. Communication check

     (a) Learner group—twelfth-grade students

     (b) Learning task—

        (1) Content area skill—essential parts of a communication

        (2) Behavioral domain—cognitive at the analysis level.

B. Evaluation

   1. Basic statement of performance—

      So that when given the following question, students will orally derive each of the two correct conclusions

     (a) Performance—orally derive

     (b) Optional statement—so that when given the following question

   2. Success level criterion standard—

     (a) Learner requirement—each of two correct conclusions

     (b) Optional statement—none

The inclusion of the test question enables the reader to determine that the thought processes required to select the two correct answers will go far beyond simple knowledge or recall and that his performance may require understanding at the analysis level. This problem was designed to require the learner to separate the problem situation into its component parts in order to select the elements which would lead to the two correct conclusion statements. There are times when a teacher will wish to convey complete information concerning the requirements of an objective; when this is the case, it is the teacher's option to determine the amount and specify the information to be provided. The use of this type of objective provides great flexibility as well as precise communication of the objective's intent. Instructional strategies of teachers should include training of the learner to think logically in order to be able to achieve the objective successfully.

The problem identification style of writing objectives requires more writing time. The time necessary to construct the test, however, would be reduced accordingly. In most practical situations objectives should be written in what can be referred to as an implied problem style.

There are two alternative implied problem styles available for use, the "goals approach" and the "outcomes approach" writing techniques. The following two examples show how the same objective might be stated using each of the approaches:

IMPLIED PROBLEM COMMUNICATION STYLE:

(1) Goals approach —
    For twelfth-grade students to be able to think analytically in order to discover essential parts of a communication so that when given an appropriate question and a list of five statements, students will be able to orally derive two correct conclusions.
(2) Outcomes approach —
    Given an appropriate question and a list of five statements, students will be able to orally derive two correct conclusions.

Obviously, there is a communication loss in the outcomes approach objective. Both objectives have lost the advantage gained from having the sample test question available. This, however, due to the defined requirements of the goals approach definition, is the only loss of communication that occurs in the first example.

The second example not only loses the information provided by the test question, but, in addition, it loses the entire basic statement of intent which includes both the specificity of the content area skill and the behavioral domain classification level. True, an objective statement written by the "goals approach" is a little longer, but length of the objective is relatively unimportant. Does it matter whether or not a student's list of objectives fills one printed page or two? No, but the loss of clarity and specificity can be disastrous. It is also true that much more information can be added to outcomes approach *performance* statements than are required by outcomes approach definitions, but in so doing, provided the information were equal, the objective writer would no longer be stating objectives by the definition used for the "outcomes approach," but would have adopted a type of goals approach.

WRITING OBJECTIVES ACCORDING TO THE TAXONOMY CLASSIFICATIONS OF COMPLEX BEHAVIORS AND SKILLS

Complex behaviors and skills refer to all learning levels beyond the simple knowledge category. These behaviors require learners to organize problems, recognize appropriate material, and use basic memory knowledge and materials in solving new problems.

Obviously, no one person can have complete knowledge, thus, each individual must be able to take that which he has and apply it to new situations. For this reason basic memory knowledge is taught in order that a student may store in his memory bank the most useful information available, based upon past experience, and then attempt, through objectives based upon intellectual abilities and skills, to apply this limited knowledge to new problem situations.

The implied problem style of writing behavioral objectives will be used in the development of the examples in this chapter. The reader should keep in mind, however, that in the development of behavioral objectives for his specific area he may wish to use the problem identification method. Bloom's *Taxonomy of Educational Objectives* is the reference used for the naming and numbering of the basic classification categories of the objective hierarchy and for the sub-categories involved in each classification. In addition, some descriptive information under each classification has been adapted from this same reference.

2.00 – COMPREHENSION:

Objectives written at the comprehension level require learners to paraphrase, translate or restate ideas from one form of communication to another. The basic idea is to be able to discuss or communicate intelligently about something. The cognitive taxonomy places comprehensive behavior into the following three categories:

CLASSIFICATION SUB-CATEGORIES	GENERAL DEFINITION	ACTION WORDS FOR EVALUATION
2.10 – Translation 2.20 – Interpretation 2.30 – Extrapolation	The ability to be able to take a written or oral communication and make use of its ideas without relating it to other ideas or materials or seeing fullest meaning.	TO: group, form, translate, read, examine, discuss, classify, interpret, describe, illustrate, prepare, estimate, represent, make summary, explain, measure, transform, change, restate, rephrase, reorder, draw, demonstrate, infer, predict, determine, extend, extrapolate

2.10 – TRANSLATION:

In translation a learner receives a specific communication and then converts the message into another form of communication. Conversion could convert one language into another language, replace words by meaningful symbols, or refer to any other conversion from one form of communication to an equivalent form. In some respects translation must become an individualized type of overt response. This is because each person receives the message, at least in part, within the framework of his own field of reference and within the context to which he is exposed to the communication. Thus, he will react or translate each communication to some other communication based upon his particular concept of parallel or equivalent form.

Example Objective:
To develop the ability of fourth-grade arithmetic pupils to translate the relationships between Roman numerals and Arabic numerals so that, when given a set of twenty Roman numerals, the students will be able to *transform* them, in writing, to Arabic numbers with at least eighty percent accuracy.

Critique:
A. Goal
   I. Basic statement of intent –
        To develop the ability of fourth-grade arithmetic pupils to translate the relationship between Roman numerals and Arabic numerals
      a. Learner groups – fourth-grade arithmetic pupils
      b. Learning task – translate the relationship between Roman numerals and Arabic numerals
         1. Content area skill – Roman numerals and Arabic numerals
         2. Behavioral domain – cognitive at the 2.10 comprehensive level (translate the relationships)
      c. Communication check complete – Basic statement of intent communicates at least at the minimum level
B. Evaluation
   I. Basic statement of performance –
        So that when given a set of twenty Roman numerals, the students will be able to transform them, in writing, to Arabic numbers with at least eighty percent accuracy
      a. Performance – transform them in writing to Arabic numbers
      b. Optional statement – so that when given a set of twenty Roman numerals

II. Success level criterion standard
  a. Learner requirement—eighty percent accuracy
  b. Optional statement—none
Rationale—This objective requires recall information and, in addition, the ability to convert symbols of one form into another form without losing the true meaning of either one.

2.20—INTERPRETATION:

The second category of comprehension, interpretation, involves the understanding of a communication with reference to the relative arrangement of its parts. The learner must not only be able to translate a communication but also must be able to comprehend the individual component parts of the communication and their interrelationships, as well as the overall meaning of the communication. If necessary, the learner must be able to rearrange the components of the communication in his mind in order to make the meaning of the message more realistic to himself.

Example Objective:

For seventh-grade science students to develop their ability to make the *interpretations* necessary to identify and classify a mixed collection of rocks as determined by the students achieving an accuracy of seventy-five percent in placing all the rocks into three basic rock classification categories.

Critique:

A. Goal
  I. Basic statement of intent—
      For seventh-grade science students to develop their ability to make the interpretations necessary to identify and classify a mixed collection of rocks
      a. Learner group—seventh-grade science students
      b. Learning task—to make the interpretations necessary to identify and classify a mixed collection of rocks
        1. Content area skill—mixed collection of rocks
        2. Behavioral domain—cognitive at the 2.20 level of comprehension (interpretations to identify and classify)
      c. Communication check—complete

B. Evaluation
  I. Basic statement of performance—
      As determined by the students achieving an accuracy of seventy-five percent in placing all the rocks into three basic rock classification categories
      a. Performance—placing rocks into three basic rock classification categories
      b. Optional statement—none

II. Success level criterion standard
    a. Learner requirement — an accuracy of seventy-five percent
    b. Optional statement — none
Rationale — The objective requires that the students perform an activity that can be objectively measured. They are required to classify rocks according to specific categories.

2.30 — EXTRAPOLATION:

A third category of comprehension is extrapolation. Extrapolation refers to a type of inference or going from one proposition considered to be true to another whose truth is believed to follow from that of the former. The learner must not only understand what the communication is, but should also be able to infer some logical consequences that might be expected to occur as a natural result of the truth of the first communication. Extrapolation requires that the learner use every phase of the comprehension category. In other words, he must recall, translate and interpret the message as well as be able to project implications based upon the truth of the proposition.

In research, sample populations are chosen from the total population or the entire universe of a particular variable. Based upon the results obtained in study of the sample population, certain implications, or generalizations, are made for the entire universe. There are, however, limitations to the number and amount of the generalizations that can be made from any given research data. Thus, it is important that the learner involved in extrapolation recognize these limits. As is the case with statistical probability, generalizations based upon samples cannot be assumed to be positive truths, but only what appears logical to infer, based upon the information available when the inference is made.

Example Objective:
For eleventh-grade economics students to learn to *extrapolate* in order to interpret the budget expenditures of the federal government so that when given a line chart showing the major budget expenditures of the federal government for the past twenty years, and ten conclusions that are purported to have been drawn from the chart, five of them correct, eighty-five percent of the students will be able to orally explain without error the five correct conclusions.
Critique:
A. Goal
    I. Basic statement of intent —
        a. Learner group — eleventh-grade economics students
        b. Learning task —
            1. Content area skill — budget expenditures of the federal government

2. Behavioral domain — cognitive at the 2.30 level of comprehension (to extrapolate)

B. Evaluation

  I. Basic statement of performance —

    a. Performance — to orally explain five correct conclusions

    b. Optional statement — so that when given a line chart showing the major budget expenditures of the federal government for the past twenty years and ten conclusions that are purported to have been drawn from the chart, five of them correct

  II. Success level criteron standard —

    a. Learner requirement — explain without error (100% accuracy)

    b. Optional statement — eighty-five percent of the students is teacher expectancy

Rationale — In this objective the student is furnished the truth about federal government expenditures for the past twenty years in the form of a simple line chart, From this information he is expected to estimate the consequences or implications that the information has with reference to the ten variables shown in the conclusions. His ability to extrapolate information is revealed by the number of correct conclusions he is able to explain by his own interpretation of the data. This objective involves recall, translation, interpretation and extrapolation.

Based upon traditional programs of public school education and the wide variety of possible testing methods available for use in the comprehension classification of information, it can be assumed that the comprehension category probably is the most widely used for purposes of education of all of the cognitive domain levels. What is the case and what should be the case, however, may be two different things. This point will be further illustrated under the section on synthesis.

3.00 — APPLICATION:

Student activities based upon objectives written at the application level must involve the solving of new problems. Such objectives require the learner to demonstrate his ability to make a transfer of his knowledge and experiences through comparison, implication, or numerically. Substitution of new numbers in a math formula or problem does not qualify as application because the problem is not a new one, but just different numbers.

This may be done through problem solving activities in which the student will independently apply his own knowledge and skills. An illustration of implied application might be taken from the old quotation "Why don't you practice what you preach?" The implication here is that, through instruction or experience, certain information has been stored and verbalized and that it should be used in true life situations.

Application is similar to comprehension but more complex. In comprehension the learner can demonstrate or use an abstraction to solve a problem when he is familiar with it or understand it well enough to follow a prescription for its use. Application requires that the learner be able to take a new problem or one that is basically unfamiliar to him and establish relationships which will enable him to select suitable methods for solving the problem. This involves the ability to explain ideas through problem solving techniques, to work with an entire concept as well as with its component parts, and, in addition, the learner must be able to develop his own strategies or procedures of operation rather than just follow someone else's previously established directions and instructions.

Application is applying knowledge to problems encountered in everyday life. For example, certain teachers may attend a workshop on behavioral objectives. They might then, through application, utilize this training in developing behavioral objectives for their pupils. The application level requires that the learner also be able to use the knowledge and comprehension levels of understanding.

In classroom situations there are many opportunities for a learner to demonstrate application or problem solving abilities that will demonstrate his ability to transfer knowledge and experiences. In accounting, students learn many definitions, relationships and other operations on a day-by-day basis. Then on a final examination, they may be given a practical problem that is new to all of them and they will be expected to bring into focus the knowledge and comprehension understanding they have obtained and to apply them to the new problems in such a manner that it will be correctly solved. The same type of illustration would be true in geometry, music, art, and almost any other area of instruction.

Bloom's taxonomy specifies that there are at least two types of variations in application problems, those that require changes in behavior and those requiring new situations. Behavior application variations include the demonstration of the choice of correct principles and their use, the demonstration and recording of the processes involved in problem solving solutions, the solving of a problem and recording of a correct abstraction. New situations may include the use of simulated situations, use of materials that are new to the learners, and/or the application of new solutions to established situations. It is highly recommended that the reader study the *Taxonomy of Educational Objectives* and Sanders'[3]

Classroom Questions: What Kind? for further insights into the application category. The taxonomy only lists one category for application as follows:

CLASSIFICATION SUB-CATEGORIES	GENERAL DEFINITION	ACTION WORDS FOR EVALUATION
3.00—Application (No sub-categories for application classification)	The ability to take a problem, idea, principle, or theory, and use it in a new situation.	TO: solve, choose, use, predict, relate, apply, diagram, draw, demonstrate, transfer, develop, employ, classify

Two examples of objectives written in the application category are:
(1) To apply the art and skill of planning and preparing meals by girls in the tenth-grade Home Economics Class so that when given ten principles for meal planning and preparation, seventy-five percent of the girls will be able to plan, cook and serve a prescribed new meal without error, based upon a written report of the procedures used in applying the ten criterion principles and subjective teacher judgment.
Critique:
A. Goal
    I. Basic statement of intent
        a. Learner group—girls in the tenth-grade Home Economics Class
        b. Learning task—
            1. Content area skill—planning and preparing meals.
            2. Behavioral domain—cognitive at the 3.00 application level (to apply the art and skill)
B. Evaluation
    I. Basic statement of performance
        a. Performance—to plan, cook, and serve a prescribed new meal and make a written report
        b. Optional statement—so that when given ten principles for meal planning and preparation
    II. Success level criterion
        a. Learner requirement—without error and subjective teacher judgment
        b. Optional statement—seventy-five percent of the girls is teacher's expectancy
    Rationale—This objective requires that the learner record the choice of correct principles and demonstrate their use in planning, preparation and serving of a meal. In addition, the learner applies new solutions to a common

situation since she has never prepared that particular meal before.

(2) For eighth-grade students to demonstrate their ability to make correct application of instructions on how to use the globe so that when given instructions on a teacher made grid and other necessary data, students can, on the first try, locate and diagram with better than seventy-five percent accuracy the movement of hurricane Inga at every six hour interval over a three day period.

Critique:

A. Goal
    I. Basic statement of intent
        a. Learner group — eighth-grade students
        b. Learning task —
            1. Content area skill — use of the globe
            2. Behavioral domain — cognitive at the 3.00 application level (to make correct application of instructions).

B. Evaluation
    I. Basic statement of performance
        a. Performance — locate and diagram the movement of hurricane Inga.
        b. Optional statement — so that when given instruction on a teacher made grid and other necessary data.
    II. Success level criterion
        a. Learner requirement — seventy-five percent accuracy on the first try.
        b. Optional statement — at every six hour interval over a three day period.

Rationale — This objective requires the learner to select and record information and solve the problem with reference to determining the path hurricane Inga will follow. Since they must do this on the first try, the objective implies that it is a new situation to which previous knowledge and comprehension must be applied in order to obtain the solution.

4.00 — ANALYSIS:

Objectives in this classification require conscious effort on the part of the learner to identify component parts of a whole and to understand the reasons for their relationships. Both teachers and students need training in understanding and using objectives in this category. As was true in the previous three categories, the use of category four also requires the utilization of categories one, two, and three.

Briefly stated, analysis is concerned with the meaning or intent of subject matter as shown by a person's ability to consciously understand the breakdown of material and the relationship of its parts. The ability to break down a communication into its parts does not imply that the person so doing can also determine the values of the parts or that he is able to make evaluative judgments. Analysis objectives are sometimes rather difficult to distinguish from comprehension and application objectives due to the fact that they contain many of the same ingredients. They do, however, require more formal solutions and a more consciously organized approach to the solution of each problem. The analysis classification is divided into the following three sub-categories:

CLASSIFICATION SUB-CATEGORIES	GENERAL DEFINITION	ACTION WORDS FOR EVALUATION
4.10 – Analysis of Elements 4.20 – Analysis of Relationships 4.30 – Analysis of Organization	Ability to break down a communication or material into component parts and detect the relationship of the parts and the way they are organized. Analysis is intended to clarify or make ideas and relations more explicit.	TO: distinguish, contrast, detect, derive, identify, organize, classify, translate, discriminate, discover, recognize, differentiate, see reasons why, see relationships, detect categories, see cause and effect, deduce, categorize, and analyze.

4.10 – ANALYSIS OF ELEMENTS:

Analysis of elements requires the learner to be able to recognize the important elements of any communication whether they are explicitly stated, implied, or inferred. Such elements can relate to facts, values, or intents. The learner should be able to distinguish between facts, values, or intents. The learner should be able to distinguish between facts and assumptions. He should be able to discriminate among any number of variables that may be of importance to any given communication.

An example of an objective written in the elements category is:

For behavioral objective workshop participants to develop the ability to analyze and critique desired level behavioral objectives so that given ten correctly stated desired level behavioral objectives, the participants will be able to derive in writing a complete critique of the goal and evaluation components in each of the objectives with one hundred percent accuracy.

Critique:
A. Goal
    I. Basic statement of intent
        a. Learner group — behavioral objective workshop participants.
        b. Learning task —
           1. Content area skill — desired level behavioral objectives.
           2. Behavioral domain — cognitive at the 4.10 level of analysis (to analyze and critique).
B. Evaluation
    I. Basic statement of performance.
        a. Performance — to derive in writing a complete critique of the goal and evaluation components.
        b. Optional statement — so that given ten correctly stated desired level behavioral objectives.
    II. Success level criterion.
        a. Learner requirement — one hundred percent accuracy in each of the objectives.
        b. Optional statement — none
Rationale — In this objective the learner is required to recognize the important elements of the ten objectives, some of which are explicitly stated such as the goal and evaluation components. These, in turn, must be broken down into their communication check components. This example is a simplified illustration of analysis based upon the identification of elements.

4.20 — ANALYSIS OF RELATIONSHIPS:

Analysis of relationships requires that the learner not only be able to differentiate among the elements of the objective, but also be able to determine some of the important relationships between these elements. This may involve the ability to determine which elements are essential to the communication being made and which elements are optional, or merely used to clarify and extend the message. An example of analysis involving relationships is:

To develop the ability of graduate students in the College of Education to be able to analyze relationships necessary for the performance of basic research activities utilizing the scientific process so that when given a list of twenty statements, each representing a potential step necessary for performing scientific research, the students will be able to analyze in writing, and without error, each of the six correct statements that are essential to the scientific process method and organize them in correct sequential order based upon their application to problem solving situations.

Critique:
A. Goal
    I. Basic statement of intent
        a. Learner group—graduate students in the College of Education
        b. Learning task—
            1. Content area skill—basic research activities utilizing the scientific process.
            2. Behavioral domain—cognitive at the 4.20 level (analyze relationships).
B. Evaluation
    I. Basic statement of performance
        a. Performance—analyze and organize sequentially in writing.
        b. Optional statement—so that when given a list of twenty statements, each representing a potential step necessary for performing scientific research.
    II. Success level criterion
        a. Learner requirement—six correct statements without error and correct sequential order.
        b. Optional statement—none
Rationale—The objective requires that the learners be able to analyze the twenty given statements and also the scientific process so that they can derive the correct six statements. In addition, they must show how the six statements relate to each other by organizing them according to their application in problem solving situations.

4.30—ANALYSIS OF ORGANIZATIONAL PRINCIPLES:

Objectives written in this classification of analysis involve a concern over the form, pattern, structure, or organization of the information that is being presented. Included in this category would be objectives which are concerned with the purposes, points of view, attitudes, techniques, and so forth, of a composer, artist, or author, as portrayed in his creations. In addition, this type of objective could be concerned with how the elements of some works are organized to produce the whole work. The ability to understand and appreciate art and music through recognition of their forms and patterns would be appropriate in this category of objectives.

Example Objective:
For twelfth-grade students to demonstrate their ability to distinguish organizational characteristics and to analyze scientific research studies so that when given ten different completed research reports,

the students will be able to orally discriminate between the form and organization of the information presented, according to pre-determined criteria, and place the reports in rank order with eighty percent accuracy.

Critique:

A. Goal

    I. Basic statement of intent—

        a. Learner group—twelfth-grade students

        b. Learning task—

            1. Content area skill—specific research studies

            2. Behavioral domain—cognitive at the 4.30 analysis level (distinguish organizational characteristics and to analyze).

B. Evaluation

    I. Basic statement of performance

        a. Performance—to orally discriminate and place in order.

        b. Optional statement—so that when given ten different completed research reports.

    II. Success level criterion—

        a. Learner requirement—rank order with eighty percent accuracy.

        b. Optional statement—none

Rationale—This objective requires the students to analyze the organization and structure of the entire research reports. In addition, the student must be able to establish some insights concerning the points of view and biases of the person who performed the investigation as well as to understand the techniques of research used in his study.

5.00—SYNTHESIS:

The synthesis category could be referred to as the level of understanding designed for creativity. This level requires learners to create a whole from component parts, or to be original and imaginative by producing a unique product. Creativity in this sense does not mean that a learner will develop something original that has never been accomplished before, but rather that he will create something that is new to himself. Objectives written at this level must give the students an opportunity to be individually independent and not too structured in their thinking. To create, compose, organize or construct, the students must have the opportunity to do their own planning.

Creative classrooms are adventurous and can cause exciting individual learning. Thus, the creative educational philosophy places a child's emotional and social development along with his cognitive learning as the central core in the educational process. Evaluation of activities in the creative classroom will be more difficult, but the goals and objectives in this area are so valuable that creative activities should be implemented with or without evaluation sophistication.

Synthesis objectives require students to use their imagination. Since even small children can be imaginative, it must be assumed that some objectives for children at any grade level should fall into the synthesis category. Naturally, early elementary children should be given simple synthesis objectives whereas secondary children can perform more complex assignments. Synthesis objectives are designed to make children inquisitive and when properly presented to and pursued by the children they are apt to be highly motivational.

Synthesis objectives are similar to, and extend from, objectives involving comprehension, application and analysis. The main difference is that they are more complete and require originality. In addition, comprehension, application and analysis objectives usually specify certain limitations in the elements of the whole variable about which they are concerned. Synthesis, however, may allow the student to build a product that requires no limitation upon the variables or resources that are used.

An important consideration that must be kept in the mind of teachers writing behavioral objectives in the synthesis area is that the students should be allowed a great degree of freedom of response in solving the goal of each objective. It is true that not all synthesis objectives will be designed to give students complete creative expression, but many will. In the case of creative expression which is restricted by specific limitations set by the objective, it is appropriate to supply objective criteria that will place the objectives in the classification of desired level or criterion-referenced behavioral objectives. If, however, the objective allows the student to be completely creative without conforming to any previously established standards, then the objective may be free from criterion statements and will probably be more appropriately stated in the minimum level behavioral classification.

Sanders stated this position very well when he described the difference between convergent and divergent thinking. If one follows his line of reasoning, objectives requiring convergent thinking require that a student converge on one correct answer after having been given several possible alternatives. This correct answer would, therefore, be known and standards for acceptance of the student's response could be readily established. Divergent thinking objectives are not only shown to offer a variety of alternatives, but can include many different answers, all of which could be correct. A simple example of a goal requiring divergent thinking is for the parents of a new born baby to select the child's name. They may choose from thousands of possible names and any name they select can be considered to be the correct one. The point is that convergent thinking objectives should be written at the desired level behavioral category. Evaluation of synthesis objectives may often be subjective since in many cases there is no standard measure of creativity.

The goals approach to writing behavioral objectives requires the statement of a specific goal and the evaluative behavior that will be necessary to determine how successful the learner is in reaching the desired goal. The goal introduces the concept of creativity and the evaluation component substantiates the goal's intent. Sanders has developed a taxonomy of questions for interpreting the cognitive domain. These taxonomy questions, with the proper adaptations, could serve as excellent guidelines for writing the evaluation components of any behavioral objective in the cognitive domain. In brief, he indicates that synthesis or creativity can be shown by written or oral reports as follows:

(1) by questions giving the learner the opportunity to practice originality;

(2) by questions requiring the learner to derive abstract relationships;

(3) by the right questions asked when involved in a new problem solving situation;

(4) by the development of goal hypotheses in problem solving situations;

(5) by use of the imagination in choosing between alternative actions in a given situation;

(6) by planning appropriate actions or activities for specific assignments; and

(7) by designing simple experiments which are new to the learner and which require imagination and creativity.

The taxonomy sub-categories are:

CLASSIFICATION SUB-CATEGORIES	GENERAL DESCRIPTION	ACTION WORDS FOR EVALUATION
5.10—Production of a unique communication 5.20—Production of a plan or proposed set of operations 5.30—Derivation of a set of abstract relations	The ability to put elements or parts together to form a united organization or whole. To arrange and combine things in such a way as to constitute a pattern or structure not clearly there before.	TO: construct, write, compose, organize, tell, relate, create, design, plan, transmit, perform, originate, predict, modify, document, propose, specify, produce, derive, develop, combine, synthesize, formulate

5.10 — PRODUCTION OF A UNIQUE COMMUNICATION:

Production of a unique communication is primarily concerned with the communication of one's ideas, feelings, or thoughts to someone else in a manner that is most meaningful to both persons. The variables of major concern in the production of unique communications are: (1) the effects to be achieved; (2) the nature of the audience; (3) the method of communication (writing, speaking, etc.); and (4) the resources which are at the disposal of the person attempting to communicate. The taxonomy indicates that objectives in this category should reveal: (1) skill in the organization of ideas in writing; (2) ability to creatively write a story or essay; (3) ability to write poems or simple musical compositions; and (4) ability to make extemporaneous speeches or to tell experiences effectively.

Examples of objectives written at this synthesis level are as follows.

A. MINIMUM LEVEL BEHAVIORAL OBJECTIVE:

For graduate school music major students to develop ability and skill to write unique verse and compose unique music so that when given six class periods for creative writing and music composition, eighty percent of the students will write a verse of 100 words and compose the music necessary for a three minute cantata that will reflect their own feelings and ideas.

Critique:

A. Goal
  I. Basic statement of intent —
    a. Learner group — graduate school music major students.
    b. Learning task —
      1. Content area skill — write unique verse and compose unique music
      2. Behavioral domain — cognitive at the 5.10 level of synthesis (creativity through writing unique verse and composing unique music)

B. Evaluation
  I. Basic statement of performance —
    a. Performance — write a verse and compose the music
    b. Optional statement — so that when given six class periods for creative writing and music composition
  II. Success level criterion standards —
    a. Learner requirement — none
    b. Optional statement — eighty percent of the students

Rationale — In this objective, stated at the minimum behavioral level, the students are to show creative skill in writing a verse, to write a musical composition, and to show skill in organizing their ideas and statements. It is classified as a minimum level behavioral objective since the learner requirement or criterion measure of performance was omitted. The learner requirement is necessary in order for an objective to be classified as a desired level or criterion-referenced behavioral objective. The teacher expectancy percentage cannot stand alone to represent the success level to be achieved by the learner.

B. Desired Level Criterion-Referenced Behavioral Objective:

For graduate school music major students to develop the ability and skill to compose unique music so that when given a written verse of 100 words and four class periods for creative composition, eighty percent of the students will compose a written three minute cantata which meets at least seventy-five percent of the criterion standards previously established by the music instructor for acceptance of musical compositions.

Critique:

A. Goal
  I. Basic statement of intent —
    a. Learner group — graduate school music major students.
    b. Learning task —
      1. Content area skill — to compose unique music
      2. Behavioral domain — cognitive at the 5.10 level of synthesis (compose unique verse — creativity).

B. Evaluation
  I. Basic statement of performance —
    a. Performance — compose a written three minute cantata.
    b. Optional statement — so that given a written verse of 100 words and four class periods for creative composition.
  II. Success level criterion standards —
    a. Learner requirement — to meet at least seventy-five percent of the criterion standards previously established by the music instructor.
    b. Optional statement — eighty percent of the students.
Rationale — The students are required to show creative skill in the organization and writing of a musical composition according to previously established criterion standards.

5.20—PRODUCTION OF A PLAN OR PROPOSED SET OF OPERATIONS:

Objectives in this synthesis category are intended to require the production of a set of plans which satisfy the requirements of a specific task. The specifics of the assignment may be furnished to the learner or he may be required to develop them himself. In either event, these criterion specifications will give the learner a measure by which to evaluate the success level of the activity he is to undertake. Objectives which furnish the criterion specification to the learner can still allow for creativity, but should always be written at the desired level behavioral objective classification. Objectives which require that the learner develop his own criterion specifications may be written in either the minimum or desired level behavioral classification.

Synthesis objectives in this category may include: (1) plans to solve a problem; (2) ability to organize a unit of instruction for a particular teaching situation; (3) ability to create alternative approaches to test hypotheses; and (4) ability to design equipment, buildings, materials, etc., according to the specific functions they must serve.

An example of an objective written in this category is:

Twelfth grade students should exhibit creativity in problem solving so that, when given a specific mission to accomplish, 90 percent of the students will be able to analyze the mission components and organize them into a written master plan that can be effectively used in achieving the desired mission. Success will be determined by the expertise and subjective judgment of the teacher.

Critique:
A. Goal
  I. Basic statement of intent
    a. Learner group—twelfth grade students
    b. Learning task
      1. Content area skill—creativity in problem solving
      2. Behavioral domain—cognitive at the 5.20 level of synthesis (organize mission components into a written master plan)
B. Evaluation
  I. Basic statement of performance
    a. Performance—written master plan
    b. Optional statements—analyze mission components and organize them
  II. Success level criterion
    a. Learner requirement—that the written master plan be approved as adequate for use according to teacher judgment
    b. Optimal statement—90 percent of the students

Rationale—In this instance, the students were required to produce a set of plans to solve problems related to carrying out a specific mission. The complete behavioral objective required the students to know, comprehend and apply information. In addition, they were required to break (analyze) the ·mission down into its component parts, know the relationships of these parts, and to synthesize them together into a whole, represented by a master plan.

5.30—DERIVATION OF A SET OF ABSTRACT RELATIONS:

According to the taxonomy, there are two different types of tasks here. First, the learner may begin with concrete data which he must bring together to classify or explain. Second, he may begin with certain basic propositions from which he must deduce other propositions or relations. The first task may be purely explanatory or require the formulation of a hypothesis that will account for or pull together all of the data that has been specified. The second task requires that the learner operate from within some prescribed boundaries such as the limits imposed by a particular theory. He has complete freedom for creativity only as long as he remains within the prescribed boundaries. Thus, the final product that the learner will develop in this category must meet strong objective standards which may be predetermined.

The development of hypotheses to be used in research projects is one example of the derivation of abstract relationships. Research is based upon certain observed data and rationale for why it should be performed.

Analysis of the important data and rationale combined with new insights submitted by the researcher are brought into focus to establish new, appropriate hypotheses that will be tested during the course of the research study. This type of creativity also would include the formulation of new theories, concepts and the ability to produce products such as mathematical discoveries. An example of a synthesis objective in the 5.30 category is:

For driver education instructors to construct new and appropriate testable hypotheses concerning factors related to automobile accidents and injuries so that when given hard statistical data concerning the accident trends in the United States for a period of ten consecutive years and twenty new hypotheses from which to choose, the instructors will orally predict correctly seventy-five percent of the hypotheses which are tenable based upon the given statistical data.

Critique:
A. Goal
    I. Basic statement of intent
        a. Learner group—driver education instructors
        b. Learning task—
            1. Content area skill—testable hypotheses concerning factors relative to automobile accidents and injuries
            2. Behavioral domain—cognitive at the 5.30 level of synthesis (construct new and appropriate)
B. Evaluation
    I. Basic statement of performance—
        a. Performance—orally predict hypotheses
        b. Optional statement—so that when given hard statistical data concerning the accident trends in the United States for a period of ten consecutive years and twenty new hypotheses from which to choose
    II. Success level criterion—
        a. Learner requirement—orally predict correctly seventy-five percent of the hypotheses
        b. Optional statement—none
Rationale—In this objective the learner is required to bring together statistical information in a meaningful manner so that he can predict hypotheses that are logically based upon the information provided. Another way to look at this objective is to envision the learner as classifying the statistical information to such an extent that he can eliminate hypotheses that do not fit the classification he has established.

The taxonomy provides a very important critique of the special problems that may be encountered in writing and testing behavioral objectives at the synthesis level. Here is a summary of those problems:

(1) Providing conditions that permit creativity or freedom of expression. This includes freedom to determine criterion specifications as well as freedom in determining other elements of the assignment.
(2) Providing time for creativity to develop and be recognized.
(3) Securing adequate sampling to insure the reliability of the product as being truly indicative of the student's ability.
(4) Evaluation by subjective standards and competent judgment (such as teacher's judgment) in complex objectives or in creative objectives where objective standards are not available or appropriate.
(5) The extent to which errors can creep into the learner's understanding of the true nature of the whole problem and its component elements.

6.00 – EVALUATION:

The highest level of understanding presented in the taxonomy is evaluation. Evaluation refers to the rendering of judgments concerning the value of various concepts relating to facts, opinions and values. This category of understanding requires the ability to use all five of the lower classifications (knowledge, comprehension, application, analysis, and synthesis). The judgments, according to the taxonomy, may be either quantitative or qualitative. Sanders indicates that the judgments may be either objective or subjective and *that many objective answers utilized in questions designed for purposes of evaluation might be more properly placed under the interpretation category. He further indicates that evaluation is apt to require some subjectivity and that subjective judgment may be preferable for the evaluation category.*

In most instances, evaluation will involve the use of some specified criteria and/or standards to determine the worth of some given variable. The major difference between evaluation and the synthesis category is that evaluation includes criterion standards and values. The inclusion of values and value judgments into the cognitive area relates the cognitive domain to the affective domain where values – interests, appreciations, likes and dislikes – are major factors.

Evaluation implies assessment; assessment implies the determination of either the value or the quality of something. Quality, in turn, refers to how well something meets its own specifically defined objectives or purposes. The assumption is made that individual parameters within a single system or population may differ widely in their quality or representativeness; therefore, appropriate values, criteria, or standards should be established which can be used to compare different facts, opinions and values, in order to make judgments concerning them.

Facts, opinions and values are very different in their own right and should be treated differently. Facts can be proved to be either true or false. Opinions are usually little more than impressions that are made without any real positive knowledge. Values are the same as opinions, in that they cannot be proved true or false, but they are characteristics which are deemed to be important and indicate commitment to an idea or behavior. *Thus, the primary concern of the evaluation category is to make judgments based upon either factual information or values.*

Evaluation objectives are relatively easy to prepare but difficult to assess adequately due to the frequency with which values and value judgments are utilized. Evaluation objectives based upon facts are, of course, easier to assess objectively, but, as was mentioned earlier, they sometimes require only interpretation of information and may be better classified in the interpretation category. Many value-oriented objectives are open ended and subject to many interpretations with no one interpretation being proved any better than the others. The taxonomy divided the evaluation classification into two categories as follows:

CLASSIFICATION SUB-CATEGORIES	GENERAL DEFINITION	ACTION WORDS FOR EVALUATION
6.10 — Judgments in terms of internal evidence. 6.20 — Judgments in terms of external criteria.	The ability to make judgments about quality, values, procedures, methods, etc. by using the appropriate criteria. Ability to compare a work with established standards, to compare theories, generalizations and facts. To be able to indicate fallacies in arguments.	TO: argue, prove, assess, judge, select, evaluate, solve, weigh values, appraise, validate, decide, compare, contrast.

6.10 — JUDGMENTS IN TERMS OF INTERNAL EVIDENCE:

Evaluation in this category is concerned with internal criteria such as logical accuracy and consistency. In this category, the learner is apt to be required to analyze a piece of work and then make judgments about its quality based upon its purpose and the criterion standards that have been established specifically for use in evaluation of that particular piece of work.

Other examples of judgments in terms of internal evidence are: (1) the ability to uncover either logical fallacies or consistencies on controversial issues; (2) the ability to judge something based upon the criteria set up for its existence; and (3) the ability to judge the accuracy of a communication based upon the evidence that is available at the time. An example of a behavioral objective in this category is:

For sophomore students to be able to make logical judgments on current world problems so that when given a one page problem statement on birth control, four possible conclusions, and six statements, the students will orally choose, without error, the two correct conclusions and the two correct statements which support the logic of the conclusions selected.

Critique:

A. Goal
    I. Basic statement of intent —
        a. Learner group — sophomore students
        b. Learning task —
            1. Content area skill — current world problems
            2. Behavioral domain — cognitive at 6.10 level of evaluation (make logical judgments)

B. Evaluation
  I. Basic statement of performance
    a. Performance—to orally choose
    b. Optional statement—so that when given a one page problem statement on birth control, four possible conclusions and six statements from which to select the two that support the logical accuracy of the conclusions chosen
  II. Success level standards—
    a. Learner requirement—choose without error two correct conclusions and the two correct statements
    b. Optional statement—none
Rationale—In this objective the learner must be able to analyze the problem statement, form conclusions from this analysis and then make judgments concerning which of the conclusions and logic statements are appropriate. This involves the ability to determine logical fallacies and the accuracy of the communication based upon the available evidence.

6.20—JUDGMENTS IN TERMS OF EXTERNAL CRITERIA:

This category requires that the learner know a certain subject area, or phenomenon, so well that he can organize or apply acceptable criteria which are appropriate for judging the variable in question. He must be able to demonstrate his ability to analyze the phenomenon in question before evaluating it. The task to be performed should represent a new idea to which the learner can apply specific criteria. In some instances, the component parts of the idea or ideas may need to be broken down, analyzed and evaluated separately before any overall judgment of evaluation can be made. An example of judgments in terms of external criteria is:

For public school teachers to demonstrate their ability to evaluate and select an appropriate method for writing behavioral objectives, so that when given two day workshops on both the goals and outcomes approaches for writing behavioral objectives and the rationale for the use of behavioral objectives in curriculum development, seventy-five percent of the teachers will be able to analyze both methods in writing, to choose the technique most efficient for their own work, and make at least two logical oral statements in support of their own conclusions and judgment. The acceptability of the analysis, choices, and statements will be determined by the expert opinion of the instructor.

Critique:
A. Goal
    I. Basic statement of intent—
        a. Learner group—public school teachers
        b. Learning task—
            1. Content area skill—appropriate method for writing behavioral objectives
            2. Behavioral domain—cognitive at the 6.20 level of evaluation (ability to evaluate and select)
B. Evaluation
    I. Basic statement of performance—
        a. Performance—to analyze in writing, choose the technique, and make at least two logical oral statements
        b. Optional statement—so that when given two day workshops in both the goals and outcomes approaches for writing behavioral objectives and the rationale for the use of behavioral objectives in curriculum development
    II. Success level criterion standards—
        a. Learner requirement—analysis, choices, and statements must be acceptable according to expert opinion of the instructor
        b. Optional statement—seventy-five percent of the teachers is teacher expectancy

Rationale—This objective required the teachers to perform activities utilizing knowledge, comprehension, application, analysis, synthesis, as well as evaluation. The analysis and synthesis of the objective allows the teachers to compare the two techniques and, through this comparison, to make a judgment as to which one of the two was most appropriate for their own use. It might be pointed out that this objective could have very appropriately been written at the minimum level rather than the desired behavioral objective level. Since the ultimate acceptance or rejection of the standard of quality by which the objective was to be considered successful consisted, in part, of a value judgment, and since values can neither be proved nor disproved, the statement of the teacher evaluation performance or behavioral activities might have been considered as appropriate evaluation for the goal as stated.

In summarizing this chapter on complex abilities and skills several points should be emphasized. First, an instructor's only commitment to the use of the different levels of understanding is that of doing justice to himself and his students. Second, it is important that teachers be able to develop objectives at each of the six classification levels, but relatively unimportant that they deliberately attempt to write for each sub-category level. Since the categories overlap to such a great degree, and since individual perfection or expertise in interpreting the taxonomy is not likely to occur too often, this type of requirement could become self-defeating. Thirdly, textbook material lends itself best to the memory level, but almost any concept can be presented at several different levels of understanding provided the instructor will take the time to plan the activity.

The different subject areas will dictate many of the specifics to be included in the behavioral objectives written for each area. It is only by use of each of the six classifications that teachers can insure their students the opportunity to develop all the necessary understandings required to think and act adequately in solving contemporary social, economic and political problems. The taxonomy should be studied independently from this text in order to use it most efficiently.

SUGGESTED PRACTICE EXERCISES

Write and critique one desired level behavioral objective for each of the five taxonomy classification levels for complex behaviors and skills. Use the following format:

I. Objective: _____

_____

_____

_____

Critique:
A. Goal
    I. Basic statement of intent —
        a. Learner —_____
        b. Learning task —
            1. Content area skill _____

            2. Behavioral domain classification level _____

B. Evaluation
    I. Basic statement of performance —
        a. Performance _____

        b. Optional statement _____

    II. Success level criterion standard
        a. Learner requirement _____
        b. Optional statement _____

C. Rationale _____

_____

_____

GLOSSARY OF TERMS

Implied Problem Communication Style: an approach or performance objective writing format that implies the level of understanding to be required by the question that will be used to indicate learner success in achieving his goal. This format does not reveal the actual question.

Performance Contracting: a commitment by some person, group, or organization to successfully achieve certain specified behavioral results with learners in return for remuneration which is scaled to reflect the amount of success obtained.

Problem Identification Communication Style: an approach or performance objective writing format that completely identifies the objective's goal, how it will be evaluated and includes the specific questions to be answered in measuring learner success.

REFERENCES

1. Benjamin S. Bloom, et. al. (ed.) *Taxonomy of Education Objectives: Cognitive Domain,* New York: McKay, 1956.

   All references, use and applications of the terms taxonomy, sub-categories, classification levels, levels of understanding and related terms refer to this book. It is recommended that the reader purchase a copy of this taxonomy for further enlightenment on developing behavioral objectives.

2. Carter V. Good, (ed.) *Dictionary of Education,* New York: McGraw-Hill, 1959, pp. 570, 414.
3. Norris M. Sanders, *Classroom Questions: What Kind?* 1st ed., New York: Harper & Row Publishers, 1966, pp. 75–93.

Chapter 8

DEVELOPING PERFORMANCE BASED COMPETENCY MODULES

> The writer does the most who gives his reader the most knowledge, and takes from him the least time.
>
> *Sidney Smith*

CHAPTER GOALS

For the reader to:

1. comprehend the essential components necessary for the systematic development of competency modules.
2. develop skill in preparing competency modules for courses of instruction.
3. become familiar with the format and content of six competency modules that have been prepared according to the systematic approach for module development outlined in this chapter.

Perhaps the most effective way to implement performance based instruction, individualized or regular, is through the development and use of competency modules. *A competency module is a written guide intended to direct the individual learning efforts of a student or group of students in any given content area.* Modules can, in this respect, be considered to be learning tools. The basic idea of the competency module is that all instruction should be related to appropriate performance objectives and that the competency module is the vehicle or tool for organizing and implementing learning activities, materials and equipment.

There are many types of competency modules, each with common and unique components. A typical competency module may include: (1) a heading page; (2) an introduction; (3) a module outline; (4) instructions for using the module; (5) an optional pre-assessment instrument; (6) a statement of the specific goals, competencies and/or objectives to be achieved; and (7) a list of learning strategies, resources, and activities that can be pursued in order to achieve the module's objectives.

The intrinsic value of a competency module lies in the selection of goals or competencies to be achieved, stating the goals as behavioral objectives, and identifying representative strategies, resources, and learning activities. All of the rest of a module's components are developed as means to implement these components.

Some competency modules are developed as learning packets in which all of the instructional strategies, content resource material, and supplementary information are included in the module so that it can become completely self-sufficient. These learning packets can be very effective, but there are several problems that occur which should be considered before a competency module developer decides to develop a learning packet. Among these problems are the following:

1. Learning packets tend to become inflexible and repetitious in their content coverage. In other words, they can become just another textbook, changed only by a window dressing introduction and chapters preceded by performance objectives.
2. The cost of learning packets, based upon offset printing costs, can exceed book publication rates by approximately one-hundred percent on a page for page basis.
3. Most content that is placed in learning packets can be distributed just as easily as class handout material. These handout materials can be collected again after they are used if necessary.
4. Frequently learning packets are found to include much copyrighted material. Permission must be obtained from the publishing companies involved prior to the use of such material. Often a charge will be made for such permission.
5. Learning packets may lose the variety of benefits that are to be found in other multi-resource materials such as library reference, filmstrips, films, guest lecturers, and professional expertise.

Staff members in educational institutions may develop different types of modules for different content areas and instructional environments, but the best competency modules, in the long run, are those which are easiest to operationalize. This means that the modules should be direct, concise, straight, clear, and specific presentations of the goals or competencies and strategies that are needed to achieve the module's intent. Introductory and other superfluous material should be kept to a minimum.

The remaining portion of this chapter will be devoted to presentation of information that can be utilized in the development of a competency module format. This will be followed by six mini-modules that have been developed from these guidelines.

Perhaps the most crucial decisions in the development of competency based educational programs are the following:

1. Full conceptualization by all persons involved concerning the purposes of competency based educational programs and the rationale concerning why the curriculum is being developed in this manner.
2. Involvement by all faculty members concerned in the decision to undertake module development.
3. Adequate in-service training in goal setting and writing behavioral objectives.
4. A sufficient amount of time to plan, implement, elevate and revise the modules being developed before staff members are held accountable for the final product.

This writer assumes that these decisions have been satisfactorily resolved and proceeds, on that basis, to an analysis of the contents of a competency module.

Module analysis involves a quasi-systems analysis procedure designed to aid in identifying the preferred choices of module components from possible alternative selections. This should be a simple, rational approach to presenting the elements of the module in a clear, concise, systematic and logical fashion. We can consider module analysis as a system that is intended to produce an outline, or plan, representing the format and explanation of the specific modular components that will be constructed.

The module format to be used should be complete to the point that it can be utilized for individual or group study and in either classroom or independent study programs. Procedurally speaking, it must be self-sufficient in every respect. Module analysis might result in the following module components:

1. Heading Page
2. Preface, Introduction and/or Rationale
3. Operational Instructions
4. Diagnostic Pre-Assessment
5. Plans for Post-Assessment, Recycling and/or Grading
6. Statement of Specific Goals (Competencies) to be Achieved
7. Mission Objective
8. Performance Objectives
9. Learning Strategies
10. Learning Resources

1. HEADING PAGE

The heading page, the front page of a module, usually presents the major items in a module's identification, coding, specification of prerequisites and additional information considered to be important by module developers. The following information is typical of that which might be used in developing a heading page.

(a) *Module Identification:*

Should include information such as course symbol, number and name.

Example:

EDACM 690 – Individual Study and Research

(b) *Coding:*

Coding will be necessary for all modules for purposes of classification, storage, retrieval, and publication. Modules may or may not be adopted for use with computers. Among factors that may be considered in coding are: (1) module symbol, number and name; (2) departments or learning area; (3) general content area; (4) specific content; (5) learner group; (6) professional use; and (7) program needs.

Example:

A. EDACM 690 – Individual Study and Research
B. Department – Educational Administration and Supervision
C. General Content Area – Accountability
D. Specific Content – Systems Development: Educational Accountability
E. Learner Group – Graduate Students
F. Professional Use – All Educators
G. Program Needs – Both Instructional and Non-Instructional Programs

An example of the heading page that may be placed on a module that represents the specific needs of an institution follows:

NAME OF UNIVERSITY

NAME OF COLLEGE

DEPARTMENT: _____

COURSE TITLE: _____

MODULE CODING: _____

GENERAL CONTENT AREA: _____

NAME OF MODULE: _____

PREREQUISITES: _____

DESIGNED FOR: _____

DATE: _____

ADDITIONAL INFORMATION
     A. _____
     B. _____
     C. _____
     D. _____

2. PREFACE, INTRODUCTION AND RATIONALE

Immediately following the heading page there should be either a module preface, introduction, rationale or some combination of these. The purpose of this modular component is to introduce the student to the content of the module and to develop at least a general perspective of the area covered in the module.

If rationales are utilized, they should be designed to give short and concise overall viewpoints of the conditions, principles, or rules underlying the need for and use of the module's specific content. The preface and/or introductions are used to state brief and concise purposes and functions of the specific content to be covered. They may also include a brief coverage of other types of information which have been carefully chosen as an aid to either motivating or better informing the student.

The importance of the objectives stated in the module can be brought out in this modular component.

3. OPERATIONAL INSTRUCTIONS

Each module should be self-containing with reference to how it is used. Thus, every module will have its own set of specific instructions outlining the steps necessary to complete all phases of the module. This information may include a check to see if the learner has completed all prerequisites. The instructions should guide the learner through all of the learning strategies designed to achieve the module's goals (competencies) and provide a final evaluation to determine the learner's success in goal achievement. Examples are shown in the modules included in this chapter.

4. DIAGNOSTIC PRE-ASSESSMENT

Instruction may be given in this component concerning how the student should proceed, where he should go, etc., for pre-testing or other assessment to determine whether or not he already has some of the competencies required in the module. From the information obtained in diagnostic preassessment, a learner will be able to concentrate his efforts on the specific skills of the module which he has not mastered.

If he is able to score high enough to fulfill the requirements of the mission objective, he may be allowed to skip that module with credit and move on to another area of his program. In many instances, the course instructor may serve as the best authority for pre-assessment activities. In these instances all that is needed under pre-assessment is the statement, "See the Instructor." Diagnostic pre-assessment instruments are not needed for all modules, particularly for graduate courses that are based upon materials and objectives not related to prerequisites and which by their very nature will be new to the student. Pre-assessment can be required of these students if part of the evaluation is to be based upon gain or improvement from the beginning to the end of the course.

5. POST-ASSESSMENT, RECYCLING AND GRADING

Post-assessment explains the plan for evaluating each objective. Plans for determining the final grade a student may receive on a module can also be presented at this point. Recycling informs the learner of any additional opportunities he will have to achieve selected objectives in the event he does not achieve an objective on the first post-assessment.

6. SPECIFIC GOALS (COMPETENCIES)

The goals (competencies) or specific intents (learning outcomes) of an instructional activity are the only part of a learning oriented program that can be said to have intrinsic value. In other words, goals are chosen for their value to the learner, whereas the only purpose of instructional strategies is to help the learner obtain his goals, and the only value of evaluation is to inform a decision maker or the learner as to whether or not he or she has been successful in achieving a desired goal.

Under this, the specific goal category, a complete listing should be made of all the programs' instructional intents which will be the basis for later student evaluation. These goals will represent the purposes of the course and can serve as a guide to potential students in determining whether or not the course has meaning for them in comparison to other elective course offerings.

7. STATEMENT OF MODULE'S MISSION OBJECTIVE

It is recognized that modules may consist of many units, each of which has the potential for being broken down into sub-goals and/or skills. The mission objective will identify the global goal of the module and some general evaluation performance which will also specify a criterion standard for determining a learner's requirement for successfully completing all sub-goals and/or skills in the module.

Example: Mission Objective

For graduate students to acquire the knowledge and skill necessary to use systems analysis techniques in the development of management plans as evidenced by their successful completion of at least 85 percent of the specific objectives stated in the module.

8. PERFORMANCE OBJECTIVES

Performance objectives represent extensions of the specific goal competencies stated in number 6, to include the behavioral outcomes expected from the learner. These outcomes are specified by a performance statement indicating the behavior, activity, or instrumentation that will be used to evaluate learner progress toward achieving the goals. In addition, the performance statement should include a criterion standard that represents the level of success required for a performance to be considered an adequate indicator of goal achievement.

The outcome performance statements and success level criteria used to evaluate goal achievement and to convert goals to behavioral objectives should not be considered to have intrinsic value. They are used as a means for determining short-range success in goal achievement at a particular point in time.

Each performance objective is sequentially stated in the same order as that of its corresponding goal statement listed in number 6.

9. LEARNING STRATEGIES

This component should designate alternative choices which students may make to acquire the knowledge, skill, or performance task competencies identified in the specific performance objectives. The alternate learning routes will normally consist of behaviors such as reading, listening, viewing, creating or constructing, observing, performing and/or free choice activities. An important concept to remember in developing the learning strategies is that strategies should provide methods for students to successfully complete the competency module through independent study as well as through classroom participation.

Based upon the objectives to be achieved, each student will be required to attend class or to make independent study commitments to the instructor prior to proceeding through course objectives. This is for purposes of coordination rather than limitation. For example, the student has the opportunity of free choice which means he can proceed in any manner of independent study he chooses provided he is able, in the end, to achieve the desired competencies. This is most likely to occur when the resources listed in a module are limited or in cases where a student is employed in a unique situation or is acquainted with unique opportunities which make free choice more appropriate to him. Obtaining the competency is the important concern, not how you obtain it.

10. LEARNING RESOURCES

In order to implement the learning strategies, each module should provide a list of human and material learning resources that can be used by individuals or groups in acquiring the needed behavior. Some competencies may be acquired through only one or two specified resources, particularly if there are only two resources available. Other competencies may be acquired through five or six resources. Persons preparing competency modules should recognize that all resources specified for alternative selection by the learners should be chosen according to their specificity in meeting the content requirements of the specific goals and objectives, rather than for their flexibility, versatility or scholarly intents. Criterion referenced measurement is based upon specific content coverage, not overviews.

In reality, it is not the rigid following of any module guideline or set of module specifications that produces the most efficient module, but rather the module developer's ability to select the necessary module ingredients and synthesize them in a manner that best serves his own and his students' interests. Competency selection, how competency attainment will be evaluated to determine success, and strategy selection are the essential components.

Module development should include all essential components that are necessary for a learner to achieve the purposes for which the module is prepared. Module flexibility should enable a teacher to utilize his or her own creativity and insights into the presentation of material in their own areas of expertise. The important thing is to remain concise and specific rather than to attempt to reveal all that one knows about a content area.

The mini-modules presented on the following pages were prepared and are being used by teachers in Duval, Clay and St. John's Counties, Florida. Parts of each module have been omitted, but enough detail remains to clearly illustrate how the contents of a module will appear if developed from the components listed in this chapter.

DEPARTMENT: Junior High Social Studies
COURSE TITLE: Geography
NAME OF MODULE: Map Skill for General Map Usage
CODING: MODULE 2
DESIGNED FOR: Seventh Grade Students

Name _____

Homeroom Section_____

Class Section _____

Instructor _____

Contributed by: Barbara Horstmeir, Teacher
Sandalwood Junior High School

I. PROSPECTUS
  A. Introduction /or rationale
     The study of the earth, as man's environment, must in many instances be studied through earth representatives due to the physical size of the earth. The best map of the earth is a globe which shows correct size and shape of the land and water areas of the earth. However, the globe is not a practical tool for the general uses of earth representation in daily needs. Therefore, flat maps are commonly used in meeting the daily needs for earth representation.
     Module 2 is designed to introduce the student to place location, hemispheres, and time zones on the earth's surface through the use of flat maps and prepare him for more complex map usage.
  B. Outline of Module 2
     1. Prospectus
        a. introduction
        b. outline
        c. operational instructions
     2. Post-Assessment and Recycling
     3. Statement of Specific Goal Competencies
     4. Objectives, Activities and Learning Resources
        a. mission objective
        b. performance objectives, activities and learning resources
  C. Operational Instructions
     Each concept presented in this module is based on the preceding concept, and is identified by a performance objective. The student will proceed from one concept to the next in the logical order presented in the module. When the desired performance level for an objective is reached by the student, he may continue on to the next objective. Evaluation shall be based on the level at which each objective was attained.
     The content material for Module 2 will be presented by:
     1. Lecture
     2. Films

3. Film Strips
4. Small Group Activities
5. Supplementary Practice Sheets
6. Models

The student should follow the operational procedures, as listed below, in completing this module:

Read the prospectus (Section I)
2. Become familiar with the specific goal competencies (Section III).
3. Read the mission objective of the module (Section IVA).
4. Study each performance objective (Section IVB).
5. Select and complete the activities you prefer as a means of achieving each objective.
6. Evaluate competency achievement through instrumentation provided by the instructor.
7. Move on to the next objective after achieving the previous objective.
8. If you fail to achieve an objective as indicated by the post-assessment, recycle the objective after a discussion with the teacher.
9. Repeat the operational procedures, 2–8, until you have achieved all objectives.

II. POST-ASSESSMENT AND RECYCLING

Post-assessment will be the means by which your achievement of each performance objective will be evaluated. Assessment activities shall follow the completion of each of the objectives' activities. Assessment instrumentation will be given the student as soon as he is prepared to be tested on the achievement of any objective.

As Module 2 is basic to all future study in this course, the student will be required to recycle any objective in which he has not demonstrated minimum competency. Recycling will be done by the student after a conference with the instructor, in which strategies shall be individually planned. The student shall recycle until he has demonstrated competency in the objective.

III. STATEMENT OF SPECIFIC GOAL COMPETENCIES

The goals of this module are the specific purposes for which this module was prepared. Each goal is of specific educational value in itself and is to be used as a stepping stone toward higher educational goals. The students of geography in this module shall:

1. Comprehend the four hemispheres of the earth.
2. Develop comprehension of latitude as imaginary, useable lines on the earth's surface.
3. Develop comprehension of longitude as imaginary, useable lines on the earth's surface.
4. Develop skill in locating positions on the earth's surface.
5. Comprehend the time zones around the earth.

IV. OBJECTIVES, ACTIVITIES, LEARNING RESOURCES AND RECYCLING

A. Mission Objective

Seventh grade students of geography should aquire competency in the knowledge of, and ability to use, latitude and longitude. Success of this goal shall be determined by the achievement of all five specific performance objectives as stated in the module.

B. Performance Objectives, Activities and Learning Resources

The performance objectives are extensions of specific goals stated in Section III, and include the evaluation of competency expected from each student and the activities to be conducted for each objective. The performance objectives are stated in the order of which they should be completed.

SPECIFIC PERFORMANCE OBJECTIVE #1

You are expected to demonstrate comprehension of the earth being divided into four hemispheres, as determined by your correctly answering each of six short answer questions on a written examination.

Activities and Learning Resources
1. class lecture
2. film strip
3. small group activity

Post-assessment and Recycling

You will be evaluated for this objective, immediately after completing the activities, by the instructor. The test shall be composed of six short answer questions which you are required to answer correctly. Recycling shall be allowed until you have reached the desired competency.

SPECIFIC PERFORMANCE OBJECTIVE #2

You are expected to comprehend latitude as imaginary, useable lines on the earth's surface, so that when given a world map you will correctly label the latitude on the map and correctly answer four short answer questions on a written test.

Activities and Learning Resources
1. class lecture
2. film strip and tape
3. practice maps and sheets
4. small group activity

Post-assessment and Recycling

Evaluation of this objective shall be distributed directly after the completion of the activities. The evaluation shall consist of one world map and four short answer, written questions. You will be required to label the latitude on the map and answer the four questions correctly. You shall recycle until you demonstrate minimum competency.

SPECIFIC OBJECTIVE #3

You are expected to comprehend longitude as imaginary, useable lines on the earth's surface, as determined by your ability to correctly designate longitude on a blank student globe and correctly answer two written essay questions.

Activities and Learning Resources
1. class lecture
2. film strip and tape
3. practice globes
4. small group activity

Post-assessment and Recycling

This objective shall be evaluated immediately after completion of the activities. Evaluation will consist of one student globe on which you will be required to designate longitude and a written test of two essay questions. This objective will be recycled until you demonstrate minimum competency.

SPECIFIC OBJECTIVE #4

You must develop skill in locating positions on the earth's surface through the latitude-longitude grid system, so that when given fifteen readings and a world map you will correctly locate and mark all fifteen readings.

Activities and Learning Resources
 1. class lecture
 2. movie
 3. practice maps
 4. small group activity

Post-assessment and Recycling

You will be administered a competency examination upon completing the activities. The examination will consist of a world map and fifteen readings. You will be required to locate and mark all fifteen readings on the map. You will recycle until you achieve minimum competency.

SPECIFIC OBJECTIVE #5

You are expected to demonstrate comprehension of the time zones around the earth, so that when given two class periods and the materials, you will construct a workable time wheel.

Activities and Learning Resources
 1. class lecture
 2. sun-earth model
 3. film
 4. small group activity

Post-assessment and Recycling

The competency examination will be given after you have completed the activities. You shall be given two class periods and the necessary materials with which you shall construct a correct, useable time wheel. You may recycle until the objective is achieved to minimum level.

Duval County Schools

DuPont Jr. High School

DEPARTMENT: Mathematics
COURSE TITLE: General Mathematics for Eighth Grade
NAME OF MODULE: Improving Math Skills in the Rational
                Number System
PREREQUISITES: Mathematics, Grades 1–7
DESIGNED FOR: All eighth grade students
DATE: August, 1973

Student Information

Name: _____

Address: _____

Phone: _____

Homeroom Section: _____

Contributed by: Linda L. Sammons

I. Prospectus
   A. Introduction and/or Rationale
      Recently, a major emphasis in education has been to make content material studied more relevant and understandable to students. This idea involves the motivation of students. If pupils can see where they will use a specific skill, in this case the set of rational numerals, the "why study this" syndrome becomes more evident to them. A purpose emerges, making the task of studying and concentrating an easier burden to bear.
      This module is designed as a guide to the learning of the basic skills needed in working problems in the rational number system, because it is an area with which every person in our society must come in contact at some time—in measuring, cooking, building, sewing, and countless other jobs. Fractions are simply part of living and working for all of us.
   B. Outline of Module
      1. Prospectus
         a. Rationale
         b. Outline of Module
         c. Operational Instructions
      2. Diagnostic Pre-Assessment
      3. Post-Assessment and Recycling
      4. Objectives, Activities, and Learning Resources
         a. Mission Objective
         b. Specific Goal Competencies
         c. Performance Objectives by Topic
         d. Activities and Learning Resources by Objective
         e. Post-Assessment and Recycling by Objective
   C. Operational Instructions (omitted)
      The procedures to be followed in completing this module are as follows:
      1. Complete the diagnostic pre-assessment inventory if you feel you already understand the competency well enough to try the performance outcome required.
      2. Read the statement of the module's mission objective.
      3. Become familiar with the specific goal competencies as stated in part IV.

4. Study each performance objective one at a time and preferably in sequence.
5. Implement the activities you feel will best help you attain success in achieving the performance objective.
6. Evaluate competency achievement through the means specified in the post-assessment.
7. Move on to the objective as soon as you complete the previous one.
8. If post-assessment indicates you have failed to achieve an objective with the minimum requirement, recycle to achieve the objective after consultation with the teacher.
9. Repeat the process steps outlined in procedures three through eight until you have achieved all the objectives.

II. Diagnostic Pre-Assessment (omitted)
III. Post-Assessment and Recycling (omitted)
IV. Objectives, Activities and Learning Resources
A. Mission Objective

For eighth grade mathematics students to acquire the knowledge and skills necessary to write and use the basic operational procedures in the rational number system. Success in achieving this goal will be determined by the attainment of each of the five competencies outlined by the specific performance objectives in the module.

B. Specific Goal Competencies

Goals, as used here, represent the specific intents or competencies for which the module has been written. Each goal is considered to be very important in learning how to work with rational numbers as you will use them in your everyday life, and is worth achieving. The learner will be asked to:

1. develop skill in interpolating rational numbers with lower denominators to those with higher denominators, and reducing them.
2. develop the ability to add rational numerals properly.
3. develop skill in subtracting rational numerals properly.
4. be able to multiply rational numbers properly.
5. know how to divide rational numbers properly.

C. Performance Objectives, Activities and Learning Resources

In this module, performance objectives represent extensions of the goal competencies, with the addition of the performance outcomes expected of you, the learner. They will indicate the behavior, activity, or type test which will be used to evaluate your level of success in achieving the goal. Further, a minimum standard that you must reach will be given.

Each performance objective is stated in the same sequential order as in the previous statement of goal competencies. Each objective is then followed by a list of activities and learning resources which will help you achieve the competency. Also, post-assessment and recycling information is given for each objective in order to further guide you through the process of achieving the objectives.

Performance Objective Number One:

You will develop skill in interpolating rational numbers with lower denominators to those with higher denominators and reducing them. Given twenty rational numbers and a higher equivalent numerator or denominator for each, 90 per cent of the students on a written test will find the missing equivalent numerator or denominator as asked and will then reduce them back to lowest terms with 80 per cent accuracy.

Activities and Learning Resources
    a. Attend classroom lecture, demonstration, and discussion.
    b. Review textbook pages _____ through _____.
    c. Complete all practice exercises on handout.
    d. Free choice activities.

Post-Assessment and Recycling
    You will be given a 20 question written test on completing the activities as described in the performance objective. You must show all computations on your paper for each problem. You will be able to recycle only one time.

Performance Objective Number Two:
    You will develop the ability to add rational numerals properly as evidenced by 90 per cent of the students using the procedure for adding rational numerals with at least 80 per cent accuracy on a written test.

Activities and Learning Resources
    a. Attend classroom lecture, demonstration, and discussion.
    b. Review visual materials presented.
    c. Review textbook pages _____ through _____.
    d. Complete all practice exercises assigned and on handouts.
    e. Free choice activities.

Post-Assessment and Recycling
    You will be given ten problems on a written test. Some will have similar denominators, some will not. Others will have mixed numbers as one of the addends. You must write all computations and reduce your final answer. You will be able to recycle only once.

Performance Objective Number Three:
    You will develop skill in subtracting rational numerals properly as determined by 90 per cent of the students using the procedure for subtracting fractions with at least 80 per cent accuracy on a written test.

Activities and Learning Resources
    a. Attend classroom lecture, demonstration, and subsequent discussion.
    b. Review textbook pages _____ through _____.
    c. Complete all practice exercises assigned and on handouts.
    d. Free choice activities.

Post-Assessment and Recycling
    Your test will consist of ten subtraction problems, some of which will involve the process of borrowing. You must show all work on paper and will be allowed to recycle only once.

Performance Objective Number Four:
    You will be able to multiply rational numbers properly as evidenced by ninety per cent of the students writing the procedure for multiplying fractions and mixed numbers correctly, given ten problems on a written test, with eighty per cent accuracy.

Activities and Learning Resources
    a. Attend classroom lecture, demonstration, and subsequent discussion.
    b. Review textbook pages _____ through _____.

    c. Review handout information sheets.
    d. Complete all practice exercises assigned.
    e. Perform free choice activities.

Post-Assessment and Recycling

    Your test is as described in the performance objective, and must include all your computations written on paper. You may recycle this objective one time only.

Performance Objective Number Five:

    You will know how to properly divide rational numbers, as determined by your correctly computing the answers to fifteen division problems with fractions and mixed numbers on a written test with eighty per cent accuracy.

Activities and Learning Resources

    a. Attend classroom lecture, demonstration, and subsequent discussion.
    b. Review handout information sheets.
    c. Complete all practice exercises assigned.
    d. Review textbook pages _____ through _____.
    e. Perform free choice activities.

Post-Assessment and Recycling

    You will be given a 15 question written test on which you must show all computations on paper for each problem. Recycling will be allowed only one time.

ORANGE PARK MIDDLE SCHOOL
GRADE 8

DEPARTMENT: English
COURSE TITLE: Language Arts 8
MODULE CODING: LIB−CC I
GENERAL CONTENT AREA: Library Orientation
NAME OF MODULE: *Using the Card Catalog*
PREREQUISITES:

1. Reasonable knowledge of the alphabet.
2. Some previous use of the library.
3. Successful completion of Language Arts 7.
4. Previously read *THROUGH LIBRARY DOORS 7*

DESIGNED FOR: Language Arts Grade 8 students.
DATE: August 20, 1973

Contributed by : William K. Turner

Introduction

Before you leave Language Arts 8 this year you will probably use the library on an average of twice a week. Sometimes this will be for selection of books for book reports and other times it will be for research about authors or projects you will be doing. The desire to find information which answers unknown questions is probably one of the reasons for libraries coming into existence.

Actually you have two choices when you go to the library. You can wander around aimlessly searching for the books and information you need or you can use all of the "helpers" found in the library which can make your "search" easier. Many people feel the only way to get any help is by asking the librarian. However, sometimes the librarian is just too busy to help everyone! Fortunately, the library contains a device which can almost take the place of the librarian as a "helper." This device is called the CARD CATALOG. Through this module you should greatly increase your ability to use the CARD CATALOG. If you do this you naturally increase your ability to use the library successfully.

Throughout this module you will be asked to perform activities specifically designed to make you a "pro" at handling the CARD CATALOG. Some of the activities will be nothing more than review. Please follow carefully each explanation, direction, and activity. Most of the time you will be working alone. I certainly will not force you to follow the module step by step. But, I will warn you that the easiest way to complete this module is step by step, activity by activity. Do the best work you can do, and enjoy USING THE CARD CATALOG.

Mission Objective

For eighth grade Language Arts students to acquire the knowledge and skill necessary to use the Card Catalog as evidenced by their successfully completing at least 90 per cent of the objectives stated in the module.

Operational Instructions

This module is designed so you can proceed step by step toward successful achievement of all module objectives. Each objective will be listed individually and the activities which you must perform listed with the objectives. Each objective includes not only the activities which are required, but also a test or activity which you must complete to show you have successfully obtained all the skills which the objective was designed for you to acquire.

Along with each objective you will see listed some enabling activities. These are the things you must do to help you achieve the objective properly. They will include some of the following:

1. lecture
2. paperback textbook reading
3. films and filmstrips
4. small group activities
5. library assignments
6. free choice activities by the learner

It may be necessary for you to work each one of the activities, or to skip some of the activities as you find them to be necessary or unnecessary. Make sure you follow all directions carefully and perform all enabling activities you feel are necessary to meet the objective.

RECYCLING

If you fail to achieve the minimum level of performance on an objective, your teacher will ask you to recycle and provide an appropriate activity. For some objectives you will have only one chance to recycle, but for others you will be given the opportunity to recycle as often as necessary. Recycling is not a crime punishable by death! If you are unsuccessful the first time try to do your very best when recycling.

PRE-TEST

Answer each question as well as you possibly can. If you score 90 per cent or above on this test you will be assigned to another module because you probably already know how to use the card catalog effectively.

1. The card catalog is always arranged in _____ order.
2. Each drawer in the card catalog contains three types of cards. They are the _____ card, the _____ card, and the _____ card.
3. Each drawer in the card catalog is labeled to show_____ _____.
4. The number on the upper left hand corner of some cards in the card catalog is called the _____.
5. The classification number used on some of the cards in the card catalog was named after _____.
6. Fiction books always contain a letter in the upper left hand corner. That letter is _____.
7. The card in the card catalog which refers you to some other drawer or some other card is called the _____.
8. Reference books are usually clearly marked with the letter_____ in the upper left hand corner.
9. If a book you are looking for in the card catalog has no card this probably means _____.
10. The cards in the card catalog always give basic pieces of information about every book. List the five basic pieces of information given for each book.
    1. _____
    2. _____
    3. _____
    4. _____
    5. _____

After you finish your test take it to your instructor for correction. After your test has been corrected the teacher will direct you to your next activity.

SPECIFIC GOALS

1. Acquire a knowledge and comprehension of the characteristics of the card catalog.
2. Be able to comprehend the differences between title, subject, and author cards.

3. Develop skill in using the card catalog.
4. Develop the ability to use "keys" found on card catalog cards.
5. Acquire a knowledge of specific facts found on card catalog cards.
6. Develop skill in alphabetizing authors, titles, and subjects listed in the card catalog.
7. Develop skill in constructing title, subject, and author cards.
8. Acquire a knowledge and comprehension of the Dewey Decimal System.
9. Be able to interpret the various categories of the Dewey Decimal System labeled in the card catalog.
10. Acquire skill in identifying cross-reference cards in the card catalog.
11. Acquire knowledge about Melvil Dewey.

OBJECTIVES, ACTIVITIES, LEARNING RESOURCES, RECYCLING

Specific Performance Objective #1
You are expected to acquire a knowledge and comprehension of the characteristics of the card catalog. Success will be determined by your ability to write a paragraph discussing the general appearance of the card catalog which is acceptable according to standards which will be listed by the instructor.
Activities and Learning Resources
    a. Visit the library and examine the card catalog.
    b. Read: *THROUGH LIBRARY DOORS 8*, Pages 1–6.
    c. Read: *MODERN ENGLISH IN ACTION*, Pages 51–55.
    d. Perform free choice activities.
Post-Assessment and Recycling
The student will be expected to turn in to the teacher the required paragraph and await its return. If acceptable, the teacher will instruct the learner to proceed to the next objective. Recycling will take place immediately, and the learner will rewrite the paragraph, correcting the paragraph as instructed by the teacher. Students may recycle this objective one time.
Specific Performance Objective #2
You are expected to be able to comprehend the difference between title, subject, and author cards found in the card catalog. Success will be determined by your ability to correctly label two author cards, two subject cards, and two title cards when shown six blank cards. This will be done with 100 per cent accuracy.
Activities and Learning Resources
    a. Read: *THROUGH LIBRARY DOORS 8,* Pages 8–11.
    b. Read through Vu-Chart on Card Catalog Cards.
    c. Perform free choice activities.
Post-Assessment and Recycling
Go to the teacher and get a ditto page with six blank cards printed on it. Fill in two author cards, two title cards, and two subject cards in the six boxes. Turn in your completed paper to the teacher for correction. If you have completed the activity with 100 per cent accuracy move on to the next objective. If you need to recycle get a new ditto sheet and have a classmate help you fill in the six cards. Then get another sheet and fill this one in yourself. You may recycle as often as necessary.
Specific Performance Objective #3
You will develop skill in using the card catalog so that when given

the opportunity you will explain orally, to the instructor, how to operate the card catalog.

Activities and Learning Resources

    a. Present small class demonstration to three other class members.

    b. Perform free choice activity.

    c. View film: *The Card Catalog.*

    d. Review reading from previous objectives.

Post-Assessment and Recycling

    Prepare a three minute presentation without notes to be presented to the teacher, explaining the card catalog and its use. Recycling will be determined by the teacher's opinion of the explanation and additional instructions will be given to the students recycling by the teacher at the time of recycling.

Specific Performance Objective #4

    You will develop the ability to use "keys" found on card catalog cards. Success will be determined by your ability to circle three keys found on a catalog card given you by the teacher. This will be done with 100 per cent accuracy.

Activities and Learning Resources

    a. Read: *MODERN ENGLISH IN ACTION 8,* Pages 54–56.

    b. Perform free choice activity.

Post-Assessment and Recycling

    Take the three keys found on the card your teacher gives you and put a red circle around each. There will be no recycle for this objective.

Specific Performance Objective #5

    You must acquire a knowledge of specific facts found on card catalog cards so that when asked to make a list you will list, with 100 per cent accuracy, five important facts found on all card catalog cards.

Activities and Learning Resources

    a. Read: *THROUGH LIBRARY DOORS 8,* Pages 1–12.

    b. Review Vu-Chart on Card Catalog Cards.

    c. Visit library and copy down facsimile of some card catalog cards.

    d. Perform free choice activity.

Post-Assessment and Recycling

    You will receive a ditto sheet from your teacher. On the sheet you will see five blanks numbered one through five. Fill in the five specific facts which appear on all cards in the card catalog. Recycling will be done immediately by reviewing all activities and taking the quiz in an oral fashion.

Specific Performance Objective #6

    You will develop skill in alphabetizing authors, titles, and subjects listed in the card catalog. Success will be determined by your ability to alphabetize a list of ten authors, titles, and subjects found in the card catalog, with 100 per cent accuracy.

Activities and Learning Resources

    a. Perform free choice activity.

Post-Assessment and Recycling

    From the list of ten titles, subjects, and authors listed on the board, you will properly alphabetize with 100 per cent accuracy, all ten titles, authors, and subjects. Recycling will occur immediately with a new list of titles, subjects and authors.

(OBJECTIVES 7 THRU 11 OMITTED)

ORANGE PARK MIDDLE SCHOOL
LANGUAGE ARTS

NAME OF MODULE: Improving Your Dictionary Skills
DESIGNED FOR: Sometimes secretive, and surprisingly sensitive,
        special seventh grade students.
DATE: September 5, 1973

Student Information

Name: _____

Team: _____

Teacher: Carol S. Broxton

Homeroom: _____

TABLE of CONTENTS

A. Introduction
    There will be many times, especially in school, when you will need to use a dictionary. You have used one many times before, I am sure, but probably your introduction to the dictionary was simplified for use in the lower grades. As a matter of fact, you probably avoid using a dictionary, if possible, because it takes so long to find what you're looking for and once you find what you want you become confused as to which definition is correct. This module will help you to become more comfortable using the dictionary by improving your skill in locating words quickly and improving your understanding of some of the types of information the main entries of the dictionary provide.

B. How to Use the Module
    This module is arranged so that you can proceed step by step toward successful achievement of all the objectives in the module. At each step you will know exactly what it is you are expected to know or be able to do, what

activities will help you, and also how you and I will know if you have been successful and therefore ready for the next step. The information you will need to complete this module will come from:

1. teacher lecture
2. small group activities
3. *Webster's New Student Dictionary*
4. class discussion
5. *Open Highways Skillbook*

The steps you should follow as you proceed through the module are:

1. Fill out the student information section on the cover.
2. Keep the module in your notebook.
3. Complete the pre-test scheduled for Thurs., Sept. 7.
4. Become familiar with the objectives in the module by reading them several times.
5. Read the over-all objective.
6. Concentrate on each objective as we schedule it in class.
7. Complete the activities assigned as a means to achieve each objective.
8. Take the test for each objective to determine your success.
9. Move on to the next objective as soon as you successfully complete one.
10. If, at any step, you are not successful, consult with the teacher to arrange for additional help and a chance for a re-test.

You are finished and to be considered a great success and a persevering person when you successfully achieved all the objectives in this module!

C. About the Pre-test

The purpose of this test is to find out how well you might already know the skills which this module should help to develop. If you already are able to do one or more of the skills in the module at a level desired by your teacher, as an indication of your success you will be allowed to skip the learning activities and proceed directly to the test or tests. YOU WILL BE NOTIFIED BY YOUR TEACHER IF THIS OCCURS. The pre-test will be given to the entire class on Thurs., Sept. 7. Since speed is a factor in determining your success in the module, the test will be timed. At the time of the test you will be provided with a student dictionary and then given oral directions to turn to certain pages and find particular information which I will be asking for. Whenever you hear the sound of a bell you MUST stop writing and wait to begin the next part of the test.

D. About Individual Tests and Re-tests

Each time you complete the learning activities for a certain objective you will be given a test to see if you have been successful. If at first you don't succeed, you do get a chance to try again. In a conference with the teacher you will find out exactly what activities you will need to do to prepare for another test.

E. What You've Always Wanted to Know About Grades But Were Afraid to Ask

Your grades will be based on the following:

1. (Absolutely wonderful) = all nine of the objectives achieved at 90 per cent accuracy or above the first time around.

2. (Better than most) = all nine of the objectives achieved with 90 per cent accuracy or above after one or more re-tests.

or

3. (Better than many) = nine objectives achieved with 85 per cent accuracy first time around.
4. (Couldn't you have tried just a little bit harder?) = nine objectives achieved at 80 per cent accuracy first time around.
5. (Disappointing for both of us) = nine objectives achieved below 80 per cent accuracy but not below 70 per cent.
6. (Frustrating for both of us) = objectives achieved at below 70 per cent accuracy.

F. Over-all Objective of the Module

This module should improve your skill in locating words quickly and improve your understanding of some of the kinds of information provided by the main entries, thereby increasing your skill in using the dictionary.

G. Specific Objectives of the Module
1. You should improve your skill and accuracy in alphabetizing so that when given a timed (3 min.) test you will correctly alphabetize, by numbering, a list of twelve words and correctly indicate by writing "yes" or "no" whether or not five lists of words are in correct order. You must score 80 per cent or above on this.
   Activities and Learning Resources
   a. Small group activities
   b. Timed contest
   c. Student dictionary exercises, pages 4a–top of 6a.
2. You should improve your skill in determining alphabetical order by first, second, third, fourth, and fifth letters. Proof that you have accomplished this will be determined by 80 per cent accuracy on a test. The test will be composed of ten lists of three words each. You will underline the letter which determines the order of the words in each list.
   Activities and Learning Resources
   a. Individual practice
   b. Boardwork (hopefully not "bored work")
   c. Student dictionary assignments for in-class exercises.
3. You should improve your ability to locate words quickly using guide words so that when given four pairs of guide words, each with a list of five entry words, you will indicate next to each word whether it would appear "on," "after," or "before" the page referred to by the guide words. You should have 90 percent accuracy on this.
   Activities and Learning Resources
   a. Individual practice
   b. Student dictionary. (Check-up 2; page 5a.)
4. You should understand the purposes for alphabetical ordering as well as the advantages of rapid recognition of alphabetical order. Proof of this will be established by your listing at least five situations where your knowledge of alphabetical ordering has been helpful to you and by explaining, in your own words, the purpose for alphabetical ordering. The teacher will be the judge of the quality and completeness of the assignment.

Activities and Learning Resources
a. Class discussion
b. Reading assignment (page 6a). Student dictionary.
5. You should acquire skill in using main entries to determine the correct forms of words. To be successful you must achieve 100 per cent accuracy when given a list of eight words and these directions: Use your dictionary to determine if the words are listed in their correct form or not. Make any corrections necessary.
Activities and Learning Resources
a. Individual practice
b. Timed contest
6. You should be able to use main entries to find out what the acceptable word breaks in writing are. To prove your success you will be given a list of ten words, each written with three different break patterns, and you will use your dictionary to find and circle the correct pattern for all ten.
Activities and Learning Resources
a. Dictionary practice. (Check-ups 3 and 4; page 6a.)
7. You should acquire skill in deciding which definition in a series of definitions is suitable for use in a particular situation. You will be given a reading selection containing ten unfamiliar words. Using a dictionary you will define in writing at least eight of the words correctly.
Activities and Learning Resources
a. *Open Highways Skillbook* (pages 14–15)
b. Class discussion
c. Small group practice
8. You should be able to distinguish between separate entries which are spelled alike. (These are called homographs.) To determine your success you will be given a list of ten sentences containing underlined words which may or may not be homographs. You will list, in writing, those which are homographs and write the correct definition of each. You must score 80 per cent or above.
Activities and Learning Resources
a. Teacher lecture
b. Student dictionary. (Check-up 5; page 7a.)
9. You should be aware that many words have variant spellings and should be able to find the most common spelling so that when given a list of six words you will refer to the dictionary and underline the words which have more than one spelling and mark with the letter "C" any of these which appear on the list in most common form. (100 per cent accuracy.)
Learning Resources and Activities
a. Dictionary (Check-up 7; page 7a.)
10. You should be able to use main entries to determine correct capitalization. Proof of this will be determined by 100 per cent accuracy on a test consisting of an uncapitalized list of ten words which you will correctly capitalize using your dictionary.
Activities and Learning Resources
a. *Open Highways Skillbook* (pages 18–20)
b. Dictionary. (Check-up 8; page 7a.)

ORANGE STREET FIFTH GRADE CENTER
ST. JOHNS COUNTY, FLORIDA

DEPARTMENT: Education
COURSE TITLE: Improving Comprehension Skills in Fifth-
            Grade Students
NAME OF MODULE: Objectives and Activities for
                  Comprehension Skills in Reading
CODING: ICSFG 525
LEARNING GROUP: Fifth-Grade Students
PROFESSIONAL USE: All Fifth-Grade Teachers
PROGRAM NEEDS: Instructional
DATE: August 14, 1973

Devised By:
Angelo Macedonia
Fifth-Grade Teacher
St. Johns County
St. Augustine, Florida

I. Prospectus
   A. Introduction
       As a teacher of fifth-grade students, I saw a rising need for fifth-
   grade Reading students to improve their comprehension skills. Reading, I felt, would be the best subject to work with for devising this
   module. If a child can improve his comprehension skills in Reading,
   it would certainly help in the further development of other subject
   matter and areas of study.
       This module is designed as a complete course to guide the
   teacher in helping to improve comprehension skills in fifth-grade
   Reading students.
   B. Outline of Module (omitted)
   C. Operational Instructions (omitted)
II. Diagnostic Pre-Assessment (omitted)
III. Post-Assessment and Recycling
       Post-assessment will consist of evaluating your students'
   achievement to determine whether they have achieved each performance objective of the module. All assessment activities will
   follow immediately upon completion of the enabling activities used
   as strategies to achieve each goal. Assessment instrumentation will
   be given to the student when he thinks he is prepared to be tested
   on the achievement of any objective.
       Recycling activities are designed to give the student additional
   opportunities to achieve selected objectives that may not have been
   achieved in his initial endeavor. The strategies or enabling activities,

to be used in recycling will be individually prescribed for each student by the instructor.

IV. Statement of Specific Goal Competencies

Goals, in the context used in this module, represent the specific intents or competencies for which the module has been written. Each goal is considered to have a specific instructional intent. In this module the student in ICS 525 (fifth-grade reading student) will be asked to:

1. Develop the ability to relate personally to Reading.
2. Develop the ability to discuss orally a book they've read.
3. Develop the ability to recognize and interpret emotional reactions of characters in a book.
4. Develop the ability to determine the main idea of a paragraph.
5. Develop the ability to recognize sequence of ideas.
6. Develop the ability to find and relate details.
7. Develop the ability to interpret figurative and descriptive language.
8. Increase their ability to develop critical reading skills.
9. Develop the ability to make inferences.
10. Develop the ability to recognize cause and effect relationships.
11. Develop the ability to compare and contrast information and ideas in a short story.

V. Objectives, Activities, Learning Resources and Recycling

A. Mission Objective

For fifth-grade Reading students to acquire the competencies necessary for using comprehension skills in Reading. Success in achieving this mission will be determined by their achievement of at least eight of the eleven specific performance objectives outlined in the module.

B. Performance Objectives, Activities, and Learning Resources

In this module, performance objectives represent extensions of the specific goals, stated in Part IV, to include the educational outcomes expected from the learner. These outcomes are specified by a performance statement indicating the behavior, activity, or instrumentation that will be used to evaluate learner progress toward achieving the goals. In addition, the performance statement will include a criterion standard that represents the level of success required for a performance to be considered an adequate indicator of goal achievement.

Each performance objective is sequentially stated in the same order as that of its corresponding goal statement in Part IV of the module. Each objective is followed by the listing of specific activities and learning resources that may be used to achieve the competency. In addition, supplementary post-assessment and recycling information is stated for each individual objective.

Specific Performance Objective Number One:

For fifth-grade students to develop the ability to relate personally to Reading so that when given a short story, which they themselves have chosen, the majority of the students will be able to list the ways the short story may or may not relate to their personal lives.

Activities and Learning Resources

a. Individual conferences with instructor.
b. Supplementary materials provided by the instructor.

    c. Activities:
        1. Students can make their story into a short skit to demonstrate
           to their classmates.
        2. After reading their short story, students can tell what a char-
           acter in the story has done that the student himself has done
           before.
    Post-Assessment and Recycling
        The instructor will evaluate this objective after completion of
    the enabling activities. All students will be required to have an
    individual conference with their instructor. The questions will be
    devised by the teacher and the students may recycle as many times
    as he sees the need to until the objective has been mastered.
Specific Performance Objective Number Two:
    For fifth-grade students to develop the ability to discuss orally a book
they've read so that when given the opportunity to have a conference with
their instructor, the majority of the students will be able to answer at least
eight of the ten questions developed by their instructor and pertaining to
the book they've read.
    Activities and Learning Resources
    a. Individual conferences with instructor.
    b. Supplementary materials provided by the instructor.
    c. Activities:
        1. Ask the students to tell what they liked most about the book
           they've read.
        2. Students may tell about their book to their classmates in small
           group work sessions.
    Post-Assessment and Recycling
        Students failing to achieve this objective will be given a work-
    sheet which asks ten to fifteen questions for which they are ex-
    pected to skim through their books to find the answers. Students
    may recycle this objective one time only if necessary.
Specific Performance Objective Number Three:
    For fifth-grade students to develop the ability to recognize and interpret
emotional reactions of characters in a book so that when asked how a character reacted to a particular situation, the majority of the students will be
able to recognize that reaction and interpret how the character handled the
situation.
    Activities and Learning Resources
    a. Individual conferences with instructor.
    b. Supplementary materials provided by the instructor.
    c. Activities:
        1. Place the student in a particular situation and ask him to ex-
           plain how he would react to it.
        2. Have the student read a short adventure story which has no
           conclusion, and ask him to end the selection.
    Post-Assessment and Recycling
        This competency will be achieved by all students applying
    their own emotional reactions to situations at home. The students
    will be asked to explain how they felt and how they reacted when
    they were punished for their wrongdoings. This competency may be
    recycled until the objective has been mastered.
Specific Performance Objective Number Four:
    For fifth-grade students to develop the ability to determine the main
idea of a paragraph so that when given a paragraph conveying the main idea

which is stated at the end of the paragraph, followed by four choices, the majority of the students will underline the choice which states the main idea of the paragraph.

Activities and Learning Resources
a. Individual conferences with instructor.
b. Supplementary materials provided by the instructor.
c. Activities:
   1. After the students carefully read a paragraph, ask them to underline one important sentence that they feel the paragraph is about.
   2. Give the students a paragraph which has the wrong main idea underlined. Ask them if the underlined sentence conveys the message contained within the paragraph.

Post-Assessment and Recycling
Various drill exercises will be administered to those failing to achieve this objective. When the instructor feels that students have mastered the competency, they may move on to the next objective.

Specific Performance Objective Number Five:
For fifth-grade students to develop the ability to recognize sequence of ideas so that when given five sentences which can be arranged in a logical, sequential order, the majority of the students will be able to number them in order, using the numerals one through five.

Activities and Learning Resources
a. Individual conferences with instructor.
b. Supplementary materials provided by the instructor.
c. Activities:
   1. Ask the students to tell how they go about making something, listing what comes first, second, third, etc.
   2. Have the students give a demonstration speech in front of their peers, explaining how something is done or the procedure for making something work.

Post-Assessment and Recycling
Each student failing to achieve this objective will be administered various worksheets provided by the instructor. Recycling will continue until the instructor feels that the student has mastered the objective.

R. B. HUNT SCHOOL
THIRD GRADE

DEPARTMENT: Reading
COURSE TITLE: Location and Study Skills
NAME OF MODULE: Objectives and Activities for
Location and Study Skills
LEARNER GROUP: Third Grade Students

DESIGNED FOR: Third Grade Teachers
DATE: August 10, 1973

Designed by:
Gwen P. Reichert
Third Grade Teacher
St. Augustine, Florida

I. Prospectus
  A. Introduction and/or Rationale
     In our fast moving world of today, a student who lacks location and study skills facility will have great difficulty in obtaining knowledge, in and out of the classroom.
     Children practice oral language habits constantly out of school, but their location and study skills must be developed almost entirely through the school curriculum. Therefore, a language program must provide a considerable number of experiences which give the student the opportunity to learn where and how to find needed information. The teacher should be sure that the students are involved in activities which provide them with reasons for using and improving their location and study skills.
     The objectives of this module are stated in approximately the order in which students would need each skill. However, deviation from this order is advisable so that a skill may be developed concurrently with a similar skill in another discipline or to concur with a class activity which calls for proficiency in a particular skill.
     Objectives stated in this module should be differentiated to fit the different capabilities and individual needs of the students. Instruction which does not meet individual needs is inefficient. The teacher will find it necessary to evaluate each child's capabilities and needs in order to carry on this unit of study.
     This module is designed to serve as a unit of study to guide and motivate students in the understanding and usage of Location and Study Skills, and is an attempt to suggest several activities and learning resources to be used in each area of study.
  B. Outline of Module (omitted)
  C. Operational Instructions (omitted)
     The operational procedures to be followed in completing this module are as follows:
     1. Carefully read the prospectus.
     2. Read the statement of the module's mission objective.
     3. Familiarize yourself with the specific goal competencies that represent the specific intents of the module.
II. Diagnostic Pre-Assessment
     The purpose of the diagnostic pre-assessment in this module is designed to assist the teacher in determining student strengths and weaknesses in Location and Study Skills. The teacher may use the Data Gathering Survey along with personal observation in order to plan appropriate strategies for implementation of each stated objective in this module. From data collected the teacher will be able to determine individual, small group and whole group needs.

DATA GATHERING SURVEY

Instructions:
   The teacher will indicate by placing an X in the appropriate space provided, whether or not the student has mastered a particular Location and Study Skill on his or her grade level. Data for selecting the answers may be gathered through verbal, written and observational means prior to the initiation of this module.

Concepts	YES	NO
1. Arranges words in alphabetical order		
2. Uses textbook aids, such as the Title Page, Table of Contents, and Index		
3. Recognizes the parts of a library catalogue card		
4. Ability to identify and explain meanings of map symbols, colors, and key		
5. Locates words and their meanings in the dictionary		
6. Ability to identify and use correct punctuation and capitalization		

Teacher Comments:

III. Post-Assessment and Recycling (omitted)
IV. Statement of Specific Goal Competencies
   Goals, in the context used in this module, represent the specific intents or competencies for which the module has been written. Each goal is considered to have a specific instructional intent that has intrinsic value and is considered to be a long-range end worth achieving. In this module the student will be asked to:
   1. Develop the ability to arrange words in alphabetical order.
   2. Develop the ability to use the Title Page, Table of Contents and the Index of a book.
   3. Develop the ability to recognize the main parts of a library catalog card.
   4. Develop the ability to identify and explain the meanings of colors, symbols and keys found on sample maps.
   5. Develop the ability to demonstrate skill in locating words and finding the meanings of the words in a dictionary.
   6. Develop the ability to identify and use correctly punctuation marks and capital letters.
V. Objectives, Activities, Learning Resources and Recycling
   A. Mission Objective
      For third-grade Reading students to acquire the competencies necessary for using Location and Study Skills. Success

in achieving this mission will be determined by achievement of at least four of the six specific performance objectives outlined in this module.

B. Performance Objectives, Activities and Learning Resources

In this module, performance objectives represent extensions of the specific goals, stated in Part IV, to include the educational outcomes expected from the learner. These outcomes are specified by a performance statement indicating the behavior, activity, or instrumentation that will be used to evaluate learner progress toward achieving the goals. In addition, the performance statement includes a criterion standard that represents the level of success required for a performance to be considered an adequate indicator of goal achievement.

Each performance objective is sequentially stated in the same order as that of its corresponding goal statement in Part IV of the module. Each objective is followed by the listing of specific activities and learning resources that may be used to achieve the competency. In addition, supplementary post-assessment and recycling information is stated for each individual objective.

Specific Performance Objective Number One:
For third grade reading students to develop the ability to arrange words in alphabetical order, so when given a list of ten words, each word beginning with a different letter, the majority of the students will relist the words in alphabetical order, as witnessed by the teacher.

Activities and Learning Resources
a. Attendance in class and small group work sessions
b. Review textbook or study materials
c. Student-Teacher Conferences
d. Supplementary materials provided by the teacher
e. Free choice activities
f. Discuss the uses of alphabetical order the students may know about: class lists, school office records, telephone directory, dictionary, telephone dial, library, rows in a theater.
g. If the students have not had prior experience with alphabetizing, you will probably want to provide a variety of practice exercises. You could begin by alphabetizing the first names of four or five students in the class. Then alphabetize the last names of the same children.
h. Have students take turn finding names in a real telephone directory.
i. ORAL: Play this alphabet game with your class. Divide into teams. When the teacher calls a team, see how quickly the students can stand and arrange themselves so that their last names are in alphabetical order.

Post-Assessment and Recycling
The teacher will evaluate this objective immediately after completion of the enabling activities. Each student will be required to complete a written test composed of ten words, each beginning with a different letter, to be relisted in alphabetical order. Students must achieve 100 per cent accuracy. The students will be allowed to recycle two or more times.

Specific Performance Objective Number Two:
For third grade reading students to develop the ability to use the Title Page, Table of Contents and Index of a book in order to locate desired in-

formation. Success will be determined by the majority of the students identifying the correct part of a book to use to locate desired information on a teacher-made test.

Activities and Learning Resources
a. Attendance in class and small group work sessions
b. Review textbook or study materials
c. Student-Teacher Conferences
d. Supplementary materials provided by the teacher
e. Free choice activities
f. Before beginning this lesson, you may want to let the students work in pairs and explore the Title Page, Table of Contents and the Index of a book, making a list of the differences. Then pool their findings and discuss them with the entire class.
g. Field Trip to visit the grave of Randolph Caldecott, illustrator, buried in Evergreen Cemetery, St. Augustine, Florida
h. As you teach other subjects, encourage the students to use the Title Page, Table of Contents and Index.

Post-Assessment and Recycling
The students will be administered a competency examination upon completion of the instructional activities. The examination will consist of short answer questions. The students are to use a specified book in order to complete the exam. The students will be asked to state the section of a book used to locate the desired information and page number on which the information was found. Students may recycle two or more times.

Specific Performance Objective Number Three:
For third grade reading students to develop the ability to recognize the main parts of a library catalog card, so when given a library catalog card, the majority of the students will identify the author, title, subject, and call number of a book, as witnessed by the teacher.

Activities and Learning Resources
a. Attendance in class and small group work sessions
b. Review textbook or study materials
c. Student-Teacher Conferences
d. Supplementary materials provided by the teacher
e. Free choice activities
f. Motivate interest by arranging for the children to tour the school library or the public library before studying this lesson.
g. Ask the Librarian to demonstrate how to make a catalog card.
h. Read to the class: *How Can I Find Out?* by Mary M. Bongirno and Mable Gee.
i. Film: *Discovering the Library* (11 min., b.w., color) Coronet Film
j. Filmstrip: *Our Library* (48 fr., color) Encyclopaedia Britannica Films

Post-Assessment and Recycling
Post-assessment evaluation will consist of successfully recognizing the main parts of a library catalog card. The post-assessment may be done by oral or written means. Students may recycle the objective two or more times.

Specific Performance Objective Number Four:
For third grade reading students to develop the ability to identify and explain the meaning of symbols, colors, and keys used on simple maps, so when given a simple map using colors, symbols and a key, the majority of the students will identify and explain the meaning of each of the symbols, colors and keys used in map reading, as witnessed by the teacher.

Activities and Learning Resources
a. Attendance in class and small group work sessions
b. Review textbook or study materials
c. Student-Teacher Conferences
d. Supplementary materials provided by the teacher
e. Free choice activities
f. Students make a map showing buried treasure using simple symbols, colors and a simple key.
g. Provide several simple maps to illustrate symbols, colors and keys.
h. Harris, Ruby M. *The Rand McNally Handbook of Map and Globe Usage.* Chicago: Rand McNally, 1959. (Pages 1–22, methods for introducing primary children to maps and globes.)

Post-Assessment and Recycling
The students will be administered a competency exam at the completion of the enabling activities. The exam will consist of a simple map using colors, symbols and a key to be identified and the meaning of each to be explained by the student. Students may recycle two or more times.

Specific Performance Objective Number Five:
For third grade reading students to develop the ability to demonstrate skill in locating words and finding the meanings of the words in a dictionary, so when given a list of five words, the majority of the students will locate the words in the dictionary and locate the meaning of each word, as witnessed by the teacher.

Activities and Learning Resources
a. Attendance in class and small group work sessions
b. Review textbook or study materials
c. Student-Teacher Conferences
d. Supplementary materials provided by the teacher
e. Free choice activities
f. Motivate interest in this lesson by having the students explore a dictionary.
g. Ask the pupils to suggest words that were unfamiliar to them. List them on the board, and have the pupils race to see who can find the words first in their dictionaries.

Post-Assessment and Recycling
This competency will be evaluated by the ability of the students to locate words in the dictionary and to find the meanings of the word. The exam will consist of a list of five words to be located in the dictionary and the meanings of each word to be located as witnessed by teacher observation. Students may recycle this objective two or more times.

Specific Performance Objective Number Six:
For third grade reading students to develop the ability to identify and use correctly punctuation marks and capital letters, so when given a paragraph with no punctuation or capital letters, the majority of the students will correctly write the paragraph, employing needed punctuation and capitalization.

Activities and Learning Resources
a. Attendance in class and small group work sessions
b. Review textbook or study materials
c. Student-Teacher Conferences
d. Supplementary materials provided by the teacher
e. Free choice activities
f. Motivate interest in using periods by writing the following on the board: therewerenospacesbetweenwordswhenwritingfirstbeganit

washardtotellwhensentencesbeganorended. Then ask the students what could be done to make the words on the board more readable.

g. Supply some copies of short stories, leaving out all the capital letters. Include in the stories some names and possibly the word "I." To avoid confusion, retain the correct punctuation in the stories, the first time; later remove the punctuation marks, also. Ask the students to rewrite the story using capital letters for all words that require them.

h. Dictate some sentences such as the following, trying not to indicate with your voice where the punctuation goes or where sentences begin and end. Have the students write the sentences correctly.

it is a warm day shall we go to the lake the swimming should be good today have you a bathing suit

i. Pupils might enjoy making up questions, which other pupils can answer with statements.

j. Read the following poem aloud to the students and encourage discussion of it: *Don't Tell Me* by Dorothy Aldis. (Concerns the question mark.)

k. To increase awareness of punctuation marks, let the students work out a spoken code for using a different noise or nonsense word for each mark. For example: comma – coo, question mark = whoop, period = bang, exclamation mark = whap. Using this code the students might read aloud passages from their textbooks.

VI. List of References and Materials (St. Johns County Learning Resource Center)

	Table of Contents	Card Catalog
Subject		
Publisher	Harper	Laidlaw
Title	New Directions in English	English 3
Pages	179–188	128–129

The Learning Resource Center has the following films:

1. *Beginning Responsibility – Books*
2. *The Library – A Place for Discovery*
3. *The Magic Book*

The Center has filmstrips and transparencies which would be helpful in teaching study skills.

VII. Glossary of Terms

Prospectus – A preliminary introductory group of statements that describe module components that are considered essential.

Supplementary Materials – Films, filmstrips, games, workbooks, worksheets, multi-level textbooks, tapes, charts, transparencies, field trips, resource personnel.

Chapter 9

THE AFFECTIVE DOMAIN: REALM OF FEELINGS AND EMOTIONS

Next to excellence is the appreciation of it.

Thackeray

CHAPTER GOALS

For the reader to:

1. be able to conceptualize the scope and nature of the affective domain.

2. become acquainted with some appropriate literature concerning the writing of objectives in the affective domain, as well as on relationships between the affective, cognitive and psychomotor domains.

3. comprehend a few basic terms that are useful in developing understandings in the affective area.

4. be introduced to a simple general theory that can be used as a working model for conceptualizing affective stimuli and responses.

5. be introduced to a theoretical basis for writing objectives in the affective domain in a practical, unthreatening and easily understood manner.

Formulating meaningful behavioral objective statements in the cognitive and psychomotor domains presents many problems, but development of affective objectives produces even greater trepidation. It is relatively easy to evaluate cognitive or psychomotor objectives through overt measurable learner behaviors. Appropriate meaningful evaluation techniques are, however, very limited for objectives written in the affective domain. Knowledge accumulated by behavioral scientists relating to evaluation of feelings and emotions still does not allow educators and researchers to state overt measurable learner behaviors that will conclusively support progress in affective areas. The approach to

166

be proposed in this text is to encourage more specific identification and definition of affective goals. This, in turn, should enable an evaluator to plan more specific and efficient evaluation.

PERTINENT LITERATURE

Kibler, Barker and Miles[1] indicate that the development of behavioral objectives for the affective domain is different from writing objectives based upon knowledge and recall owing to the difficulty in observing and measuring feelings and emotions.

Ojemann[2] stated that affective educational objectives should bring changes in the learner and that these changes are internal; thus, they cannot be seen. The only way to determine if a learner has acquired a specified emotional pattern is to observe his behavior in specified situations. He further pointed out that behavioral objective writers tend to omit goals in the affective domain because objectives in this area are harder to state in behavioral terms.

Harrow[3] wrote, "One must always keep in mind that behavior may be conceptualized as falling into one of three learning domains, but in reality when observing a child's behavior, it is usually a combination of all three." She further stated, "A learner's behavior does not fall neatly into one of the three separate compartments of the learning domains. The learner behaves as an integrated whole and the behavioral objective writer must isolate the particular behavior which at the moment is the prime concern."[4]

Eisner[5] indicated that some educational outcomes such as appreciation cannot be measured. Krathwohl[6] stated, "At all levels of the affective domain, affective objectives have a cognitive component." This would mean that there is a relationship between the cognitive and affective domains that prevents their being entirely separate from each other. The feelings a learner has toward obtaining knowledge will affect his achievement in this area. The more knowledge a learner has about a subject, the more likely he is to appreciate or have a good feeling toward it.

Piaget[7] wrote:

> . . . there is a close parallel between the development of affectivity and that of the intellectual functions, since these are two indissociable aspects of every action. In all behavior, the motives and energizing dynamisms reveal affectivity, while the techniques and adjustment of the means employed constitute the cognitive sensorimotor or rational aspect. These is never a purely intellectual action, and numerous emotions, interests, values, impressions of harmony, etc., intervene, for example, in the solving of a mathematical problem. Likewise, there is never a purely affective act, e.g., love presupposes comprehension. Always and everywhere, in object-

related behavior as well as in interpersonal behavior, both elements
are involved because the one presupposes the other.

Harrow's[8] work extends this togetherness of the domains into the
psychomotor areas.

Eiss and Harbeck[9] wrote "At the present state of our knowledge
about the affective domain, it may not be possible to suggest behaviors
that invariably will serve as indicators of the achievement of a given
affective objective, or to provide numerical values between overt behaviors and desired goals . . . . It is only in the psychomotor that the
credibility gap is fairly closed between behavior and objective." They
referred to the credibility gap as the lack of certainty that overt measurable learner behaviors often identified should be accepted as evidence
that the goal of the desired objective has been achieved. These two
writers also indicated that in the affective area, the attempt to formulate
measurable learner objectives often results in objectives that are trivial
and often do not represent the goals that the teacher is trying to achieve.

Beatty[10] refers to feelings and emotion in behavior and suggests
that educators have been too much concerned with intellectual behavior
in children when the key issue might well be the affective and emotional
behavior of the learner. This article supports Harrow's, Krathwohl's,
and Piaget's statements about the relationship between the affective and
cognitive domains. Esbensen[11] states, "Perhaps the most important difference between the psychomotor and cognitive domains on the one
hand, and the affective domain on the other, is the difference between
can do and will do." This is interpreted as meaning that cognitive objectives assume a learner may not be able to accomplish a certain goal,
whereas affective objectives assume that the learner can accomplish the
goal, but may not choose to do so of his own volition.

General and research literature concerning both the affective
domain and the writing and use of behavioral objectives abound with
perplexities of coping with and evaluating behaviors relating to feelings
and emotions. The above citings were not intended as a summary of
literature on the subject, but were chosen to present a brief overview
showing that problems do exist and must be considered.

DEFINITION OF TERMS

A brief, general definition of terms which are basic to understandings developed in the affective area may be helpful to the reader. From
these general definitions, behavioral objective writers should develop
more specific operational definitions for each term before using it.
This will insure that each objective will be more specific and will be used
in the proper context.

(1) Affective Domain: *The sphere of influence that involves behaviors caused by feelings or emotions.*

(2) Interests: *A perceptual condition which combines both cognitive and affective consciousness into a type of feeling.* This feeling can be either temporary or permanent, based upon the quantity and quality of experiences which have created it. The term itself is a type of continuous variable in which the feeling of interest may constantly change based upon the phenomenon to which it is applied.

(3) Appreciation: *Emotional awareness of the significance of anything.* Appreciation involves an interest in the worth or value of the variable; it indicates a person's identification with the way something has been created or expressed. Appreciation may be indicated by a person's response to the variable in part or as a total being.

(4) Attitudes: Attitudes may best represent the mean expression or verbalization of affective terms. Many attempts to define attitudes have been made during the past thirty or forty years. Definitions have ranged from terms such as "emotionalized tendency," "predisposition to perform, think, perceive, and feel," "readiness to react toward a situation, person, or thing," to statements that would indicate that attitudes are little other than verbalizations of feelings and emotions. For the purpose of this text, it is proposed that attitudes be defined as *emotionalized dispositions utilized in the information processing aspects of behavior which will cause a person to think or behave either positively or negatively toward a particular variable.* No one attitude covers everything, but each distinct variable may create its own emotion in the learner and emotions concerning component parts of a variable may differ in their positive or negative tendencies. The resulting behaviors produced by each attitude will, at least in part, be determined by the conditions present at the time and in the context of each new situation.

(5) Values: Values are derived through an accumulation of interests and appreciations and the formation of attitudes concerning different phenomena; they are formed over long periods of time. Examples of values are open mindedness, social tolerance, intellectual curiosity, and moral standards. With reference to the educational processes, values are developed or taught by what we do, what we say, and what we observe. In other words, values are taught by personal examples, through class discussion, and by other interaction with the environment.

In this country, it is construed that public educational systems should be interested in developing a sense of values in students. Along with this, students should be taught to choose between alternative values or to make value judgments. This supports the theory that education must be concerned with the whole child so that each one may develop to the fullest. All students have some value consciousness concerning general as well as specific concepts. As is the case with attitudes and appreciation, students will demonstrate some behaviors to indicate value judgments.

Teachers and administrators should recognize, however, that students will not act out all of their values, have the same values, or even necessarily react to the same values in the same way.

Based upon these conclusions, it would be possible to define value by several different characteristics. The definition could be quite burdensome and long. In this text, however, values will simply be defined as *any quality or trait deemed worthy enough to be socially, morally or psychologically desirable.*

(6) Adjustment: Good[12] defines adjustment through several categories—emotional, personality, social and many others. These indicate that the area of adjustment must be diagnosed before a proper definition can be formulated. Three definitions, two psychological and one social, will suffice for the purposes of this text: (a) the process of finding and adopting modes of behavior suitable to the environment or to changes in the environment; (b) favorable, neutral, or unfavorable adaptation of an organism to external and internal stimulation; (c) the process by which individuals or groups accept, compromise, or acquiesce to social forces or one another.

Based upon these explanations, adjustment will be defined as *the adaptation of a person which will enable him to deal more effectively with his environment.* The nature of the area of concern will then provide a frame of reference in which a more specific operational definition can be produced based upon a specific application of the term.

GENERAL THEORY

Affectively speaking, people are probably more nearly alike at birth than at any other time of life. Perceptions of the environment are more nearly neutral at birth than it is possible for them to be throughout the rest of life. The newborn learner has little awareness of himself or the world around him. He has limited interests and appreciations; he probably has no fixed attitudes or values. In addition, he has had to make few adjustments to the world at birth.

Virtually all of a learner's cognitive development, feelings and emotions, and voluntary movement must be developed as part of the growing process. Perception in regard to feelings and emotions is what the affective domain is all about. There are many ways of perceiving feelings. In the human, feelings are always present, but fortunately for the individual they usually do not show externally. Feelings can be good or bad, positive or negative, strong or weak, for or against and many other combinations of extremes. Usually they do not show unless they are stimulated by some specific situation. Feelings in the affective domain often refer to interests, appreciations, attitudes, values, and adjustments, and are the reason for defining these terms early in the text. Interests represent feelings that are less strong and less stable than other feelings such as attitudes. Attitudes are less strong and stable than values and so it is with other affective terms; they can be placed in hierarchical order.

Feelings are both common and unique. There is virtually no limit to the number of variables about which a learner may develop feelings. A learner's feelings will greatly affect his performance in almost any given activity, provided they are strongly felt. Weak feelings are easier to change than strong feelings. Stronger feelings, however, are also subject to change if correct and sufficient stimuli are used. Perhaps an easy, though over simplified, way to understand the development of feelings is through a general theory which can serve as a working model for developing understandings and objectives in the affective domain.

Learning theory indicates that learning begins when some stimulus causes an organism to react. The stimulus may be internal or external. Eventually, a person becomes aware of the stimulus. Awareness, in turn, causes some form of feeling such as interest or disinterest which will result in an individual deciding to pursue the activity or to discontinue the contact. If the original awareness creates substantial curiosity or interest to pursue the activity, it may continue until an attitude is developed or until values have been established.

Affective contact can be said to take place on a pleasure-pain continuum according to the feeling which is produced. There are three distinct possibilities which can occur when affective contact is made. We may feel pain (withdrawal), indifference (neutrality) and pleasure (attraction). These sensations, perceptions, and behavior reactions can be placed on a continuum.

In simple terms, the pleasure-pain theory may be viewed graphically as in the chart below. A stimulus can develop a response of pleasure, pain or indifference depending on a wide variety of factors, including the individual awareness of people.

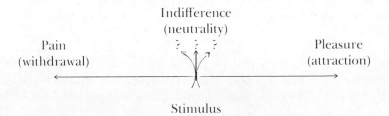

It may be assumed that the further along the continuum a feeling moves toward either polar extreme and away from the point of neutrality, the greater will be the amount of either pleasure or pain that is experienced. The general theory may be revised into a working model which may be more useful in evaluating affective terms such as interest, appreciations, and attitudes.

At birth, as well as subsequently, there exist certain drive mechanisms such as thirst and hunger, but, through stimuli and their reinforcement, learning occurs and more complex motivational systems develop, including those within what we call the affective domain. As the human being develops he is able to process information (stimuli) at increasing levels of complexity. Within the complexity, information processing and motivation systems, such as feelings, interests, attitudes and appreciations, are developed.

This working model may be illustrated this way:

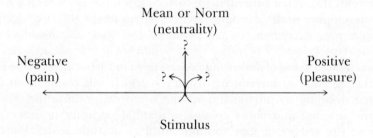

In this chart "pleasure" and "pain" have been replaced by the words "positive" and "negative" which are more closely associated with affective terms—attitudes and interests. A stimulus occurs at what we might call the mid point or point of neutrality. This point might well represent the intenseness of a learner's feelings at birth. Immediately, this stimulus will pass from the cognitive to the affective self and become associated with positive, negative or neutral responses. For the sake of brevity, we will hereafter only refer to the feeling called attitude. It can be easily established that interests, appreciations, and other affective terms may apply to the theory just as appropriately as attitudes, although the polar objectives might change according to concept usage. This change would be similar to changing pain to negative and pleasure to positive.

The concept, image, object, or activity providing a stimulus will tend to move toward the positive pole in the case of a favorable response and toward the negative pole if the response to the stimuli is unfavorable. *The task of the teacher is to provide learning strategies which will help the student gain the maximum positive and the minimum negative experiences.* The outcomes of these experiences must then be identified through observation of behavior change for purposes of evaluation.

The chances of observing a behavior change are at least in part dependent upon the strength of the affective response following the stimulus activity. In other words, how strong, whether positive or negative, a behavior will become will depend partially upon the following criteria:

1. Intensity of the stimulus
2. Duration of the stimulus
3. Consequences of the feelings
4. Whether the feelings provided are always positive or negative.
5. Whether the object of the feeling affected is near or remote.
6. Nature of the stimulus.

We might assume that an attitude is not in most instances made up of feelings obtained from just one stimulus. In many instances there will be repeated stimulus situations which gradually are coordinated to establish an overall attitude toward a specific concept. This means *that a firmly established attitude may be composed of many component parts which individually may be quite different in the feelings they convey, but collectively establish the positive or negative position of the overall concept.*

For example, a competency module, as outlined earlier in the text, is a written instructional guide intended to direct the individual learning efforts of students in a given content area. Major components of a module may become sub-concepts in developing student attitudes toward use of competency modules. Affective domain sub-concepts or components should include at least the following:

1. A statement of specific goal competencies
2. Specification of behavioral objectives
3. Pre-Assessment
4. The instructional strategies and learning resources
5. Post-assessment
6. Recycling.

Students will encounter these sub-concepts repeatedly as they utilize competency modules in competency based instructional programs. Each concept can be interpreted as representing a potential stimulus that will produce a feeling that can produce a certain amount of either positive or negative response. The difference between the total of all positive responses and all negative responses will determine a student's attitude, positive or negative, toward the use of competency modules.

In reality there are many other factors which may tend to shape a student's attitude toward the use of instructional modules. The whole of a student's module experiences may, in addition, be a greater influence on attitude development than just the accumulation of his isolated sub-concepts. The point is, however, that this illustration does emphasize the fact that attitudes, hence feelings and emotions, are composed of impressions made by more than one stimulus concerning the same concept.

This illustration can also be used to emphasize the point that *the interests, beliefs, appreciations, and attitudes which people have will result in their eventually having preferences which, in time, may be seen as values and adjustments.* In this illustration we have the following relationships:

interests are to appreciations
as
appreciations are to attitudes
as
attitudes are to values
as
values are to adjustments

It is not necessary that we prove this or that these relationships remain fixed at all times. The purpose is achieved if the reader can conceptualize such relationships in preparing to write behavioral objectives in the affective domain.

The problem presented to the behavioral objective writer in evaluation, regardless of the behavioral level he chooses to change, is to determine an overt behavior that will be an expression of something the student chooses to do for himself. A secondary problem in evaluation is to plan and establish the appropriate situations that will permit the student opportunities to express himself and make choices in a natural situation. The key question in each observation becomes whether or not the student is willing to choose the behavior for himself rather than his ability to perform the action. The *willingness* to perform places the objective in the Affective Domain.

The problem involved in the overall changing of most feelings is often the inability to isolate one feeling from a host of other feelings to which it is attached. Feelings are often based upon faulty stimulation or evidence and are thus subject to emotional irrationality which further complicates any analysis of their development.

There are several factors which should be identified as being part of the conceptualization of this general theory. We need to be specific about our goals, objectives, concepts and terms. A teacher, if successful, must employ strategies which will provide experiences which are pleasurable or positive in the mind of the student. These positive experiences will create positive interest, appreciation, belief, attitudes or values on the part of the learner. Conversely, negative experiences will produce the reverse effect.

Finally, instruments or behavioral situations must be provided which will furnish data concerning the status or direction of movement of the affective components being studied. People with negative beliefs and attitudes will tend to avoid those concepts they view negatively. People with positive beliefs and attitudes will seek out those activities which give them pleasure. The movement in direction or preferences shown by learners is really what the affective domain is all about; evaluation with valid observation is extremely difficult.

GLOSSARY OF TERMS

Affective Domain: a behavioral area that consists of all behaviors which describe changes in interests, attitudes, values and the development of appreciation and adequate adjustment. It consists of both motivational and perceptual factors.

General Theory: in this chapter, general theory refers to the development of a set of general facts and suppositions which represent a systematic view of possible affective domain relationships. This general theory can be used to establish hypotheses that can be used as a working model for evaluation of affective domain variables.

Pleasure-Pain Theory: refers to the concept that the human animal is capable of mentally interpreting a stimulus activity as being either pleasurable or painful or equidistant between these two feelings at a point of neutrality. The degree of pleasure or pain is supposed to fluctuate according to characteristics of the stimulus received.

REFERENCES

1. Robert J. Kibler, Larry L. Barker, and David T. Miles, *Behavioral Objectives and Instruction,* Boston, Allyn and Bacon, Inc., 1970, p. 98.
2. Ralph H. Ojemann, "Should Educational Objectives Be Stated in Behavioral Terms? Part II," Elementary School Journal. 68, (February, 1969), pp. 229–235.
3. Anita J. Harrow, *A Taxonomy of the Psychomotor Domain: A Guide for Developing Behavioral Objectives,* New York. David McKay Company, Inc. 1972, p. 30.
4. Ibid, p. 37.
5. Elliott W. Eisner, "Educational Objectives: Help or Hindrance?" *School Review,* 75 (Autumn, 1967), pp. 250–260.
6. David R. Krathwohl, B. S. Bloom, and B. B. Masia, *Taxonomy of Educational Objectives,* 1st ed., (Handbook II: Affective Domain), New York, David McKay Company, Inc., 1964, p. 54.
7. Jean Piaget, *Six Psychological Studies,* New York, Random House, 1967.
8. Anita J. Harrow, *op. cit.,* pp. 37–39.
9. Albert F. Eiss and Mary Blatt Harbedk, *Behavioral Objectives in the Affective Domain,* (National Science Teachers Association) Washington, National Education Association, 1969, p. 4.
10. Walcott H. Beatty, "Emotion: The Missing Link in Education," adopted from a speech at the conference on Issues in Human Development, Present and Future, at the Institute for Child Study, University of Maryland, April 20, 1968.
11. Thorwald Esbensen, *Using Performance Objectives,* Published by the State of Florida, Department of Education in cooperation with the Bureau of Educational Personnel Development, U.S. Office of Education, Office of Publications and Textbook Services, Knott Building, Tallahassee, Florida, p. 29.
12. Carter V. Good, editor. *The Dictionary of Education,* New York: McGraw-Hill Book Company, Inc., 1959, p. 12.

Chapter 10

THE AFFECTIVE
TAXONOMY

> Our feelings were given us to excite to action, and
> when they end in themselves, they are cherished
> to no good purpose.
>
> *Sandford*

CHAPTER GOALS

For the reader to:

1. comprehend the classification and sub-category levels of the *Taxonomy of Educational Objectives. (Handbook II: Affective Domain).*

2. understand possible limitations in using the taxonomy to write behavioral objectives at specific classification and sub-category levels.

3. comprehend practical relationships that exist between a goal statement of intent and objectives stated in the taxonomy at each of the five classification levels.

According to the *Taxonomy of Educational Objectives, (Handbook II: Affective Domain)*[1] the major components of the Affective Domain would appear to be: (1) the levels of hierarchy termed *receiving, responding, valuing, organizing,* and *characterization by a value complex;* and (2) selected commonly used affective terms such as *interest, appreciation, attitudes, values, and adjustment.* Adapting information from this taxonomy, we can visualize these major components and the sub-category levels of the hierarchy as shown in Figure 10–1.

Interests have a behavioral range of meaning from the first to the third hierarchy level extending along the continuum from awareness to actural preference for an object or event. Appreciation is shown to mean anything from willingness to pay attention to the actual desire for something. Attitudes and values then have similar hierarchical values; they both indicate anything from behavior that shows willingness for response to behaviors indicating that values have been formed. Finally, the word adjustment has the broadest interpretation—extending all the way from behaviors indicating willingness to respond to behaviors indicative of the characterization of a value complex.

176

Range of Meaning	Hierarchy Classification Levels	Sub-category Taxonomy Continuum
↕ ADJUSTMENT, ↕ APPRECIATION, ↕ INTERESTS	1.0 Receiving	Awareness 1.1 Willingness to receive 1.2 Controlled or selected attention 1.3
↕ ADJUSTMENT, ↕ VALUE, ↕ ATTITUDES, ↕ APPRECIATION, ↕ INTERESTS	2.0 Responding	Acquiesence in responding 2.1 Willingness to respond 2.2 Satisfaction in response 2.3
↕ ADJUSTMENT, ↕ VALUE, ↕ ATTITUDES, ↕ APPRECIATION, ↕ INTERESTS	3.0 Valuing	Acceptance of a value 3.1 Preference for a value 3.2 Commitment 3.3
↕ ADJUSTMENT, ↕ VALUE, ↕ ATTITUDES	4.0 Organization	Conceptualization of a value 4.1 Organization of a value system 4.2
	5.0 Characterization by a Value Complex	Generalized set 5.1 Characterization 5.2

Figure 10–1 Range of meaning for common terms along the hierarchical classification continuum.

Traditionally, educational programs are geared to the first two affective classifications, receiving and responding. The first, or lowest, level, receiving, does not actually provide for affective learning change. This classification only begins learning through receiving a communication and is, therefore, not an affective response that can be evaluated. Attempts to evaluate receiving should be based upon evaluation of cognitive information or knowledge rather than affective response.

According to the working model for evaluation, feelings are developed after stimulus has been received. The stimulus is then transferred into existing cognitive patterns accompanied by possible positive or negative affective reactions. The point is that receiving precedes any reaction to a communication; therefore, it would be impractical to attempt to evaluate behavioral responses which have not yet occurred. In the event that one were to assume that all stimuli and initial response occupy the same time span, the depth and intensity of the affective behavior may not be significant enough to identify or measure.

It is important to recognize that there is no problem in accepting the receiving classification as part of the affective taxonomy. It is a necessary sequential part of feeling development just as is the lowest classification level, reflex movements, in Harrow's[2] *Taxonomy of the Psychomotor Domain.* Psychomotor behaviors are defined as all observable voluntary human motion. Reflex movements are performed without conscious decision upon the part of a learner. They are not, therefore, voluntary movements, but are rightfully accounted for in the taxonomy in order to give a better overview of the entire movement domain.

The affective taxonomy was developed as an aid to people who wish to develop affective goals and objectives. *The primary purpose of a discussion of the receiving category is to elicit the thought that the receiving classification level is not amenable to the development of affective behavioral objectives. Thus, it is not recommended that a teacher write any affective behavioral objectives for the receiving classification.* This classification level can be useful in the development of goals which will benefit the higher levels of response. It is recommended that if the receiving classification is used at all, its use should be limited to goal development. In the event objectives are stated for the receiving classification, the goals should be stated as cognitive intents, since they will be evaluated by cognitive measures.

Willingness to respond, the second sub-category in the Responding Classification level, is the first or lowest category that can be used for specification of objectives in behavioral terms. The first sub-category at this level, acquiescence in responding, does not indicate any feeling or emotion on the part of the learner. A learner may respond or acquiesce as required to a given situation, command or question. This compliance does not, however, mean that he has responded with feeling or that the response was based upon interests or appreciations held by the learner. In fact, he may have responded in a desired manner although his feelings and natural inclinations were opposed to the required behavior.

Most behavioral objectives written according to the classification scheme provided by the affective taxonomy should probably be written at either the responding or (valuing) classification levels. Learners can elicit behaviors that indicate: (1) willingness to respond; (2) satisfaction in response; (3) acceptance of a value; (4) preference for a value; and (5) commitment. It is anticipated that teachers, whether in elementary, secondary or higher education, will develop most of their affective behavioral objectives from these two classification levels.

The sub-category, conceptualization of a value, is the only component of the fourth and fifth classification levels, organization and characterization by a value complex, in which it appears it might be meaningful to write behavioral objectives. Even these attempts should be limited and are probably more suitable for psychology, learning theory, and evaluation specialists.

The affective changes and responses required by the organization and characterization of a value complex classification probably require too long a period of time to accomplish or evaluate during a short-range educational period. This complexity allows many variables, other than those relating to classroom instruction, to influence the learner, which prevents evaluation involving sound cause and effect relationships.

The behavioral objective writer must remember that evaluation is for the purpose of determining how successfully a learner achieves goals which have been established. In addition, the procedures for achieving these goals represent the strategies the teacher has developed to provide meaningful learning experiences.

Thus, behavioral objectives are not developed to determine the status of a learner's behavior or a value set already established before the teacher sees the child. Rather, they represent goals and evaluation performances designed to determine learner behavior which has been *changed* through exposure to a particular teacher, content and contextual situation.

Set values and adjustments occur over the lifetime of a learner. Changes of significant intensity and duration and the ability to evaluate them—including establishment of reliability and validity for the evaluation instruments—as well as controlling essential variables are usually beyond the scope of a teacher's influence on a learner. The teacher may help develop some new interests or appreciations and even aid in the learner's formulation of attitudes, whatever they really are; but developing and evaluating any higher levels of behavior are normally not feasible undertakings. However, this is not to rule out such undertakings in special programs, directed by well qualified persons over extensive time periods.

Again, it is emphasized that goals, and strategies to achieve them, can and probably should be stated for all levels of the taxonomy because goal achievement is still valuable. Failure in ability to evaluate success does not mean failure in bringing about positive change in the right direction, but only inability to meaningfully evaluate it most of the time. The differences between goals and evaluation performances should be kept in mind. Thus, behavioral objectives written for the two highest classification levels, as well as for the lowest level, of the taxonomy may not be worth the time and effort when viewed on realistic and practical bases.

Krathwohl[3] states that *the biggest problem in classification of affective domain objectives is making them specific.* In other words, most of the terms are too vague and the range of meaning for each term is too wide. Thus, each behavioral objective writer will need to state the goal and evaluation components in terms that will best illustrate the exact interpretation that is being made of them. The intent of the goal should be clearly pointed out by the evaluation activities to be performed.

In Chapter V of the taxonomy, Krathwohl states objectives at all five levels of the taxonomy. His intention is to have it understood that each of the objectives is intended to describe student behavior to be obtained. These statements best represent goals or general objectives, but are definitely not behavioral objectives in the sense that they specify a specific evaluation of outcome performance, criterion standards and conditions. Maybe they are not intended to be behavioral objectives in this sense.

Based upon the information provided in Figure 10–1 and the example statements from the field of art that are listed in the taxonomy, it is possible to illustrate how they might be stated as goals based upon the hierarchical classifications:

1.1 Awareness
   For students to become conscious of the use of shading to portray depth and lighting in a picture.
   Rationale:
   To become conscious of something only requires an awareness, not a response. It does not require learner willingness or selected attention; therefore, it is classified in the 1.1 subcategory. It can be assumed to be a desirable goal and have strategies developed to achieve it, but need not be converted to a behavioral objective designed to measure affective change.
1.2 Willingness to receive
   To increase fifth grade student's tolerance for bizarre uses of shading in modern art.

Rationale:

Tolerance for a communication infers that a person is not only aware of the message but willing to receive it. This willingness to pay some attention or to encounter the communication places the goal in the 1.2 sub-category. It is a desirable goal but need not be converted to a behavioral objective designed to measure affective change.

1.3 Controlled or Selected attention

For eighth grade art students to watch for instances in which shading has been used to create a sense of three-dimensional depth at the same time that it indicates something about the lighting in a picture.

Rationale:

To watch for something indicates that selected attention is being given some variable that is not being given to other variables. Thus, this goal is placed under the sub-category 1.3. The goal is desirable but need not be evaluated for affective change or stated as a behavioral objective.

2.1 Acquiescence in responding

For sixth-grade students to obey their teacher's request to look for instances in art where shading has been well used.

Rationale:

To obey is to comply which places this goal under the 2.1 sub-category for acquiescence in responding. This does not require any learning or behavioral change since the student does not necessarily choose the act for himself. The goal need not be stated as a behavioral objective.

2.2 Willingness to respond

For eleventh-grade art students to voluntarily look for instances of good art where shading, perspective, color, and design have been well used.

Rationale:

To volunteer indicates a willingness to respond or perform a behavior by a learner's own choice. This places the goal under sub-category 2.2. This goal can be meaningfully converted into a behavioral objective.

2.3 Satisfaction in response

To increase tenth-grade students' enjoyment in finding instances of good art where shading, perspective, color and design have been well used.

Rationale:

Enjoyment of an activity indicates that the learner is getting satisfaction out of his response to some stimulus which places the goal under the 2.3 sub-category. The hierarchical order of 2.3 and 2.2 could easily be reversed since satisfaction may in many instances precede willingness. It is of no serious consequence since the important concept is to know the difference. As is the case with the cognitive domain, some affective objectivities can be placed into more than one classification or subcategory. This goal can be converted into a meaningful behavioral objective.

3.1 Acceptance of a value

To develop in seventh-grade students a willingness to accept the worth of modern art as being the unique enjoyment that an individual receives from viewing it.

Rationale:

To accept the worth of an object is the same as acceptance of a value which places this goal under the 3.1 sub-category. It is adequate for conversion into a behavioral objective.

3.2 Preference for a value

For ninth-grade art students to seek out examples of good art for their own personal enjoyment.

Rationale:

To do something for personal enjoyment indicates a value has previously been placed upon the activity. To actually seek out the activity indicates a preference for this value. This goal can be converted to a meaningful behavioral objective.

3.3 Commitment

For twelfth-grade art students to pledge to obligate at least one hour of their spare time each week to improve their local communities' attitudes toward art.

Rationale:

To pledge to obligate means to commit. Commitment means that values have been accepted and are preferred which places the goal under sub-category 3.3. This goal is adequate for conversion into a meaningful behavioral objective.

4.1 Conceptualization of a value

For twelfth-grade art club students to desire to make an evaluation of art works which they have created and appear to be appreciated.

Rationale:

To evaluate a piece of art requires a determination of the interrelationship of values which have been developed. A person must be able to conceive both the good and bad features of art. This conceptualization of the plus and minus characteristics of the object places the goal under sub-category 4.1. This goal is suitable for conversion into a behavioral objective.

4.2 Organization of a value system

For college seniors to choose art as one of life's dominant values.

Rationale:

To choose art indicates a preference and commitment for a value. To choose art as a dominant value shows that the desirable and undesirable features have been conceptualized and organized into some type of hierarchy in which art tends to dominate or is placed near the top. The goal must qualify for sub-category 4.2. It is not likely that this goal can be met through change brought about in one year or by any one teacher, but will have roots established in many previous years of experience. It is not recommended that teachers try to formulate objectives at this level, but concentrate primarily on the goal and strategies to achieve it.

5.1 Generalized set

For art major students to tend to view all problems primarily in terms of their aesthetic aspects.

Rationale:

This goal would include the generalization of selected values into controlling tendencies forming a set. To tend to view all problems in terms of aesthetic aspects means that the art major students are so committed to aesthetic interests that aesthetic aspects of problems have become the dominant way of looking at things. This places the goal into the 5.1 sub-category. It is not recommended as being practical for conversion into a behavioral objective, but can be pursued as a goal.

5.2 Characterization

For art major students to develop a philosophy of life based upon aesthetic values.

Rationale:

This goal requires receiving, responding, valuing, and organization of values. It also includes the generalization of selected values (aesthetic) into a controlling tendency, or set, with a subsequent integration of the sets into a philosophy of life. This places the goal into the 5.2 sub-category. A philosophy of life will be developed over a lifetime and will be influenced by a learner's total environment. Again, this goal can be pursued, but is not practical for conversion into a performance objective.

It should be emphasized at this point that each of the illustrations listed under the five major affective classification levels represent goal statements only, not outcomes or objectives. In the goals approach to writing behavioral objectives it is first necessary to establish and spell out specific goals before any attempt is made to specify outcomes. In their present form, the goals that were stated as illustrations would only need to have the evaluation activities spelled out and joined to the goal statements in order for them to become acceptable behavioral objectives.

These illustrations point out some of the difficulty in stating objectives which occur because of language or word meaning problems which may develop at different classification levels. In many instances, it is wise and necessary for the classroom teacher to classify her objectives in order to insure correct learning strategies and evaluation.

The biggest problem in classification of affective objectives remains that of making them specific. Specific goal statements for each subcategory classification level can be stated. Considerable doubt must remain concerning whether or not teachers should attempt to achieve complex objectives in the affective domain. This basically refers to (1) valuing; (2) organization; and (3) characterization by a value complex. The following list gives a few of the reasons for this concern:

1. Evaluation is very difficult to establish.
2. Teachers must be highly dedicated to the achievement of these objectives in order to devote the time and energy necessary to provide learning activities and evaluation experiences required, in addition to those specified for achievement and evaluation of cognitive intents.
3. Achievement of higher level affective objectives may require years to attain rather than just the weeks involved in a normal teaching situation.

The best summary of this chapter would be for each learner to study the affective taxonomy from which this chapter was adapted. Additional insights will be gained from reading the taxonomy.

GLOSSARY OF TERMS

Affective Taxonomy: refers to the *Taxonomy of Educational Objectives* (Handbook II: Affective Domain.)

Higher Level Affective Objectives: specifically refers to classification levels four and five, Organization and Characterization by a Value Complex, of the affective taxonomy.

REFERENCES

1. D. R. Krathwohl, B. S. Bloom, and B. B. Masia, *Taxonomy of Educational Objectives* (Handbook II: Affective Domain), New York, David McKay, Inc., 1968, p. 37.
2. Anita J. Harrow, *A Taxonomy of the Psychomotor Domain: A Guide For Developing Behavioral Objectives,* New York, David McKay, Inc., 1969.
3. D. R. Krathwohl, B. S. Bloom, and B. B. Masia, *Taxonomy of Educational Objectives* (Handbook II: Affective Domain), New York, David McKay, Inc., 1968, pp. 64–67.

Chapter 11

EVALUATION PROBLEMS: AFFECTIVE DOMAIN

We must not let go manifest truths because we cannot answer all questions about them.

Jeremy Collier

CHAPTER GOALS

For the reader to:

1. be cognizant of several evaluation problems that inhibit teachers and researchers in the development of behavioral objectives in the affective domain.

2. comprehend the concepts of evaluation by direct, indirect, and transmitted relationships.

3. comprehend four evaluation designs that may be used in determining the degree of success to which affective goals are achieved.

4. become familiar with specific affective domain evaluation problems related to measurement techniques and data collection.

5. become familiar with several data gathering techniques that may be used to help evaluate the success of affective goal achievement.

Evaluation to determine success in achieving goals in the affective domain involves a constant search to find both overt and covert responses which indicate either positive or negative feeling toward some object or activity. Positive responses are interpreted as representing pleasurable or good feelings, negative responses represent painful or bad feelings. It is possible, however, at times, to interpret the absence of negative responses as an indication of at least moderately good feelings.

Several problems present themselves when evaluation is required of affective goals. First, if affective goals are to be fulfilled and evaluated, they must, as is the case with cognitive objectives, be clearly and specifically defined. Behavioral change strategies or experiences must be provided to help the learner achieve the desired change. Finally, there must be some acceptable method for evaluating the extent to which learners reach their prescribed goals.

Evaluation suggests obtaining accurate observational data representing learner change and relating this data to appropriate standards which have been built into the objective. Accurate and valid observational data are hard to obtain and frequently there are no meaningful standards for comparison. Thus, in many instances, evaluation of affective goals must remain suspect.

In education there are many performance activities such as applying mathematical skills, reading, and identifying memory facts that are easily converted into behavioral objectives. These activities can be self-containing and can be stated and evaluated in a closed-ended style. There are, however, other behavioral activities (such as some of the ones found in the affective domain as well as objectives found at the higher cognitive levels) which require critical thinking and creativity and which may frequently be better and more easily stated if they are left open ended. Overt performances for evaluation of some of these goals are almost impossible to identify. Thus, it appears to be somewhat foolish to state criterion standards or how well or successful one must perform something which was not properly identified in the first place.

Each goal or type of change activity must be viewed in its own contextual situation, and both the goals and evaluation components of an objective will vary or be flexible according to the behavioral change level of the desired response. Successful writing and use of affective behavioral objectives may well depend upon the specificity of the goal defined and the development of many open-ended behavioral objective statements.

A second problem is that, unlike objectives in the cognitive domain, most affective changes cannot be evaluated immediately. This should have great significance for teachers who are writing objectives for students they will teach and evaluate over a relatively short period of time. Attitudes, values, adjustments, and other deep rooted personality characteristics are developed slowly. Only the very lowest levels of affective objectives can be measured immediately, while the more complex affective levels may take a lifetime to completely develop and evaluate.

A third problem concerns the specificity of behaviorial objective requirements. *Affective objectives which are too general have very little value. However, if evaluation of these same objectives becomes too specific, it will become too restrictive unless the objectives are broken down into several distinct goals and each goal has its own unique evaluation component.* The goals approach writing technique advocates the use of several distinct goal statements whenever possible in order to improve the validity and reliability of evaluation performances.

A fourth problem is that *overt measurable learner behaviors used in the evaluation of affective objectives are hard to observe.* A most effective way might be to record each student on "candid camera" for the major portion of each day. Students can't be followed around, however, so contrived responses must be used which include direct questioning, questionnaires, and observation of subject-matter-related behaviors. The results of these techniques must sometimes be viewed as having only marginal validity and accuracy. In some instances, the attempt to specify appropriate evaluation of outcome behaviors to indicate change has resulted in changing the originally intended goal rather than evaluating its attainment.

On the first page of this chapter appears the following quotation: *"We must not let go manifest truths because we cannot answer all questions about them."* This statement is close to the philosophy of goals approach advocates. Once a desirable goal has been chosen, strategies should be developed for its achievement. It should, also, be converted into a performance objective if appropriate evaluation is possible. The evaluation performance should also include a criterion standard, provided a meaningful one is known. However, the goal and performance outcome are not discarded just because there is no known criterion standard. Likewise, a desirable goal is not thrown away just because a performance outcome is not readily apparent to evaluate it. Since the goal includes the only intrinsic value to be found in an objective, it still remains important, along with the strategies developed to help achieve it.

A fifth reason affective objectives are difficult to evaluate is that *little confidence is placed in many of the learner responses which are available.* The validity and reliability of many tests and rating scales in the past have been subject to serious doubt. They have, however, been improving in recent years. Direct responses from students, whether written, verbal, or demonstrative, which might supply valuable information can very easily become unnatural or dishonest based upon the student's recognition of what the teacher wants rather than what the student really feels.

RATIONALE FOR AN APPROACH TO AFFECTIVE EVALUATION

Criterion referenced measurement is based upon the idea that the *quality of an educational endeavor should be determined by reference to how well it achieves its goals as defined in its own specifically stated objectives.* There should be a one to one relationship between the goal and evaluation performance on a behavioral objective. In other words, when the outcome performance which will be used to determine success in achieving the goal is determined, it should define or really represent an exact or close interpretation equivalent to the goal. Evaluation components should also be direct overt measures of goal attainment if possible and should be indirect or covert measures only when direct measurements are impossible to achieve. The pleasure-pain and positive-negative general models represent only two types of polar extremes which can be placed upon a continuum intended to represent a good-bad sequence. Other polar terms might include happy-sad, excess-ascetic or, in fact, any two terms representing opposite meanings which are specifically meaningful to the problem at hand.

The use of transmitted relationships in the field of evaluation is another technique which should be applied only when direct, one-to-one relationships are not feasible. For example, transmitted relationships can be represented as follows:

A is valuable for the sake of b.

B is valuable for the sake of b.

C is valuable for the sake of d.

Thus,

A is also valuable for the sake of c and d.

B is also valuable for the sake of d.

In order to better illustrate the use of transmitted relationships in the field of evaluation, we will assign names to the letters used above. Let us say that "a" is a consultant who is employed to give an inservice training workshop on how to write behavioral objectives to a group of principals called "b." Later the principals give a similar workshop to their teachers named "c." These teachers then write behavioral objectives in their content areas to improve the achievement of their students referred to as "d." It is assumed not only that the teachers wrote behavioral objectives for their students, but that the principals developed objectives for their teacher workshops and the consultant developed objectives for the workshop for principals.

How well the principals achieved the objectives established by the consultant might be a direct evaluation of the consultant's efforts. Likewise, how well the teachers achieve the objectives of the principal and how well the students achieve the objectives of the teacher can be a direct evaluation of the principal's and teacher's efforts. By the transmitted relationship concept, how well the teachers and students achieved their objectives would also be considered data for the evaluation of the consultant's efforts — the teacher's achievement more directly than that of the students. In addition, the student achievement under this concept would also be an indirect evaluation of the efforts of the principals.

In this type of transmitted relationship, the further the final end is from the original end, the less valuable it can be considered as an evaluation tool. This is because no direct cause and effect relationship can be established owing to the introduction of many new variables. Thus, the end in view for the consultant was achievement of his own objectives by the principals. Once this end was obtained, it became the means to achievement by the teachers, and as soon as this was successful it no longer had any value except as a means to improving learner achievement.

Since effective evaluation must sometimes involve indirect assessment of responses that are not overtly observable, measurement by transmitted type relationships is sometimes unavoidable. This type of evaluation can be very incomplete and leaves much to be desired and can be really meaningful only when all of the sub-goals are stated, evaluated, and defined to represent all of the general goal. It can, however, serve well and be better than no evaluation at all if a person is forced into that position. Goals approach advocates prefer, whenever possible, first to define general goals into more specific goals and then to evaluate the individual sub-goals, attempting to achieve a close one-to-one relationship between the goals and their evaluation components.

Applying the transmitted relationship evaluation concept to the affective domain, we might say that values are broad, global, and firmly set types of goals developed from many interests, appreciations, and attitudes. Attitudes are narrower goals than values which are composed from many interests and appreciations. Appreciations are still more refined than attitudes; interests are more specific goals than any of the other three.

Practically speaking, it appears that any goal, such as values, which requires more time to change than is available should be reduced in most instances to more refined goals before it is stated as a behavioral objective. The same is true, to a lesser degree, of attitudes and/or other affective terms. In each instance, we attempt to measure that which is the direct end of the means provided. When this is not possible, as is frequently the case particularly in the affective domain, that evaluation is utilized which appears to be the most nearly representative of the direct approach.

EVALUATION DESIGNS

Evaluation design for affective objectives can be essentially the same as that which is used in evaluation of cognitive and psychomotor achievement. Four models, two traditional and two new, will be presented at this point.

(A) BEFORE-AND-AFTER APPROACH (GAINS MODEL)

Evaluation for change in the affective domain can be accomplished by focusing attention upon several different uses of data. The most frequently utilized approach is to measure students' gains. This usually requires a previous observation of behavior which is used as a starting point and then a final behavioral observation of the same nature to determine if the student has improved his performance. Frequently, the improvement will refer to the direction of the shift rather than any quantitative measurement. Utilizing our working model based upon positive, indifferent, and negative response, we can envision gains in several ways, based upon some type of pre and post test. First, any change from a lower positive rating to a higher positive rating would be considered a gain. Change from higher negative level to a lower negative level and change from negative response to positive response would represent gains.

This evaluation model can be utilized on either an experimental or non-experimental basis according to whether or not comparisons are desirable. Longitudinal and cross sectional time studies to illustrate changes occurring over various time spans can be adopted when appropriate. The greatest advantage of this model, particularly in experimental programs, is that all students are used as their own control and are subject to the same outside variables which cannot be controlled by the study. It is important to remember that it is the gain, amount of improvement, or shift in direction that is significant when this model is utilized. This model is particularly useful with certain types of attitude scaling techniques.

There is no difference in using the gains model in the affective or cognitive domains. In the cognitive domain we often measure student reading achievement at the beginning and ending of a school year with the difference between the first and second test representing the amount of learning change. We can, in the same manner, administer an affective rating scale before and after the application of strategies designed to change affective behavior. The difference or the amount and direction of change recorded between the first and second rating scale observations would indicate positive or negative affective learning change.

(B) AFTER-TEST-ONLY APPROACH (SINGLE TEST MODEL)

In this model, the *teacher assumes either that all of the students are equal and matched on important characteristics or that this type of equality is not necessary for the evaluation data he or she wishes to collect.* This model requires no test before the beginning of the instructional period. The teacher proposes to evaluate her goals and objectives by measuring the effect of the chosen variable upon the learner, based upon final performance rather than upon gains from one evaluation period to another.

This model, like the before-and-after model, may be used for either experimental or non-experimental situations. When used in experimental situations, the sample of learners should be either randomly assigned or matched on essential characteristics. The important evaluation characteristic of this model is how high (positive) or low (negative) the learner scores. In other words, how well he or she performs. This model has many uses and is also adaptable to attitude scaling techniques.

Again, the relationship between cognitive and affective application of this design is apparent. Teachers develop many cognitive objectives which require achievement at a pre-determined level. Seldom do they give a pre-test to determine knowledge before the change strategies are applied. Upon completion of all enabling activities or change strategies, students are tested to see if they can perform at the required criterion success level. Affective objectives and evaluation instruments can be applied under the same rationale. The degree to which a student has a certain trait at the end of the enabling activities is what is considered to be important, rather than how much he improved from a previous rating.

(C) PEER-GROUP-EXPECTANCY MODEL

"All extremes are error. The reverse of error is not truth, but error still. Truth lies between the extremes."—Cecil

This quotation does not completely fit the general theory or the working evaluation model outlined in the previous chapter, but according to the Peer-Group-Expectancy, evaluation design may apply in the majority of instances.

Aristotle applied a theory that would support Cecil's contention by applying the same idea to the *Doctrine of the Golden Mean* which was the central doctrine of classical ethics. One illustration of the use of the Golden Mean is as follows:

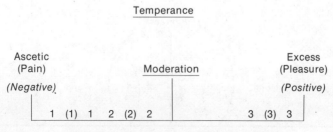

Figure 11-1 Doctrine of the Golden Mean.

This figure reveals how moderation as the Golden Mean might be influenced by the individual or group to which it is applied. The variable of application is temperance. In this instance (1) represents three Protestant ministers, (2) represents school teachers, and (3) refers to professional actors. It might be assumed that ministers would be on the ascetic side of temperance, school teachers close to the arithmetic mean, and professional actors on the side of the continuum termed as pleasure. The recording of such observations in real life situations would not necessarily be cause for alarm or incorrect. In other words, no criterion standard could be chosen that would truly represent the correct mean for all three groups.

The peer-group-expectancy model is an abrupt departure from traditional evaluation schemes and must be thoroughly understood before it is employed. This model can utilize independently the basic design features of either the before-and-after model or the after-test-only model. The significant change in this model is found in the conceptual framework within which the collected data are analyzed. This approach is not primarily concerned with gain in student performance or how high and well he performs. *Its basic concern is that behavioral observations recorded for each student fit into a range of observations which are considered to be normal for that individual and/or his peer group.*

To illustrate, we can refer back to our working model. According to the working model continuum, a stimulus painful to a learner might produce a low score or negative measurement. If the stimulus produces a pleasure experience, the scores or measurements will be positive. Furthermore, we can establish the fact that this working model will apply quite handily to the before-and-after and after-test-only evaluation models.

Figure 11–2 gives a new perspective characterized by what might be referred to as the *peer-group-expectancy mean.* This mean is based upon the norm or mean of a given variable for a given time, place, situation, context, or population.

This mean or norm is different from the absolute mean of an object or the arithmetic mean which is equidistant from both extremes. It is

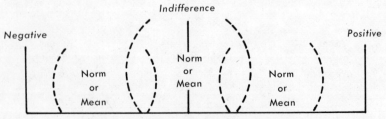

Figure 11–2 Peer-group-expectancy mean.

derived from the realities that may exist within the context of any given variable and situation. *It refers to a mean or norm that is relative to any individual or group. It refers to a mean or norm that is right for the learner and is neither too little nor too much for him. This mean indicates that the good may be found anywhere along the continuum.* The situational reality implies that the correct mean will be relative to the characteristics of a group or individual, the variable to which it is applied, and the context within which it is used, and that this mean always will be determined in this manner.

, Why should a learner be expected to be overjoyed at the prospect of conjugating verbs, learning a Latin vocabulary, reading Chaucer, working trigonometry problems, or memorizing the important dates in ancient history? Isn't it much more practical and just as useful to assume that what we really want is for each learner to appreciate, show equal interest, or have as good an attitude toward each of these variables as is normal for other members of his or her peer group?

The same assumption can be applied to other areas of behavior — such as discipline. Do we really want each learner to be docile, inhibited, and undemonstrative? If so, much of the overt responses needed for affective evaluation will be lost. Is it not more desirable that he exhibit these traits to the degree that can be considered normal for his peer group?

Returning to the peer-group-expectancy mean, its essential characteristics are basically the same as those of the Golden Mean. It is possible in the measurement of feelings that too much conformity is expected concerning that which is considered to be good, right, or positive. It has often been stated that a purpose of the school is to discover and develop individual abilities, interests, and talents in order to produce good citizens who are well adjusted to American society. Thus, it is quite possible that the question which should be asked with reference to evaluation is not "How much did they gain?" or "How high did they score?" but rather "Did the learner score within a mean or norm range which is characteristic of a group of his peers?" This in the final analysis may be a better indication of social adjustment than how positive the score appears to be on a test which may not be valid and which could have questionable reliability. At least the child would be normal according to whatever the test does measure.

Educators must be concerned with both conformity and radicalism. In the cognitive domain particularly, students should be encouraged to be creative and to do original thinking. Feelings which are too radical or feelings which are marked by a considerable departure from those which are traditional or normal can be the forerunners of serious emotional conflict, or may constitute less severe problems. For example, extremely high attitudes toward study may be considered as a "good" unless the learner has become a bookworm at the expense of other values. High attitudes toward sports can be "good" unless it is carried to the point of causing the learner to decrease in achievement in other areas. Such is the case with both high and low scoring achievement. It is not as important in self-concept to know that a student scored a negative or positive score as it is to know how negative or how positive. It should be pointed out that achievement above or below the expected-peer-group mean does not mean anything by itself. It does, however, provide valuable data for both individual and group diagnostic analysis.

It is commonly agreed by most educators that individuals differ in their aptitudes to learn particular types of subject content at different cognitive levels. Perhaps five per cent have superior abilities to learn and perform cognitive behaviors with greater ease and efficiency. Perhaps five per cent of the learners have a deficiency for certain cognitive behaviors. For example, some learners are musically inclined, and other learners have virtually no aptitude in this area. Some learners are athletically gifted; others have little control over the types of movement that are necessary for certain athletic events.

Researchers and behavioral scientists have established the fact that there is a close and almost inseparable relationship betwen the behaviors attributed to the cognitive, psychomotor, and affective domains. Thus, knowledge and ability to perform cognitive and psychomotor behaviors should be strong motivating forces to aid learners to have high interests, appreciations, and attitudes toward certain variables. The lack of knowledge and ability or natural aptitude to perform certain cognitive and psychomotor behaviors could easily produce negative feelings toward selected variables.

If these assumptions are true, we can anticipate that approximately five per cent of the learners have a natural potential to exhibit affective behaviors toward selected variables which are above their peer-group-expectancy norm. In addition, five per cent of the learners may have a natural tendency to exhibit affective behaviors toward selected variables which are below the norm for the peer group.

There will naturally need to be some subjective judgment as to what the range of the peer-group-expectancy mean should be. This, however, need not constitute too great a concern, since concern is centered on the distribution of scores rather than positiveness or negativeness. Examination of deviant cases which appear through viewing the total group may be all that is necessary. Being deviant will not necessarily mean that the feeling is harmful or bad, but will give the teacher some cause to individualize her attention for a learner until she determines whether or not a problem exists.

Deviant cases which are highly positive may indicate that a student has the potential to become a leader, master craftsman, or great contributor toward the variable in which he is highly motivated. In this instance, he should be encouraged and given additional opportunities to make progress in the area, provided this does not negatively affect him in some other way. Learners who are deviant in a highly negative manner should receive special attention to relieve the negative feelings or to substitute other variables for the ones toward which they are so poorly adjusted.

What about the rest of the learners? What about the large majority which fits within the peer-group-expectancy mean, whatever percentage that is chosen to be? Must it be said that education has failed them, that they are bad, or misfits, or have a poor attitude? Is it possible to just recognize that they are normal and that teachers are doing at least an average job of meeting their affective needs?

Another implication of the peer-group-expectancy approach to product evaluation in the affective domain is that it allows a teacher another way to determine success. This can be particularly helpful with reference to appreciations and attitudes. Figure 11-3 illustrates this point for one concept.

Traditionally, teachers have attempted to measure the success of appreciation and attitudes by way of behavioral observations which they hope may be highly positive, as would be the case with the four circled x's in Figure 11-3. If such positive behavior were established, the activity could be referred to as having been successful. By this same type of rationalization, if the behavioral observations were within the norm range it might be assumed that the appreciation training had not been as successful as it should be. If most or all of the responses are negative, a teacher would need to re-examine both her goals and instructional strategies as well as her evaluation measures. These negative responses may still be normal for the group, but the question should be raised as to why this is the case.

The concept of the peer-group-expectancy model will defend the viewpoint that the absence of negative characteristics for appreciations and attitudes may establish success just as adequately as the presence of positive characteristics. There are several reasons which will lend support to this argument. First, when teachers choose the goals and behavioral performance activities for use in evaluation, they generally

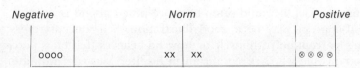

Figure 11-3 Peer-group-expectancy success alternatives.

choose a small sample group of goals and activities from a vast array of possibilities, most of which are probably not even known. Thus, the learner's failure to perform the particular outcome or outcomes chosen may represent a poor or inadequate choice of goals and outcomes rather than the failure of a child to appreciate music, for example; not only does the child have the opportunity to react negatively toward the goals and outcome performances chosen by the teacher, but he also has the opportunity to react negatively toward all of the many instructional strategies dictated by the teacher's planned training experiences.

Another feature of the peer-group-expectancy mean is its flexibility. The concepts, learners, polar extremes categories and signs (+ or −), mean or norm interval, and other components can be readily changed according to the judgment of the teacher. She need only refer to the practical realities of each situation and then plan her goal with its evaluation accordingly. It is not intended that the peer-group-expectancy approach replace the gains and after-test approaches. In many instances, it can be sufficient by itself, particularly in view of the present state of affective evaluation. The peer-group-expectancy approach should be considered as an ideal evaluation method to go along with either of the other two approaches and may produce some much needed evaluation information and interpretation data that are greatly needed, but which, if not anticipated, may otherwise be lost or not readily available. The use of this model is limited only by the type of data a decision-maker or teacher desires, depending upon pre-determined objectives. No model is best for all purposes.

(D) NO-NEGATIVE-RESPONSE MODEL

The no-negative-response model was alluded to in the peer-group-expectancy model and is closely related to that concept, but may best be utilized as a separate type of evaluation design. Simply stated, it merely contends that the *absence of negative responses can be just as meaningful as the presence of positive behaviors.*

In education desired behavioral responses are full of "do's" and "don'ts." "Do this" and "don't do that" confronts a learner from the time he is born until he goes into the better world beyond. For example, many students are considered discipline problems because of the overt behavior they display. The absence of such behaviors or a reduction in the number of such behaviors can be just as strong an indication that a behavioral goal has been reached as would be some positive behavioral response. In fact, it would often be more practical and realistic.

Self-concept may be a good illustration. Self-concept refers to a person's perception of himself or how he believes that he is perceived by other people who are significant in his life. A learner will often behave in a manner that will maintain his image or enhance his perception of himself. Thus, he may misbehave or become a discipline case because of his own perceived image and demonstrate many negative characteristics. In this case, a teacher's desired goal for the child might well be the absence of negative responses rather than the performance of any positive overt behaviors. Evaluation then can be determined through an absence of certain prescribed responses.

Another learner may be intimidated, inhibited, or almost completely withdrawn from classroom participation. The teacher may wish this learner to do something, to perform some positive, overt response. Evaluation to determine the success of a teacher's reaching a goal established for this learner will require direct observation of specified performance behaviors. In either case, whether too outgoing or too withdrawn, evaluation can be determined by direct observation. Therefore, the absence of negative observations as well as the presence of positive observations can become very meaningful.

DATA GATHERING TECHNIQUES

It is not intended that this chapter recommend in detail the techniques or instruments which should be used in gathering data. There are many texts already available which list the names of standardized and other instruments for gathering data in the affective domain. The purpose of this section of the text will be to comment briefly on various techniques which have, in the past, been used for evaluation or instrumentation purposes.

Data collection refers to the types and sources of information to be collected. Valid information can be objective or subjective. All data collected and analyzed in evaluation should be limited to the requirement of the objectives. The identification of the type of performance which is appropriate for use in evaluation is crucial.

There are four primary possibilities for gathering data representing learner behavior. These methods involve listening to what the learner has to say, reading what he is able to write, observing what and how he can demonstrate or perform, and observing to determine the absence of negative behaviors. Teachers writing behavioral objectives must determine which of the four possibilities is most appropriate for the response desired of the students as a result of the experience he or she has provided.

There are several techniques used for gathering information. Among these are the following:

A. Personal Observations

Direct observations of a learner's behavior will provide much valid data concerning feelings and emotions. These observations should be as factual and quantitative as possible. Spontaneous behavior is a desirable type of observation. A temper tantrum is definitely negative, whereas laughter most probably denotes pleasure. All behaviors in between should represent data which will fit into a working model for evaluation.

Absence of a behavior as outlined in the no-negative-response evaluation design can be included under personal observations. The problem is to observe the indicator behaviors under natural conditions or contrive situations in which the student will truly make responses based upon his own feelings and emotions.

B. Rating Scales

Rating scales differ from objective testing in that they have no single correct or incorrect answer. Rating scales include the measurement of interests, attitudes, values, creativity, motivation, and other affective traits. Most rating scales are based upon theory similar to the general theory or pleasure-pain concept and are directly applicable to the working model outlined in this text.

Well constructed rating scales include observations of behavior which are relevant to the particular variable being studied. Scaling techniques furnish hard data of a quantitative nature. They are considered to be better than surveys and questionnaires for evaluation of attitudes, values, and motivations. The Thurston and Likert scaling techniques are probably the most widely used at this time.

C. Interviews

Advantages of the interview technique are: (1) the interviewer is able to obtain more confidential information; (2) questions need not be previously structured; and (3) both the interviewer and learner can make value judgments through this type of personal interaction. Interviews are normally conducted through face-to-face contact.

Interviews can be conducted for individuals or groups and may be analytic or in depth. The biggest disadvantage of this technique is that the learner may tell the interviewer only what he thinks the interviewer wants to hear.

D. Performance Demonstrations

This technique is probably most applicable to situations in which the teacher desires for the learner to show an interest, appreciation, or attitude through his choice and performance of either specified or free choice activities.

E. Surveys

Surveys are good for both individual and group studies. These instruments ask direct questions or determine opinions. They usually will be based upon some type of positive-negative reactions such as like or dislike or approve or disapprove. The responses requested may be either open- or closed-ended. A disadvantage of surveys is that they may not be taken seriously or the respondents may give false information.

F. Check Lists

This technique is very simple and can be useful in recording the presence or absence of an event. Check lists usually attempt to determine: (1) limited characteristics of a population; (2) learner preferences; (3) interests; and (4) other factual information regarding the correct condition of specified variables.

G. Charts and Graphs

Charts and graphs represent visual description in the presentation of data more than a technique for data gathering. They tend to serve a descriptive function involving analysis, classification, quantification, and evaluation limited to very narrow characteristics of the population. They are particularly useful in showing percents, frequency of events, and numerical totals.

PROBLEMS RELATED TO MEASUREMENT TECHNIQUES AND DATA COLLECTION

Among the more acute problems relating to measurement are how to establish standards for effective performance, how to make valid behavioral observations which are real indicators of affective changes, how to conduct and record a behavioral measure so that the student will be either unaware of the observation or unaware of the behavior desired by his evaluator, and how to determine the type or types of evaluation which will be most useful.

Standards or criterion measures for positive or negative tendencies in affective evaluation do not lend themselves to the determination of tendency strengths as much as to indicating directions such as positive or negative. When possible, tendency strength should be determined because it might be just as important to know how negative an attitude is as to know whether it is positive or negative. This is particularly true in determining the necessity for corrective experiences. Present evaluative instruments in general do not allow for the determination of evaluation standards other than norms or standards based upon the instruments involved, and not too much significance can be placed on many of the instruments which have been developed.

Making behavioral observations as change indicators involves, insofar as possible, obtaining measures of the student's overt behavior or what he says he feels or thinks. This latter type of indicator may refer to written or oral response. Usually it will be considered wise to secure both types of response if possible. A variety of both "doing" and "saying" responses in each category are desirable if they are possible to obtain.

This will enable the evaluator to see clusters or patterns of responses, each one serving as a check upon the others.

One purpose of any type of observation is to determine whether or not program strategies increase the number, intensity, and/or direction of student responses toward the desired pole or norm. The teacher's primary task in planning evaluation activities will be to determine, within the proper context or frame of reference, what specific feelings and behaviors are worth observing as indication of positive or negative influence. Secondly, the teacher must decide how, under normal conditions, a student might be expected to show reaction. *Criteria which may show strong positive feeling for any object or concept might include:* (1) *desire to talk about it;* (2) *desire to purchase or acquire the object;* (3) *desire to involve others in it;* (4) *desire to write about the topic (read, further study, attend lectures);* (5) *desire to continue a relationship with it in some other appropriate capacity; and* (6) *countless other indicator responses.* At the same time, strong negative feeling will tend to reverse these desires. The stronger the feeling, the easier it will be to evaluate.

One problem is that observations of feelings will frequently fall somewhere within the indifference or norm range and may not be readily observable in what students do. This problem can be eliminated for observations which are judged to best fit into the peer-group-expectancy or no-negative-response evaluation models. The fact that teachers cannot observe either strong positive or strong negative feelings may in the long run mean only that the learners are normal.

GLOSSARY OF TERMS

After-Test-Only Approach: An evaluation design requiring only one test or measurement to be administered to a sample population and that test at the end of the treatment period.

Before-And-After Approach: An evaluation design requiring a measurement before the beginning of treatment in a study and again at the end of the study.

No-Negative-Response Model: An evaluation concept that is designed to determine the presence or absence of negative overt measurable learner behaviors rather than to detect the presence of positive behaviors. In this concept the same values are placed upon absence of negative response and presence of positive response.

Overt Measurable Learner Behavior: Any learner behavior that is both open to view and capable of being measured.

Peer-Group-Expectancy Mean: An adaptation of the Doctrine of the Golden Mean in classical ethics. Simply stated, it refers to a mean or norm that is considered normal for any peer group concerning any variable in question at a given time, place, situation, or context.

Peer-Group-Expectancy Model: An evaluation concept that is designed to determine learning success by whether or not recorded overt measurable learner behaviors fit into a range of observations considered to be normal for each individual based upon his own peer group.

Transmitted Relationship Evaluation: Evaluation that is not direct, does not establish a one-to-one relationship between a goal and its evaluation component, and for which no results (effects) that are obtained are specifically traceable to specific factors (causes) that produced them.

Chapter 12

IDENTIFYING AFFECTIVE GOALS

> The man without a purpose is like a ship without
> a rudder—a waif, a nothing, a no man.
>
> *Carlyle*

CHAPTER GOALS

For the reader to:

1. understand the difference between writing affective goal statements for abstract and specific intents.
2. comprehend the process of utilizing a *systematic approach* to goal setting prior to the development of specific affective behavioral objectives.
3. develop skill in writing unique affective behavioral goal statements.

Earlier in this text it was pointed out that under the goals approach technique it is not advisable to state evaluation performances based upon general goals. Evaluation of goal attainment was shown to be more meaningful if evaluation performances represent as close a one-to-one relationship as possible with the goal to which they are applied. The problem of abstract goals, lack of goal specificity, has prevented educators from achieving better program accountability. Lack of goal specificity is particularly destructive in the development of behavioral objectives in the affective domain.

SETTING AFFECTIVE GOALS

General goals represent global statements of clusters of many specific goals which have not been objectively identified. A specific goal is the specific intent of a course of action. These specific intents are the primary reasons for implementation of a behavioral change program. Thus, the specific goals, frequently unidentified, are the ends toward which behavioral change should be focused, have intrinsic value and are the types of goals which should be converted into behavioral objectives.

Evaluation performances to determine success in achieving abstract affective goals are extremely difficult to determine. This is because most true indicators of abstract feelings are covert and not open to direct observation. Evaluation of more specific affective goals is much easier since specific goals more often can be measured by overt performances. It appears that common judgment would dictate that accountability should not be attempted for indefinite goals and evaluation measures which cannot be seen or correctly interpreted in a direct manner.

Attitudes and values are examples of abstract goals. No one appears to know conclusively what attitudes are, only that attitudes represent an accumulation of feelings over a period of time and that values seem to be formed through placement of worth on well-formed attitudes. Feelings, such as interest or cheerfulness, are much more concrete and specific and can be evaluated much more easily through overt performances such as the willingness to do something or the appearance of a smile.

The problem, then, of goal setting and identification is that of breaking abstract or general goals down into more specific goals in order to understand and evaluate them better. One method of doing this is to use a systematic approach for determining specific goals from various levels of goal abstraction by a process of division. An objective taken from a pilot school study carried out in a Florida school in 1970 can be used to illustrate the goal setting approach.

One of the preliminary objectives of the study was:

> To change in a positive direction any negative or low attitude which pilot school teachers may have toward their present school situation as determined by a five concept semantic differential scale administered before and after change strategies are applied.

The abstract or general goal of this objective was "to change in a positive direction any negative or low attitude which the pilot school teachers may have toward their present school situation." Attitudes represent an abstract term for feelings; and "present school situation" is also too general. It can be surmised that the five concepts to be used in the semantic differential scale were supposed to define further what was really meant by attitudes. These concepts were: (1) teaching educationally disadvantaged students; (2) parent interest and cooperation; (3) services provided by county staff; (4) emphasis on self-concept; and (5) local school leadership.

These goals were not spelled out as specific intents, but are derived by implication from the proposed evaluation instrumentation. Thus, the general goal could be envisioned to include five more specific goals or intents as shown in Figure 12–1. If the consultants employed to provide in-service training and other expertise had not intervened, the objective would have been stated as proposed and change strategies would

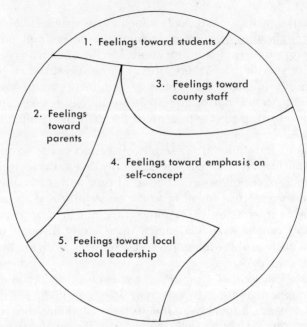

Figure 12-1 General goal (attitude) containing five subsidiary goals.

have been developed for only the concepts stated in the evaluation rating scale.

Goal identification can be further illustrated by placing these goals in a systems framework utilizing subsystems, subsystem components, and sometimes interim components as follows:

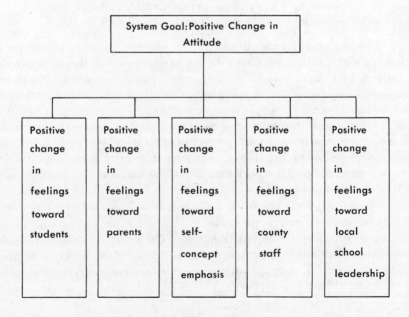

SUBSYSTEM GOALS

A complete goal statement and behavioral objective can be stated for each of the subsystem goals which will be more specific than the one stated for the system goal of positive attitude change. Each goal in turn can be better matched with its evaluation component than is possible when using the general goal.

Through interaction with faculty members in this pilot school, the consultants were able to determine that there were several other concepts or potential goals which should be included in determining the attitude of teachers toward their school situation. Each of these additional concepts was significant to that particular faculty at that particular point in time. These additional concepts were:

1. individualized instruction
2. faculty group planning activities
3. educational change and innovation
4. evaluation of educational practices
5. in-service training activities
6. nongraded organizational structure
7. graded organizational structure
8. fellow faculty members
9. action research projects
10. school-community relationships
11. school philosophy

The additional concepts identified under the same general goal increased the number of pertinent subsystem goals from five to sixteen. Figure 12-2 graphically illustrates this increase and their relative importance to successful attainment of the general goal of positive attitude change.

The significance of this expansion of subsystem goals within the framework of the more global abstract goal is easy to see. First, since all of these concepts would contribute to the formation of teacher attitudes toward their present school situation, the general goal and its evaluation will be much more complete. In fact, the evaluation may be considered to be three times more efficient. Second, the subsystem goals will be more specific and will provide the opportunity to have more specificity in each of their evaluation performances. Third, and most important under the theory that goals are the desired ends, the strategies for change will be developed to achieve many more goals than under the original objective.

In other words, it might be assumed that if, on the pre-test, teacher feelings were found to be high for three of the concepts, the need and emphasis would have been to concentrate change strategies on the two

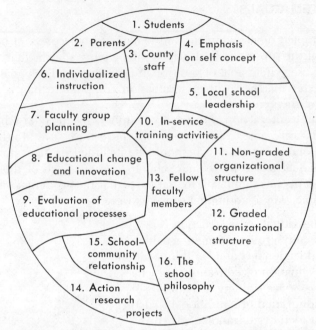

Figure 12-2 General goal (attitude) increased from five to sixteen subsystem goals.

lower rated concepts in order to improve overall attitudes. Under the revised sixteen concept definition of attitude, it may be assumed that as many as nine concepts may have been rated high on the pre-test and strategies would be developed for improvement of seven concepts. Since attitudes are thought to represent the intensity and duration of many accumulated feelings, the broader coverage should ultimately prove to be more effective.

Under the sixteen concept definition, the subsystem goal breakdown would be as shown on the opposite page.

Complete goal statements could be written for each of the sixteen concepts by the goal writing technique outlined in Chapter 3. These goals could then be converted into objectives by the addition of an evaluation component. In reality the goal statements developed from these subsystems will still be more abstract than desired. Although they are more specific than the original abstract goal. This points out the fact that there may be several levels of abstraction and that the least abstract or most specific level possible should be sought before developing final program objectives.

Assuming this to be true, subsystem component goals must be

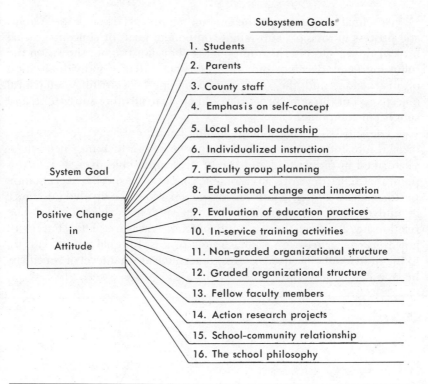

Subsystem Goals

1. Students
2. Parents
3. County staff
4. Emphasis on self-concept
5. Local school leadership
6. Individualized instruction
7. Faculty group planning
8. Educational change and innovation
9. Evaluation of education practices
10. In-service training activities
11. Non-graded organizational structure
12. Graded organizational structure
13. Fellow faculty members
14. Action research projects
15. School-community relationship
16. The school philosophy

System Goal

Positive Change in Attitude

identified within the framework of each subsystem goal. Such identification will change the goal setting system as shown on the following page.

As was the case with the system goal, each subsystem goal can be broken into subsystem components as illustrated for the subsystem, individualization of instruction. These components represent steps or the more important functions with which a teacher might become involved in individualization of his instructional activities.

The sixteen subsystem goals represented concepts which were much more specific than just the term "attitude" for the identification of a person's feelings toward a general goal. By the same line of reasoning, the eight subsystem component goal concepts are much more specific representations of the rather general term "individualization of instruction." Goals written for the subsystem component concepts will be more specific interpretations of what teachers' feelings are directed toward; and evaluation performances to determine success in achieving these goals will again become more specific and meaningful. Thus, by relating these new concepts to Figure 12–2, it can be seen that subsidiary goal number six would now be divided into eight parts representing the setting of more refined goals.

As a final illustration of the goal setting process through the systematic process of division, subsystem component goals or concepts can be broken down into interim components. This illustration, shown on the following page, develops only one subsystem, that of individualization of instruction, and the subsystem component of writing behavioral objectives; but the same process would apply to all other subsystems and subsystem components.

The subsystem component, writing behavioral objectives, has been broken into four very specific concepts or tasks which may need to be performed in the writing and use of behavioral objectives. It is at this point that there develops a reasonable chance to be specific in evaluation performances. Even the interim components could be divided into more definitive concepts. It then would be even easier to establish a one-to-one relationship between the goal and outcome measure. This chapter is, however, concerned with establishing a process for goal setting. It is up to the individual objective writer to determine at what level of specificity he is to be held accountable.

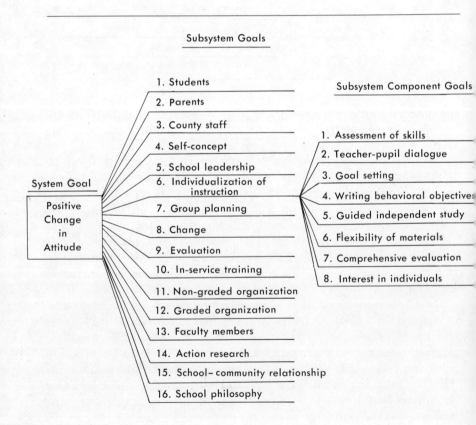

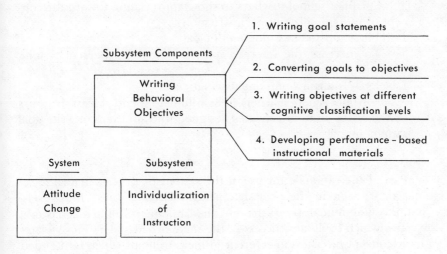

Interim Components

Another factor which is important is the situational context within which the objective writer must function. The person's role, time available, financial support, and other contextual constraints must be considered in determining the final objectives to be operationalized. In addition, it must be assumed that all systems, subsystems, subsystem components, and interim components will be ranked according to necessity and practicability. Thus, no teacher or other educator should undertake to develop goals or objectives which are beyond reasonable expectation for the situational context within which they function. Once the final operational goals are set, behavioral objectives should be established from which instructional and administrative strategies to achieve them are developed.

In the pilot school setting used as a reference for illustrating the goal setting and identification process developed in this chapter, goals would have been established for four levels of abstraction. Behavioral objectives could have been written for each level, although not recommended or necessary at any level except that of the functional tasks referred to as interim components. The four levels of goals might be stated as follows:

Level 1.—System Goal:

To change in a positive direction any negative or low attitude that the pilot school teachers may have toward their present school situation.

Level 2.—Subsystem Goal:
   For pilot school teachers to show appreciation toward the concept of individualization of instruction.
Level 3.—Subsystem Component Goal:
   To increase the interest of pilot school teachers in writing behavioral objectives.
Level 4.—Interim Components Goal:
   For pilot school teachers to be willing to spend at least six hours of their free time in activities designed to train them to write goal statements.

Part of the rationale for use of the systematic process in goal selection can be seen in the goal statements written at these four levels. First, the system goal is very general and can only result in a behavioral objective which evaluates success in the same broad sense. This violates a basic concept of criterion-referenced measurement which is intended to measure specific content coverage. The specific conceptual content of a general goal is not identified; thus, the evaluation component is restricted for the same reason.

The subsystem goal is also rather nebulous since the term appreciation is also vague and overt evaluation performances will be difficult to determine. The subsystem component goal involving interest in writing behavioral objectives is more specific in both its content and behavioral intent. Interests are better understood and evaluation activities are easier to determine. Willingness to spend time, as depicted in the interim component goal, refines the desired behavior to a very specific level. In addition, the specific content coverage, writing goal statements, narrows substantially the concept of writing behavioral objectives.

Secondly, this goal selection method has illustrated a goal setting process which can be useful in writing behavioral objectives by use of the affective taxonomy. This was accomplished by identifying the possible stages in the development of an abstract term, attitude. Attitudes were refined to appreciations, narrowed to interests, and finally restricted, in this example, to willingness to respond, which is the 2.1 sub-category level of the affective taxonomy.

Finally, it must be emphasized that the same process would be equally effective even if the goals statements are not taxonomy oriented. Many teachers and other educators will never adopt the taxonomy as the basis for developing their objectives. These people will not desire or, possibly, may not have need or ability for deep involvement in affective goals. They will wish to formulate goals and attempt to evaluate them within the framework of their classroom situation. Such persons can benefit greatly through restricting their evaluation attempts to goals which have been very specifically defined.

GLOSSARY OF TERMS

Interim Goal: a written statement of the intent of an activity representing a sub-function of a subsystem component in a system.

Subsystem Component Goal: a written statement of the intent of an activity representing a major sub-function of a subsystem in a system.

Subsystem Goal: a written statement of the intent of an activity representing a major division of a system.

System Goal: a mission statement of the intent or purpose for which a system is developed.

Chapter 13

WRITING AFFECTIVE GOALS AND BEHAVIORAL OBJECTIVES

> There is no road to success but through a clear strong purpose. Nothing can take its place.
>
> *T. T. Munger*

CHAPTER GOALS

For the reader to:

1. understand the necessity for stating affective goals as specific intents that can be evaluated by an activity that approaches a one-to-one relationship between the goal and evaluation components.

2. develop skill in converting affective goals into affective behavioral objectives without use of a taxonomy.

3. comprehend the use of the peer-group-expectancy and no-negative-response evaluation designs in writing behavioral objectives in the affective domain.

Once a goal statement has been formalized, it is essential that a performance objective writer correctly match his goal with a relevant evaluation statement. The evaluation statement should truly define success in achievement of the goal or match the goal in as close a one-to-one relationship as possible. The chart which follows shows that evaluation components include the identification of (1) a correct type of performance, (2) meaningful success level criterion standards, and (3) optional statements which indicate given conditions, or the situational contexts which are necessary for effective evaluation.

WRITING AFFECTIVE GOAL STATEMENTS WITHOUT USE OF A TAXONOMY

This entire book is predicated upon the idea that the goals, rather than evaluation outcomes, have intrinsic value and represent the desired ends to be achieved. The goals approach requires that, whenever possible, general goals be broken down into specific goals before they are converted into behavioral objectives. This facilitates and makes more meaningful the selection of relevant evaluation measures to determine success in goal achievements. It also facilitates establishment of specific accountability and the overall communication of an objective's intent.

The chart below again illustrates the requirements of a goals approach behavioral objective. In this technique, behavioral objectives are formalized through the use of two explicitly stated major components, goals and evaluations. Thus, a completed behavioral objective statement should convey the exact intended goal and how it will be evaluated for success.

LEARNING ORIENTED OR BEHAVIORAL OBJECTIVE

MINIMUM LEVEL PERFORMANCE OBJECTIVE	DESIRED LEVEL OR CRITERION-REFERENCED PERFORMANCE OBJECTIVE

Goal—Identifies
  1. Learner (learner group)
  2. Learning task
    (a) Content
    (b) Behavioral domain
Evaluation—Identifies
  1. Performance, instrumentation, or activity
  2. Optional statements
	Goal—Identifies
	  1. Learner (learner group)
	  2. Learning task
	    (a) Content
	    (b) Behavioral domain
	Evaluation—Identifies
	  1. Performance, instrumentation, or activity
	  2. Success level criterion standards
	  3. Optional statements

Under this objective writing technique, all behavioral objectives must include a goal and a performance activity. This is represented by the minimum level classification. Optional statements are not a requirement, but an option. The purpose of the minimum level classification is to provide for the statement of objectives for which there are few objective success level criterion standards which would be appropriate. There may be affective objectives that will need to be stated in this classification.

All behavioral objectives should be stated at the desired level classification if meaningful criterion standards are available. If it is impossible to state a meaningful evaluation performance, strategies are still developed and carried out to achieve the goal. When only performance outcomes are available for evaluation, strategies are developed to achieve the goal and evaluation is accomplished either objectively or subjectively by evaluation of the outcome performance in relation to goal achievement. In the event that all evaluation components are available, strategies are developed to achieve the goals and complete evaluation will be accomplished using both performance and success level criterion standards.

Behavioral objectives written in the affective domain are stated with exactly the same precision and communication requirements, no more and no less, as were the objectives written for the cognitive domain in Chapters 3, 4, 6, and 7. The learning task has two components: (1) content area identification, and (2) behavioral domain classification. Content area specifies the specific content, subject, or object toward which behavioral change is directed. The behavioral domain classification specifies the level of affective behavioral change which is intended.

The writer of each affective goal statement should perform a communication check, which is only a mental exercise, to determine whether or not he has identified the specific intent which is his desired end. This self-checking critique helps the writer develop greater proficiency in specification of intents.

Affective goal statements can be developed by two methods, as was the case with cognitive goals. They can be developed with or without the use of the affective taxonomy. *Following are several examples of goal statements written by teachers, based upon their own initiative and understanding, without any knowledge or reference to the taxonomy.*

1. Gregory Smith will improve his attitude toward selected concepts considered essential for safe driving at night
   Critique:
   a. Learner – Gregory Smith
   b. Learning task –
      (1) Content area – selected concepts considered essential for safe driving at night
      (2) Behavioral domain – improve his attitude places this objective in the affective domain
2. Teachers on the Jackson High School faculty should learn to appreciate (approve, enjoy, commend) the writing and use of behavioral objectives as part of their teaching strategy
   Critique:
   a. Learner Group – teachers on the Jackson High School faculty
   b. Learning task –
      (1) Content area – writing and use of behavioral objectives as part of their teaching strategy
      (2) Behavioral domain – to appreciate (approve, enjoy, commend) indicates affective domain

3. Driver training students should develop an interest in concepts considered to be necessary for safe night driving
   Critique:
   a. Learner—driver training students
   b. Learning task—
      (1) Content area—concepts considered to be necessary for safe night driving
      (2) Behavioral domain—should develop an interest in is indication of affective domain

4. James Anderson should develop both an interest in and preference for selected works of art
   Critique:
   a. Learner—James Anderson
   b. Learning task—
      (1) Content area—selected works of art
      (2) Behavioral domain—interest and preference designate the affective domain

5. Bradley Senior High School students should develop loyalty toward their school and its published standards concerning student dress, hair care, and the use of psychologically or physically addictive health hazards
   Critique:
   a. Learner Group—Bradley Senior High School students
   b. Learning task—
      (1) Content area—school and its published standards
      (2) Behavioral domain—loyalty is an affective domain concept

6. Mrs. Alice Higginbotham should develop an interest in learning both how to write and use behavioral objectives
   Critique:
   a. Learner—Mrs. Alice Higginbotham
   b. Learning task—
      (1) Content area—write and use behavioral objectives
      (2) Behavioral domain—develop interest is an affective domain assignment

7. Members of the administrative staff should learn to appreciate the use of systems analysis techniques in the development of educational programs
   Critique:
   a. Learner Group—each member of the administrative staff
   b. Learning task—
      (1) Content area—use of systems analysis techniques in the development of educational programs

      (2) Behavioral domain—learn to appreciate indicates the affective domain

8. Preschool children should learn to enjoy developing skilled movements
   Critique:
   a. Learner Group—preschool children
   b. Learning task—
      (1) Content area—developing skilled movements
      (2) Behavioral domain—learn to enjoy is an affective domain concept

9. To improve James Johnson's tolerance for the personal viewpoints of his classmates regarding a variety of types of art forms
   Critique:
   a. Learner—James Johnson
   b. Learning task—
      (1) Content area—personal viewpoints of his classmates regarding a variety of types of art forms
      (2) Behavioral domain—tolerance is an affective domain concept

10. Sixth-grade students should be willing to listen respectfully to announcements and speeches made in their classroom by outside speakers
    Critique:
    a. Learner group—sixth-grade students
    b. Learning task—
       (1) Content area—announcements and speeches made in their classroom by outside speakers
       (2) Behavioral domain—willing to listen respectfully indicates the affective domain

11. High school seniors should exhibit positive feeling toward further pursuit of education
    Critique:
    a. Learner group—high school seniors
    b. Learning task—
       (1) Content area—further pursuit of education
       (2) Behavioral domain—exhibit positive feeling is an affective concept

12. Seventh-grade boys should receive satisfaction in participating in group singing
    Critique:
    a. Learner group—students
    b. Learning task—
       (1) Content area—participation in group singing
       (2) Behavioral domain—receive satisfaction indicates affective domain

AFFECTIVE OBJECTIVES WRITTEN WITHOUT USE OF A TAXONOMY

Taxonomies do not generate or determine appropriate behavioral objectives. This is primarily accomplished through goal setting. Taxonomies can, however, help assure a variety of behavioral goal levels and assure that the evaluation performance outcomes to be required of learners are appropriate for the intended goal. In view of this hypothesis it must be assumed that use of a taxonomy in behavioral objective development is a means rather than an end. The end is the goal sought by the learner.

Taxonomies aid objective writers to focus evaluation activities on desired levels of behavior which may not otherwise be detected. Each taxonomy consists of orderly hierarchical classifications of learning behaviors, based upon the premise that learners need to be exposed to all behavioral levels although not necessarily to the same extent.

Many problems exist when people attempt to write behavioral objectives according to a taxonomy. These problems include: (1) understanding the taxonomy itself, (2) there is no distinct and complete separation of the hierarchical levels of behaviors, and (3) teachers are often just interested in meeting an immediate need as they see it and are not really concerned with where a certain behavior fits into a taxonomy.

Based upon the stated assumptions and the many contextual situations in which teachers write behavioral objectives, there must be means for stating objectives other than by use of a taxonomy. Perhaps the most practical approach is to use a simple direct process. This process is to identify needs, recognize the problems they create, determine a specific goal, and convert the goal to a behavioral objective by adding a reasonable common sense evaluation component.

CASE STUDY:

It is very important that any goal selected be real, practical, and worthwhile, and truly represent the need from which it is derived and the exact intent of the program. For example, consider any one of three different children who have been diagnosed as having problems relating to self-concept. One child habitually exhibits aggressive behavior. He may do this through aggressive language, rebellion to authority, or some other overt action such as annoying another child. The second child exhibits overly submissive behavior. He is very unobtrusive and undemanding. He imitates others a lot and may in return be the object of their overly aggressive behavior. The third child is neither aggressive nor submissive but tends to withdraw completely from participation in his social environment. The specific needs, respectively, are (1) reduction of aggressive behavior, (2) reduction of submissive behavior, and (3) reduction of withdrawal behavior. These needs should be stated as goals or specific intents and should serve as the basis for the development of a behavioral objective.

In each situation, the teachers diagnose the learner as having a problem in self-concept. According to the prevailing practice of stating general rather than specific goals, each teacher in these genuine life case studies formulated a behavioral objective based upon a general goal.

In all three instances the learner was administered a rather standardized type self-concept rating scale to determine his feelings about himself prior to the beginning of correctional strategies. At the completion of a rather lengthy time period, the rating scales were again administered and revealed in each instance that the learner involved had made significant positive change in self-concept; thus, the evaluation of the behavioral objective of each project indicated that the teachers' strategies were a success.

Normally, the story would end at this point and everyone would live happily ever after. This study, however, occurred in an experimental school situation and was subject to an unusual amount of consultant observation which is not readily available in conventional school programs.

Each of the three learners had been selected by needs assessment and problem identification techniques. Thus, in the final analysis success must realistically be determined by whether or not the specific needs of each individual had been eliminated or reduced. In other words, the question asked was,"is what is the case the same as what ought to be the case?"

Further study of the three children revealed the following information:

A. Overly aggressive learner

Direct observation indicated that despite the improvement shown on the rating scale, the overly aggressive child was still overly aggressive. In fact, it appeared that the extra attention this learner received had possibly been interpreted by the child as a reward for his attention-getting, aggressive behavior. He was, in fact, at least as big a discipline problem at the end of the program as he was when he was selected for study.

This indicated that although his problem may have involved self-concept, the term is too general and involves too many variables to be effectively changed and evaluated by the self-concept scale used. Since the original diagnosis was based upon overly aggressive behavior, the goal would have been better if it had been stated specifically to reduce his aggressive behavior. The objective developed from this goal would then have included an evaluation component which would provide both easy and direct evaluation to determine success in goal achievement. In the final analysis, the program for this learner was considered to be unsuccessful and the objective not appropriate in the first place.

B. Overly submissive learner

Post-study observation of the overly submissive child revealed essentially the same information as that found in the overly aggressive child, but in reverse. He still neglected to assert himself, took more abuse from his peer group than was desirable, and exhibited approximately the same overall behavioral characteristics as he did before strategies were applied to improve his self-concept.

Again, it was determined that this child's program had actually failed. The goal selected and the behavioral objective stated were found to be faulty. The specific goal should have been for the child to become less submissive and the objective could easily have evaluated this type of goal.

C. Withdrawn learner

The withdrawn learner was the only one of the three who appeared, after post-study direct observation, to have really achieved success. Prior to application of the teachers' change strategies, this child virtually never participated in any formal classroom activities. Also he did not participate in informal playground activities.

By the time the teacher administered her post-test rating scale, this learner was volunteering to answer questions, participating in activities requiring him to come to the front of the room and playing games rather regularly with classmates.

This child's program was considered a success, not because of the goal, stated objective, and rating scale evaluation, but because his observed and diagnosed need had been met. It was probably a case of good teacher perception and strategy which brought about desirable results despite a poor selection and statement of a behavioral objective.

Summarized as one objective, the original objectives were stated this way:

To improve the student's self-concept as determined by a positive shift in the rating obtained on an appropriate self-concept rating scale that is administered on a before-and-after test basis

Critique:

Goal: To improve the student's self-concept
 1. Learner—student
 2. Learning tasks—
   (a) Content area—self-concept
   (b) Behavioral domain—affective (self-concept)

Evaluation: As determined by a positive shift in the rating obtained on an appropriate self-concept rating scale that is administered on a before-and-after test basis
 1. Performance—instrumentation requiring writing remarks on a self-concept rating scale
 2. Success Level criterion standard
   (a) Learner requirement—shift in a positive direction
   (b) Optional statement—none

Objective Classification: Desired Level

Rationale: Both the goal and evaluation components of this objective communicate desired information, but no objective has much worth if it is not meaningful for the specific situation in which it is to be used.

This general objective would have become much more effective if, in each situation of use, it had been replaced by specific objectives such as the following:

A. Overly aggressive learner

For James White to reduce the number of incidents in which he exhibits acts of aggressive behavior. Success will be determined by a reduction of at least forty percent in the number of aggressive acts he performs as recorded on a frequency chart representing a time period from diagnosis to completion of the behavioral change program.

B. Overly submissive learner

For Sandra Jane Smith to develop self-confidence in asserting herself in interpersonal relationships with her peer group as determined by a checklist which reveals at least a twenty per cent increase in the number of incidents in which she is observed either to protest other learners' actions or take an affirmative stand on her own position. Comparisons will be made between the first three months and last three months of the behavioral change program.

C. Withdrawn learner

For Bobby Mitchell to acquire a willingness to participate in normal peer group activities as determined by his successful achievement of each of the following behavioral outcomes:

1. to volunteer for a classroom assignment at least twice during a six week period
2. to follow specific teacher instructions in a manner that is considered normal for his peer group
3. to agree to accept responsibility for one part in a class play

Each of these objectives is more specifically oriented toward the learners' observed need than was the general objective stated previously. The communication check critique factors were easily developed for both the goal and evaluation components of the objectives. In each incident there was built into the objective a closer one-to-one relationship between the goal and evaluation component than was possible in the more generally stated self-concept objective using a rating scale for instrumentation.

In summing up the case studies, we would have to say the self-concept change program was a failure because the only behavioral changes which could really be acceptable to meet the original observed needs were less aggression, reduced submission, and the development of a more outgoing behavior, respectively. In this instance, the general goal selected resulted in behavioral objectives which were in error in allowing the evaluation statement to designate a paper and pencil test as a means of determining changes in behavior which were not measurable in such terms. If the goals had been more specific, individualizing the program for each child's needs, this error would not have occurred.

CONVERTING GOALS TO OBJECTIVES

In an earlier chapter four evaluation designs were introduced. Two of the designs, the after-test-only and gains models, are conventional designs. Two new designs, the peer-group-expectancy and no-negative-response designs, were also introduced. The purpose of the remaining portion of this chapter will be to convert the non-taxonomic goals stated earlier in this chapter into behavioral objectives with primary emphasis being placed on the peer-group-expectancy and no-negative-response designs. Only the evaluation components of the objectives will be critiqued.

GAINS MODEL

Gregory Smith will improve his attitude toward selected concepts essential for safe driving at night so that when administered a seven concept semantic differential rating scale, on a before and after basis, and scaled from −3 to +3, he will attain a post-test score indicating more positive feeling toward six of the seven concepts.

Goal: Gregory Smith will improve his attitude toward selected concepts essential for safe driving at night

Evaluation Critique:
  (a) Performance — the writing required to complete the semantic differential rating scale being used for instrumentation
  (b) Success level criterion — attain a post-test score indicating more positive feeling toward six of the seven concepts
  (c) Optional statement — and scaled from −3 to +3
  (d) Objective classification — Desired or Criterion-referenced

Rationale: This objective is not intended to be classified according to the taxonomy, but is written merely for the purpose of illustrating an objective which has both a goal and an evaluation component. This can be considered to be a desired level objective since, in addition to the goal, it specifies a performance and a success level criterion standard. Optional statements are not necessary for an objective to be stated at the desired level, but are used to communicate additional information which is optional on the part of the behavioral objective writer.

AFTER-TEST-ONLY

Teachers on the Jackson High School faculty should learn to appreciate (approve, enjoy, commend) the writing and use of behavioral objectives as part of their teaching strategy. Proof that this goal has been accomplished will be determined by at least fifty percent of the teachers, by their own volition, writing and using behavioral objectives as part of their instructional strategies in at least one content area.

Goal: Teachers on the Jackson High School faculty should learn to appreciate (approve, enjoy, commend) the writing and use of behavioral objectives as part of their teaching strategy

Evaluation Critique:

(a) Performance—by their own volition, writing and using behavioral objectives as part of their instructional strategies
(b) Success level criterion—at least fifty per cent of the teachers—*in at least one content area*
(c) Optional statements—none
(d) Objective classification—Desired or Criterion-referenced

Rationale: This objective was written, as was the previous objective, to illustrate an objective that has both a goal and evaluation component. It is stated at the desired level with both a performance and criterion standard. In the goal component, the behavioral objective developer attempted to clarify the meaning attached to appreciation by further defining the term to include meanings such as approve, enjoy, commend.

PEER-GROUP-EXPECTANCY DESIGN

The peer-group-expectancy evaluation design is very flexible and can serve almost any purpose desired by the teacher. It should be remembered, as has been pointed out previously, that the selection of an appropriate goal is the most important ingredient of the objective. Goal selection would be similar regardless of the evaluation design. The peer-group-expectancy model can take advantage of either the gains model, single test model, or no-negative-response model and incorporate them into the evaluation if necessary.

The major evaluation difference in the peer-group-expectancy model is found in the selection of the success level criterion standard, particularly the student requirement. The evaluation performance may be the same as in the gains and single test models, but the standard of expectancy does not require high positive rating, just those ratings which appear to be normal. Normal in this instance depends upon the value judgment of the educator writing the objective. Examples of behavioral objectives written by this design are:

A. Driver training students should develop an interest in concepts considered to be necessary for safe night driving. Indication that this goal is accomplished will be based upon a semantic differential rating device that includes seven concepts and at least five bi-polar adjectives. Success will be determined by all of the students receiving a score within the normal range of their peer group as determined by subjective teacher analysis.

Goal: Driver training students should develop an interest in concepts considered to be necessary for safe night driving

Evaluation Critique:

    (a) Performance—instrumentation involving a writing activity using a rating scale

    (b) Success level criterion—all students receiving a score within the normal range of his peer group as determined by subjective teacher analysis

    (c) Optional statement—includes seven concepts and at least five bi-polar adjectives

    (d) Objective classification—Desired or Criterion-referenced

Rationale: To "develop an interest in" clearly refers to feelings. The student requirement calls for a score related to a group that is considered to be normal for the group. A question could be raised, and rightly so, asking why the peer-group-expectancy model should be used for this type of objective. The purpose here is to stress the point that objectives may be developed not only for different levels of abstraction, but also to perform different services for the teacher other than to evaluate learner progress. Affective evaluation is shaky at best; therefore, any insights into the development of goals and objectives in the affective domain should probably be encouraged.

    Flexibility is desired for both curriculum building and daily instructional planning. The four evaluation models provide one type of flexibility. The teacher's manipulation of the evaluation performance and student requirement provides another type of flexibility. It may be assumed in the stated objective that the driver training instructor had reason to believe that the normal scores for the students should cluster around a point that would be positive in value. His purpose may have been to study further all students who achieved scores that deviated radically from those which appear to be normal for the group as a whole. It could be for many other reasons known only to the teacher developing the objective. In any event, a teacher may build in flexibility to serve his own purposes as well as those of the learners.

    The reader should also have identified the fact that this objective used the after-test-only design in addition to the peer-group-expectancy design. In fact, the making of positive scores on six of the seven concepts could have been included and have been considered the major design feature, rather than the peer-group-expectancy design. Again, it may improve the interests of the instructor in developing affective objectives to realize he has the choice of one or both design possibilities.

B. James Anderson should develop both an interest in and preference for selected works of art as determined by his scoring within the normal range of his peer group in recorded case study observations which include personal discussions, written questionnaires, and rating scales. All observations must be within or above the norm range established by the observations taken from all class members.

Goal: James Anderson should develop both an interest in and preference for selected works of art

Evaluation Critique:
> (a) Performance — performance on case study observations including personal discussions, oral interviews, written questionnaires, and rating scales
> (b) Success level criterion — scoring within the norm range of his peer group as established by the teacher
> (c) Optional statement — none
> (d) Objective classification — Desired or Criterion-reference

Rationale: Again this illustrates that teachers should have the flexibility of utilizing their own creativity in choosing the success level criterion standards. Only the teacher knows all of his own purposes and intents for utilizing the evaluation data to be collected.

C. Delinquent Bradley Senior High School students should develop loyalty toward their school and its published standards concerning student dress, hair care, and the use of psychologically or physically addictive health hazards. Given an appropriate two day short course, a copy of the published standards, and a follow-up observation period of six weeks, the delinquent students will move closer to the peer group norm set by the nondelinquent student population in terms of fewer violations of the standards.

Goal: Delinquent Bradley Senior High School students should develop loyalty toward their school and its published standards concerning student dress, hair care, and the use of psychologically or physically addictive health hazards

Evaluation Critique:
> (a) Performance — will move closer to the peer group norm (wearing proper clothes, grooming hair properly and reduction of smoking, drinking, or taking drugs) set by the nondelinquent student population.

(b) Success level criterion—fewer violations of the standards
(c) Optional statement—Given an appropriate two day short course, a copy of the published standards, and a follow-up observation period of six weeks
(d) Objective classification—Desired or Criterion-referenced

Rationale: This objective clearly illustrates the evaluation of goal achievement by the peer-group-expectancy design. The delinquent students are expected to live up to the peer group norm range established by the non-delinquent student population.

D. Mrs. Alice Higginbotham will develop an interest in learning how both to write and use behavioral objectives as evidenced by her willingness to volunteer her free time for in-service training activities designed for this purpose at least as frequently as does the average of the other staff members.

Goal: Mrs. Alice Higginbotham will develop an interest in learning how both to write and use behavioral objectives

Evaluation Critique:

(a) Performance—volunteering her free time for in-service training activities.
(b) Success level criterion—at least as frequently as does the average of the other staff members
(c) Optional statement—none
(d) Objective classification—Desired or Criterion-referenced

Rationale: Again we have stated an objective with an evaluation designed to evaluate success by reference to the norm of a peer group rather than to total amount of achievement. It can be assumed that one teacher has been selected as needing to develop more interest in learning how to write behavioral objectives. Thus, the objective was written specifically for her and some strategy was employed to make her willing to volunteer for the activity. The peer-group-expectancy model was chosen by the principal because of its usefulness or its ease of application to individuals.

E. Members of the administrative staff should learn to appreciate the use of systems analysis techniques in the development of educational programs. Success will be determined by at least six of the nine department heads voluntarily developing a management plan for their own departmental program. The quality of each management plan will be adjudged by the superintendent and school board to be within a prescribed quality norm range based upon the parameters of each individual program.

Goal: Members of the administrative staff should learn to appreciate the use of systems analysis techniques in the development of educational programs

Evaluation Critique:

    (a) Performance—voluntarily developing a management plan for their own departmental program

    (b) Success level criterion—at least six of nine: and each will be adjudged to be within a prescribed quality norm range based upon the parameters of each individual program

    (c) Optional statement—none

    (d) Objective classification—Desired or Criterion-referenced

Rationale: It can be assumed that all staff members received some training in systems analysis, but it was left up to each person to either use or not use systems analysis processes in developing his own departmental program. The choice of the combination peer-group-expectancy and after-test-only evaluation design would probably be based upon what appeared to be functional in the context of each staff member's own situation.

F. Preschool children should learn to enjoy developing skilled movements as evidenced by each child's eagerness to practice and play games requiring skilled movement activities at least as frequently as other members of the peer group when given freedom of choice opportunities.

Goal: Preschool children should learn to enjoy developing skilled movements

Evaluation Critique:

    (a) Performance—eagerness to practice and play games requiring skilled movement activities

    (b) Success level criterion—at least as frequently as other members of the peer group when given freedom of choice opportunities

    (c) Optional statement—none

    (d) Objective classification—Desired or Criterion-referenced

NO-NEGATIVE-RESPONSE DESIGN

The no-negative-response idea is: when it comes to the behavioral characteristics of learners in the affective domain, there are positive and negative learner behaviors. The first three models—gains, after-test-only and peer-group-expectancy, were primarily based upon a desire for learners to exhibit feelings in some overt manner. The no-negative-response model is based upon a desire for learners not to exhibit certain feelings in an overt manner.

This concept is simply the use of the other side of the coin. Often it may be easier for a teacher to enumerate behaviors she does not desire than it is to observe positive behaviors in a natural situation or to establish realistic contrived behaviors in special situations. If negative responses are apt to be more natural than positive responses, capitalize on them. Thus, the absence of a negative response can be equally as meaningful as the presence of a positive one.

Examples of behavioral objectives written by the no-negative-response model are as follows:

A. To improve James Johnson's tolerance for the personal viewpoints of his classmates regarding a variety of types of black art forms so that when given the opportunity to participate in five different group discussions, he is able to state his beliefs in each group without making any negative remarks concerning the viewpoints held by other persons in the group.

Goal: To improve James Johnson's tolerance for the personal viewpoints of his classmates regarding a variety of types of art forms

Evaluation Critique:
  (a) Performance—verbally participate in five group discussions
  (b) Success level criterion—without making any negative remarks concerning the viewpoints held by other persons
  (c) Optional statement—so that when given opportunity to participate in five different group discussions
  (d) Objective classification—Desired or Criterion-referenced

Rationale: Objectives using the no-negative-response evaluation design are ideal for certain types of individualization. Adaptations of this objective might well fit into the program of a teacher who has diagnosed a particular need for either an individual student or group of students. The term "to improve" in the goal statement reveals that negative responses had been detected and the student requirement of no negative remarks would indicate improvement.

B. Sixth-grade students should be willing to listen respectfully to announcements and speeches made in their classroom by outside speakers. Proof that this goal is achieved will be determined by observations of student verbal and non-verbal behaviors during three presentations in which ninety per cent of the students exhibit no behaviors which are considered discourteous or inattentive, or in any way show lack of esteem for the speaker.

Goal: For sixth-grade students to listen respectfully to announcements and speeches made in their classroom by outside speakers

Evaluation Critique:
  (a) Performance—observations of student verbal and non-verbal behaviors and student listening

(b) Success level criterion—to listen with no display of dis-courteous, inattentive or other behavior showing lack of esteem for the speaker according to subjective analysis of teacher

(c) Optional statement—none

(d) Objective classification—Desired or Criterion-referenced

Rationale: The three methods used to observe students' overt learn-ing behaviors are (1) to listen to what they say, (2) to read what they write, and (3) to observe how they perform. In this ob-jective the teacher had to listen to what they said and observe their movement performance.

C. High school seniors should exhibit positive feelings toward further pursuit of education so that when they are given a checklist of ten positive items and ten negative items from which they are to select ten items that best represent their own feel-ings concerning furthering their education, they will check only the ten positive items.

Goal: High school seniors should exhibit positive feelings toward further pursuit of education

Evaluation Critique:

(a) Performance—check items on a check list

(b) Success level standard—check only the ten positive items

(c) Optional statement—so that when they are given a check-list of ten positive items and ten negative items

(d) Objective classification—Desired or Criterion-referenced

Rationale: This objective is a different kind of no-negative-response technique than were the two objectives stated previously. The first two objectives required observation of motor-movement and oral responses. This objective requires a writing perform-ance on instrumentation provided by the teacher. This re-sponse, as was the case in the previous two, requires the learner to check all positive and no negative responses.

D. Seventh-grade boys should receive satisfaction in participating in group singing as evidenced by ninety per cent of the boys being present at all special group singing opportunities without mak-ing any negative verbal or non-verbal disturbances.

Goal: For seventh-grade boys to find satisfaction in participating in group singing

Evaluation Critique:

(a) Performance—physical presence at group singing op-portunities and display of positive behaviors

(b) Success level criterion—ninety per cent is teacher expect-ancy and no negative verbal or non-verbal disturbances is student requirement

    (c) Optional statement — none

    (d) Objective classification — Desired or Criterion-referenced

Rationale: It may be presumed that the seventh-grade boys either had been missing singing activities or were creating too many disturbances for the best interest of the girls and singing group as a whole. The teacher decided to commit herself to developing some strategies that would help the boys find greater satisfaction in group singing. Again, the evaluation was to be based upon the absence of negative responses as the student requirement. In addition, she added a positive teacher expectancy statement as a guide for a goal of her own.

Chapter 14

WRITING GOALS AND BEHAVIORAL OBJECTIVES FOR LEVELS OF THE AFFECTIVE TAXONOMY

> In the works of man as in those of nature, it is the intention which is chiefly worth studying.
>
> *Goethe*

CHAPTER GOALS

For the reader to:

1. develop an understanding of how to write affective goal statements according to *classification levels of Krathwohl's Taxonomy of Educational Objectives: Affective Domain.*

2. understand why teachers should primarily write affective behavioral objectives at the 2.2, 2.3, 3.1, 3.2, and 3.3 sub-category classification levels of the affective taxonomy.

3. acquire skill in writing behavioral objectives at the 2.2, 2.3, 3.1, 3.2, and 3.3 sub-category classification levels of the affective taxonomy.

The behavioral objectives to be illustrated in this chapter will be based on Krathwohl's *Taxonomy of Educational Objectives.*[1] Not all of the taxonomy classifications, however, will be used owing to the impractical aspects of their application into classroom or teaching situations as well as the impractical nature of the evaluation which would be required. These objectives are not any more difficult to write than the ones illustrated; but they may not be appropriate for meaningful evaluation or practical to carry out once stated. Desired goals for the classifications should be stated and strategies developed to achieve these worthwhile ends. Nobody should avoid trying to achieve a desired goal just because it cannot be well stated as an objective or because success cannot be evaluated accurately.

Behavioral objectives are stated in terms of desired goals and observable behaviors which can be used to evaluate how effectively a learner has reached the desired goals. In the affective domain, observable learner behaviors refer to changes in feelings and emotions. Thus, any learner behavioral change should be seen as a response to a feeling or emotion, and to be valid this response should be chosen by the learner at his own volition.

Classification levels for receiving—(1.1), (1.2), and (1.3)—do not appear to meet the requirements of being a feeling or emotion, and the responding level, (2.1), does not indicate that the learner chooses the response of his own volition or because of any particular feeling for the act. As was pointed out by Krathwohl,[2] the receiving classification level may be more cognitive than it is affective. It is necessary for a stimulus to be received before it can be responded to, and for that reason the position is well taken that this classification should be included as the bottom level in the affective hierarchy.

At the same time, it does not appear that this rationale justifies the time and energy it takes a teacher to prepare and evaluate low level objectives which can only indicate knowledge and feelings which were already in existence at the time of the stimulus rather than a change in response due to the stimulus. At level 2.1, acquiescence in responding to the action may be performed from duty or fear rather than from true feeling or from a change in feeling.

Classification levels 4.0, Organization of a Value System, and 5.0, Characterization by a Value Complex, are also not recommended for development and use by classroom teachers. These levels should be excluded because of the time element and the inability to establish cause and effect relationships as well as the fact that they are rather abstract concepts. It can be assumed that most values will require months or years to form and that the determination of the interrelationships and organizational hierarchy of values will take even longer. In addition, the values formed will be subject to so many influences outside the teacher-learner environment that positive behavioral responses might be attributed to any number of causes other than the teachers' goal and instructional strategies. Since these levels are best evaluated when broken down into their component parts, which consist of behaviors in the responding and valuing categories, they may just as well be stated and evaluated in these two categories.

There are perhaps only two situations which would merit the development and use of behavioral objectives at the two highest classification levels. First would be in instances where teachers were teamed vertically for organization, planning, and teaching purposes. In addition, these vertical teams would have the same students in common throughout their elementary and/or secondary school years. Thus, short-range objectives to develop interests and appreciations could be developed as a first phase in the program which would gradually be replaced by objectives requiring the development of attitudes, values, and adjustments which could be planned for and evaluated at different time intervals in the school program.

The second situation which may substantiate use of the organization and characterization by value complex classification categories is in instances where the special expertise of the developer of the objectives and the situational context in which they are to be carried out are conducive to obtaining meaningful data. Expertise here refers to insight and ability as an evaluator, rating scale developer, or behavioral psychologist, or to a team of such experts. The situational context refers to the time the learners will be exposed to treatment and the ability to control selected variables which may influence the learner either positively or negatively. These two situations probably will apply less than one per cent of the time.

The elimination of the eight sub-category classifications of affective domain objectives from classification levels 1.0, 2.0, 4.0, and 5.0 not only reduces the teacher's task in behavioral objective development, but helps insure that objectives written for the remaining five sub-categories will probably be more meaningful and better evaluated. Primary emphases in writing behavioral objectives in this chapter will be focused upon the following sub-category classifications:

2.2 Willingness to respond;
2.3 Satisfaction in response;
3.1 Acceptance of a value;
3.2 Preference for a value;
3.3 Commitment.

The evaluation model chosen for each objective will be selected from the four evaluation models outlined earlier in this text.

WRITING GOALS BY THE TAXONOMY

The second method for writing affective goal statements is to utilize the taxonomy to insure learners of affective learning at different behavioral classification levels. Goals developed by this technique are illustrated by the following:

1. Pilot school teachers must be willing to spend an adequate amount of their free time in activities designed to train them to write goal statements
   Critique:
   a. Learner group — pilot school teachers
   b. Learning task —
      (1) Content area — activities designed to train them to write goal statements
      (2) Behavioral domain — willing to spend an adequate amount of their free time indicates the 2.2 classification level of the taxonomy
2. To increase the number of pilot school teachers willing to

spend their free time in activities designed to train them to write goal statements
Critique:
a. Learner group—pilot school teachers
b. Learning task—
   (1) Content area—writing goal statements
   (2) Behavioral domain—willing to spend their free time indicates the 2.2 classification of the affective taxonomy
3. The pilot school teachers must appreciate and gain satisfaction from the writing and use of goal statements
Critique:
a. Learner group—pilot school teachers
b. Learning task—
   (1) Content area—writing and use of goal statements
   (2) Behavioral domain—appreciate and gain satisfaction represent the 2.3 classification level of the affective taxonomy
4. To increase the appreciation and satisfaction of twelfth-grade students in utilizing competency modules as part of their instructional resource materials
Critique:
a. Learner group—twelfth-grade students
b. Learning task—
   (1) Content area—utilizing competency modules as part of their instructional resource materials
   (2) Behavioral domain—appreciation and satisfaction indicate the 2.3 classification level of the affective taxonomy
5. Duval County teachers should see and accept the value of bi-weekly three hour professional development opportunities
Critique:
a. Learner group—Duval County teachers
b. Learning task—
   (1) Content area—bi-weekly three hour professional development opportunities
   (2) Behavioral domain—accept the value places this goal at the 3.1 classification level of the affective taxonomy
6. To increase in a positive manner the attitude of Duval County teachers toward their present school situation
Critique:
a. Learner group—Duval County teachers
b. Learning task—
   (1) Content area—present school position
   (2) Behavioral domain—attitudes can place this goal at several classification levels, including the 3.1 level of the affective taxonomy

7. Eleventh-grade art students should develop a strong feeling for increasing their artistic values and insights
   Critique:
   a. Learner group—Eleventh-grade art students
   b. Learning task—
      (1) Content area—artistic values and insights
      (2) Behavioral domain—strong feeling for value places this goal at a higher level than mere acceptance of a value. Thus, it can be considered to be at the 3.2 classification level of the affective taxonomy

8. Eleventh-grade art students should increase their appreciation for accepted values found in selected works of art
   Critique:
   a. Learner group—Eleventh-grade art students
   b. Learning task—
      (1) Content area—selected works of art
      (2) Behavioral domain—to increase appreciation for accepted values indicates a beginning level of value acceptance; thus, an increase indicates movement to at least the next highest classification level of the affective taxonomy, which is 3.2

9. Twelfth-grade American History students should acquire commitment to appropriate current, social, economic, and political problems that affect their own community
   Critique:
   a. Learner group—twelfth-grade American History students
   b. Learning task—
      (1) Content area—current, social, economic, and political problems that affect their own community
      (2) Behavioral domain—commitment refers to the 3.3 classification level of the affective taxonomy

10. Twelfth-grade American History students should increase their commitment toward at least one current, social, economic, or political value which affects their own town or community
    Critique:
    a. Learner group—twelfth-grade American History students
    b. Learning task—
       (1) Content area—current, social, economic, or political value which affects their own town or community
       (2) Behavioral domain—increase commitment indicates at least the 3.3 classification level of the affective taxonomy

Owing to evaluation, time, and cause and effect problems, it is not recommended that teachers attempt to write objectives for the classification levels 4.0, Organization of a Value System, and 5.0, Characterization by a Value Complex. Thus, no goals will be illustrated at these levels for objective writing purposes. Teachers should, however, feel free to attempt to develop strategies designed to attain goals at these levels and not worry about evaluating them. The goal writing process will still remain the same.

CONVERTING TAXONOMIC GOALS TO TAXONOMIC BEHAVIORAL OBJECTIVES

The goals approach to writing performance objectives is a process approach. Thus, there is no difference in converting goals to objectives regardless of whether or not they are learning, non-learning, taxonomic, or non-taxonomic. The goals previously stated according to the taxonomy will now be converted to behavioral objectives according to their classification level.

2.0 RESPONDING

It is assumed that behavioral objectives written at this and higher classification levels are based upon the premise that the learners have already been sensitized to the learning content in question or that the teachers' instructional strategies will provide adequate stimulus for the learners to make the desired response. In other words, the learner will have been aware of something, that the phenomenon or variable in question has not alienated him to the point of seeking to avoid it, and that he has been or can be made to become conscious of the object to the point that he will focus his attention upon the selected variable when appropriate stimuli are applied.

Objectives stated at the responding level require learners to act out of personal satisfaction. The affective taxonomy places responding behavior in the following three categories.

CLASSIFICATION SUB-CATEGORIES	GENERAL DEFINITION	ACTION WORDS USEFUL IN PLANNING EVALUATION
2.1 Acquiescence in responding	Requires 1.0. Initially involves receiving. May also initially react out of compliance, later out of willingness and satisfaction	To: obey, be willing to follow, spend, find place in, be sensitive to, volunteer, be eager, commend, sense, seek out, agree, play, enjoy, accept responsibility, read, participate, comply, approve, augment, discuss, practice, applaud.
2.2 Willingness to respond		
2.3 Satisfaction in response		

2.1 ACQUIESCING TO RESPONDING

The first sub-category of responding, 2.1, acquiescence in responding, is not recommended for teacher use. As previously stated, this category may refer to learner compliance rather than voluntary, natural, positive, or negative feeling. Since behavioral objectives are designed to produce learning and the overt measurable learner responses to be evaluated should definitely be natural or indicate real feeling, there appears to be little point in preparing goals and evaluation activities for objectives at this level.

2.2 WILLINGNESS TO RESPOND

The major difference between sub-category 2.1 and sub-category 2.2 is that in the latter category the learner is willing to make a voluntary response rather than to respond through obedience. This willingness to volunteer indicates pleasure or good feeling although the motive for having such feeling may or may not be known. In other words, the "willingness to respond" may have either intrinsic or extrinsic value, depending upon whether it is a natural end within itself or only a means to achieving some other reward or end.

Behavioral objectives in the responding classification are very easy to write, particularly with reference to the goal statements. A working knowledge of the levels of the affective domain and the specifically identified learning content or unit being developed is all the information a teacher needs to write effective goal statements. Krathwohl[3] provides adequate lists of anticipated student outcomes which can serve as guidelines for the development of evaluation statements. Some of these outcomes have been stated as goals in Chapter 10. The action words, listed along with the general definition and classification of sub-categories, can be used in the development of goal statements as well as for an objective's evaluation component.

Example behavioral objectives which serve as illustrations in this chapter will consist of one goal statement attached to one of the behavioral evaluation design approaches. These objectives are artificial and presented for illustrative purposes only. Do not assume that any of the examples of objectives are the best illustrations that can be presented. The writer does not claim the necessary subject matter expertise to provide examples in a variety of educational program areas. However, use of the after-test-only and Gains evaluation designs is intended to provide the teacher with enough information on evaluation technique and methodology to enable him to write affective behavioral objectives in their areas of subject matter competence.

When students have completed this text they should have no difficulty in separating an objective's goal from its evaluation components. Thus, after the statement of each objective illustration, only the evaluation component will be restated for critiqueing purposes.

Examples of behavioral objectives written at the 2.2 "willingness to respond" level are:

A. AFTER-TEST-ONLY DESIGN

Pilot school teachers must be willing to spend an adequate amount of their free time in activities designed to train them to write goal statements. Proof that this goal is achieved will be determined by ninety per cent of the teachers volunteering and completing six hours of necessary in-service training when alternative opportunities are provided during after school hours.

Evaluation Critique:
1. Performance—volunteering for the necessary in-service training activities
2. Success level criterion standard
   (a) Learner requirement—to complete at least six hours of training
   (b) Optional statement—ninety per cent is the teacher's expectancy (the goal of the administrator or person developing the objective for the teachers)

Objective Classification: Desired level or Criterion-referenced

Rationale: The goal statement required that the teachers be willing to perform the specific learning content tasks. Thus, the evaluation performance required a performance which would allow the teachers a choice of compliance or noncompliance. Volunteering indicated a willingness to achieve a goal.

The basis for the success level criterion, an adequate amount of free time, was also established in the goal statement. This was interpreted in the evaluation component to mean that anything under six hours of training would not meet the required standards or that they must volunteer and complete 100 per cent of the specifically defined time requirement. Having achieved both an acceptable performance and criterion standard, the objective was placed into the desired level objective classification. The teacher expectancy in the optional statement does not fulfill the requirement of a success level criterion standard alone. However, the learner requirement can stand alone without the optional statement.

The reader should note that the learner is the teacher. This is the type of objective that a principal might use with a faculty, and in this case the principal becomes the instructor or teacher. In classroom situations the learner would refer to the students. The goal and evaluation components in this objective imply the 2.2 responding level of the affective taxonomy by use of the terms willing and volunteering. Such reinforcement is desirable for best communication of an objective's intent.

B. GAINS MODEL

To increase the number of pilot school teachers willing to spend their free time in activities designed to train them to write goal statements as determined by an increase of at least twenty percent in the number of teachers who volunteer and complete a minimum of six hours goal writing training during their off duty hours.

Evaluation Critique:
1. Performance—volunteer and complete goal writing training in off duty hours
2. Success level criterion standard
   (a) Learner requirement—An increase of at least twenty percent of all teachers who complete a minimum of six hours training
   (b) Optional statement—none

Objective Classification: Desired level or Criterion-referenced

Rationale: This objective is essentially the same as the previous one, but was revised due to a change in the circumstances present when stated. The goal was changed from *must be willing to spend an adequate amount of their free time* to *increase the number of pilot school teachers willing to spend their free time.*

The evaluation component was changed to conform to the fact that evidently a few teachers had volunteered during the previous year which established a type of "before-test" from which gains could be determined. The success level standard was changed to indicate that success must involve an increase of at least twenty percent of the teachers who receive six hours training.

The basic rationale for placing this objective into the 2.2 classification level is the same as was stated in the 'after-test-only" approach. The rationale behind the statement of the objective by the gains approach was purely a choice of the principal based upon the information he had available. First, he had information from the year before which could serve as the pre-test. Due to the availability of this data he stated the goal to show an increase in the number willing rather than just to be willing as was the case in the "after-test-only" approach.

The major factor for the reader to consider here is that the writer of the objective has a freedom of choice in deciding how to write his intended goal and in determining his own evaluation design. He will make these decisions based upon the type of data he has available and the evidence he desires to produce concerning learning outcomes.

2.3 SATISFACTION IN RESPONSE

The next level in the affective hierarchy, but still classified as a sub-category of response, is emotional behavior which expresses satisfaction or enjoyment. Almost any affective term can be used with this sub-category classification; therefore, it is assumed that teachers will write many objectives which are intended to express satisfaction. Examples of objectives written at the 2.3 "satisfaction in response," level are:

A. AFTER-TEST-ONLY DESIGN

The pilot school teachers must appreciate and gain satisfaction from writing and use of goal statements so that when given adequate training in goal setting, identification, and use and a group self-evaluation session involving free oral response, the majority of the teachers will voice approval and commend the writing of goals as a basis for establishing behavioral objectives in their own content areas.

Evaluation Critique:
1. Performance—Teachers will voice approval and commend during a group self-evaluation session by oral response
2. Success level criterion standard
   (a) Learner requirement—none
   (b) Optional statement—so that when given adequate training in goal setting, identification and use. In addition, the term majority can be considered to be the teacher expectancy

Objective Classification: Minimum level performance objective
Rationale: Again the goal statement identified the level of affective development desired through the use of the terms *appreciate* and *gain satisfaction.* The evaluation component required both the willingness to respond and a response that would denote satisfaction. No attempt was made to quantify how well or to what degree the response had to be made as a criterion or learner requirement. "How well" would be determined by subjective interpretation which is often the most practical method.

Some writers would argue that the word "majority" was the criterion standard. This term, however, indicates the number of teachers who should make the response rather than the depth or degree of satisfaction obtained. This objective illustrates that the minimum level behavioral objective can be useful despite the fact it has no distinct success level criterion standard.

Evaluation Critique Number Two:
This objective was deliberately stated at the minimum performance objective level to emphasize a situational reality. Many times teachers cannot think of or do not know an appropriate criterion to state as the learner requirement. Since the goal is considered to be desirable, an objective is stated at the minimum level and strategies designed to obtain the goal regardless of a lack of evaluation sophistication.

A better evaluation component might have required a percentage of the teachers to write goal statements for the content of some of the subject areas they teach, without any instructions from someone else to do so. This would have been a more positive way to express appreciation and satisfaction. However, practically speaking, objectives must be written at the level of competency of the objective writer and the best effort of any teacher should be considered as acceptable, provided it communicates a true evaluation performance, until experience provides the teacher with new insights. It might also be assumed that the criterion might be the subjective opinion of the principal who will hear the voiced approval.

B. GAINS MODEL

To increase the appreciation and satisfaction of twelfth grade students in utilizing competency modules as part of their instructional resource materials. Proof that this goal has been achieved will be evidenced by seventy-five per cent of the students scoring at least twenty per cent fewer negative responses on a twenty-five item rating scale administered before and after the use of instructional modules in two of their courses.

Evaluation Critique:
1. Performance—written responses on a twenty-five item rating scale administered before and after using instructional modules
2. Success level criterion standard
   (a) Learner requirement—twenty per cent fewer negative responses
   (b) Optional statement—seventy-five per cent of the teachers

Objective Classification: Desired level or Criterion-referenced
Rationale: The rationale is similar to that stated for the previous examples. The evaluation response is, however, changed to a writing activity involving the use of an especially constructed rating scale. It must be assumed that the scale is appropriate for the desired level of response. The scale should also be both valid and reliable with reference to content as well as behavioral level. It is also assumed that the rating scale will be administered on a basis in which the students are willing to be

evaluated and have no reason to state anything other than their true feelings.

3.0 VALUING

Value was earlier defined as something "deemed worthy enough to be desired due to social, moral or psychological factors." In order to qualify for the valuing hierarchical classifications the feelings or emotions must have advanced to a stage where the behavior is felt to have substantial worth and the feeling has been internalized to the point that attitudes are being developed. The difference between the three-sub-category levels of valuing represent the difference in the internalization of the attitudes or values.

This classification of behaviors is widely used by educational practitioners, but objectives developed for attitudes are not always well defined and the evaluation measures are difficult to validate. "Ideal" attitudes are difficult to develop in learners since they are based upon values which are inconsistently held by society as a whole. Thus, in many instances no one "ideal" attitude can be or should be expected to be held by most students. In these cases the norm representing the feelings held by a learner's society or community, in general, may become more ideal than an attitude based upon the judgment of one individual. This concept gives additional support to the use of the peer-group-expectancy mean.

Behavioral objectives in this classification will in most instances refer to a program goal which includes the term "attitude" or "value." Other expressions, however, can be just as appropriate. The three sub-category levels of this classification are 3.1 acceptance of a value, 3.2 preference for a value, and 3.3 commitment, and are graphically illustrated as follows:

CLASSIFICATION SUB-CATEGORIES	GENERAL DEFINITION	ACTION WORDS USEFUL IN PLANNING EVALUATION
3.1 Acceptance of a value 3.2 Preference for a value 3.3 Commitment	Requires 1.0 and 2.0. Initially involves receiving and responding. Includes the process of accepting the worth of an object, idea, or a behavior. Attempting to promote it as a value and to develop a commitment.	To: be loyal to, see value in, discuss, debate, prefer, favor, accept, seek out, show commitment to, feel strongly about, theorize, relinquish, compare, organize, specify, increase amount or numbers, assist, help, increase proficiency, deny, argue, support, obligate, pledge, agree to, show faith, trust, or confidence in, or respect obligation to

3.1 ACCEPTANCE OF A VALUE

This sub-category classification refers to the acceptance of the worth of an object, idea or behavior. These values or attitudes become associated with the beliefs held by an individual, but are not firmly enough established at this level to have become set or fixed. The definition for attitude illustrates the acceptance sub-category by stating that attitudes are a disposition to think or behave, but does not go far enough to state that the belief is positive enough to assure the performance of the behavior. Attitudes and values in this classification are consistent enough to be identified through measurable learner behaviors. This is most frequently accomplished by various types of attitude rating scales.

Examples of behavioral objectives showing acceptance of a value are:

A. AFTER-TEST-ONLY DESIGN

Duval County teachers should see and accept the value of bi-weekly, three hour professional development opportunities so that when administered a semantic differential attitude scale, composed of sixteen concepts toward which they should be concerned, ninety per cent of the teachers will achieve at least a +1 rating for twelve of the sixteen concepts.

Evaluation Critique:
1. Performance—instrumentation involves writing answers on a semantic differential rating scale
2. Success level criterion standard
   (a) Learner requirement—to achieve at least a +1 rating for twelve of sixteen concepts
   (b) Optional statement—teacher expectancy is that ninety per cent will accomplish the learner requirement

Objective Classification: Desired level or Criterion-referenced

Rationale: It is assumed that the writer of this objective performed a goal setting analysis to at least the level of subsystem goals. Such an analysis could have identified sixteen concepts about which the teachers could be or become concerned. The goal was stated under the global topic of values, but the evaluator preferred to break values for the professional development opportunities down into more specific concepts which could be evaluated both individually and collectively by the semantic differential device.

Instrumentation provided by the rating scale can furnish ample evidence of both performance and feeling. Since all concepts are important in determining global value, achievement of +1 on twelve concepts probably justified the assumption that teachers see value in the bi-weekly professional development opportunities. In other words, it is assumed that the intensity and duration of negative feelings toward any four of the concepts would not be greater than the positive feelings for the other twelve.

B. GAINS MODEL

To increase in a positive direction the attitude of Duval County teachers toward their present school situation as determined by each teacher's showing a positive shift of at least a .5 on fourteen of sixteen concepts built into a semantic differential attitude scale.

Evaluation Critique:
 1. Performance — writing answers on a sixteen concept semantic differential attitude scale
 2. Success level criterion standard
    (a) Learner requirement — a positive shift of at least a .5 on fourteen of sixteen concepts
    (b) Optional statement — teacher expectancy would be each teacher or one hundred per cent

Objective Classification: Desired level or Criterion-referenced
Rationale: Essentially the same as the previous example except that the use of the word "increase" in the goal statement caused a shift in evaluation design from "one test" to "before" and "after" tests. Increase indicates that one must have a starting point that is known. Analysis of the ratings achieved for each individual concept will help determine which concepts need the greater continuing strategy emphasis.

3.2 PREFERENCE FOR A VALUE

The difference in the level of internalization of a feeling determines the difference in the three sub-categories of attitudes or values. The difference between acceptance and preference can be illustrated by rdering bacon and eggs for breakfast in a restaurant but accepting cereal as a substitute when the bacon and eggs are not available. In this instance, it can be assumed that the person has accepted for breakfast foods both bacon and eggs as well as cereal, but if he almost always orders bacon and eggs, he prefers them to the point of pursuing them at breakfast time. Examples of objectives showing preference for a value are:

A. AFTER-TEST-ONLY MODEL

Eleventh-grade art students should develop a strong feeling for increasing their artistic values and insights as determined by seventy-five per cent of the students indicating on the following checklist that they occasionally seek out at least four of the stated activities.

(1) frequently asks questions pertaining to art
(2) occasionally attempts to help other people understand artistic concepts and values
(3) helps organize or joins an art club
(4) goes out of his way to seek works of art
(5) writes letters to political, social, news or other influential sources on the behalf of art
(6) actively participates in conducting art shows and displays
(7) forms close relationships with peer group associates who are interested in art
(8) subscribes to or reads books, magazine or materials which are art oriented
(9) tends to look at life in general from an aesthetic viewpoint
(10) visits art museums when the opportunity presents itself
(11) initiates conversations frequently concerning art
(12) shows appreciation for art through willingness to point out strengths and discrepancies in works of art
(13) has his own art collection
(14) achieves intellectual, social, or emotional satisfaction from artistic pursuits
(15) desires to show creative expression of himself through art
(16) supports artistic endeavors for personal enjoyment

Evaluation Critique:
    1. Performance – writing on a checklist
    2. Success level criterion standard
        (a) Learner requirement – to seek out at least four of the activities indicated on a sixteen item checklist
        (b) Optional statement – teacher expectancy is that at least seventy-five per cent should meet the learner requirement

Objective Classification: Desired level or Criterion-referenced
Rationale: Strong feelings for values and insights imply the 3.2 subcategory as does the fact that they select certain activities as a response to having a preference for them. The behavioral objective is classified as desired level behavior since it has a student requirement as part of the success level criterion standard. One caution must be taken by teachers writing af-

fective behavioral objectives, particularly the type that are evaluated by instrumentation such as that provided in this objective. The student should not see the objective or know how success will be evaluated in advance. Knowledge of the teacher's desires may result in a student purposely providing evaluation data that he or she thinks will be pleasing to the teacher.

B. Gains Model

Eleventh-grade art students should increase their appreciation for accepted values found in selected works of art as determined by an increase in their proficiency to compare and debate the relative merits of selected works of art. This increase will be determined by teacher observation of student change from the beginning to the end of the school year.

Evaluation Critique:
1. Performance—orally comparing and debating
2. Success level criterion standard
   (a) Learner requirement—no objective criterion, but quality of change based upon teacher observation could be considered a standard
   (b) Optional statement—none

Objective Classification: Minimum level performance objective

Rationale: The willingness of the student to utilize the highest classification of cognitive behavior, evaluation, and to express his feeling of support for certain selected works of art seems to place this objective in the 3.2 category. It shows more than acceptance of a value. The objective is classified as a minimum level behavioral objective since it has no specifically identified learner requirement other than approval by the teacher's subjective judgment. This may be considered a subjective criterion according to the expertise of the teacher. It makes no real difference which level the objective is placed in because the student behavior will still be the same.

3.3 Commitment

Value commitment means that the internalization of a feeling or emotion has reached the stage that a person feels obligated to show faith, trust, confidence, obligation, loyalty or a pledge to do something. Any learner who performs a behavior which is indicative of com-

mitment may be thought of as holding values toward that particular
variable which may be classified at the 3.3 sub-category commitment
level. The more commitment the learner has for something the more he
may be expected to promote it. The more the learner promotes something the higher he may be expected to value it.

Usually the learner's promotion of a value will include, among other
behaviors, some attempt to sell, convince or change someone else's
viewpoint concerning the value. In this respect the learner's promotion
of the value may take on the characteristics of a compelling impulse to
act in relationship to the value. Examples of behavioral objectives showing commitment for a value are:

A. AFTER-TEST-ONLY MODEL

Twelfth-grade American History students should acquire commitment for appropriate current, social, economic and political problems
that affect their own community as measured by fifty per cent of the
seniors seeking out opportunities for active involvement in at least one
such problem. Involvement may include activities such as:
1. attending meetings and speaking for or against an issue,
2. participating in peaceful demonstrations to show loyalty,
3. organizing a group to assist those with the same attitudes about a
   specific problem,
4. writing letters stating their beliefs to the proper authorities, and
5. taking the time to study the problem in depth in order to become well versed in all phases of the issue involved.
Evaluation Critique:
   1. Performance—to seek out opportunities and to become
      actively involved in social, economic or political problems
   2. Success level criterion standard
      (a) Learner requirement—one problem
      (b) Optional statement—teacher expectancy is for at least
          fifty per cent of the seniors to meet the learner require-
          ment
Objective Classification: Desired level performance objective
Rationale: Commitment in the goal refers to valuing. Generally
   speaking, evaluation activities would appear to require a reasonable amount of time and energy on the part of the student
   which would probably require that he have enough faith in the
   undertaking to feel an obligation to do so. This objective could
   easily be converted to a minimum level objective by not stating
   the amount of time or the specific number of activities or problem involvements the students must actually participate in.

B. GAINS MODEL

Twelfth-grade American History students should increase their commitment toward at least one current, social, economic, or political value which affects their own town or community, so that when given an appropriate written pre- and post-test questionnaire, the seniors will indicate at least ten per cent more involvement in current local issues according to the post-test results.

Evaluation Critique:
1. Performance — written performance on pre- and post-test instrumentation
2. Success level criterion standard
    (a) Learner requirement — ten per cent increase in involvement according to questionnaires administered.
    (b) Optional statement — the given in this instance involved appropriate pre- and post-test questionnaires

Objective Classification: Desired level

Rationale: Commitment refers to valuing in the affective domain. Evaluation of commitment must be accomplished by measurable observations of a student's behavior which indicate loyalty, confidence, or dedication to something considered to be worthwhile. This dedication should indicate a substantial investment of time and energy on the part of the learner. It is assumed that the survey questionnaire will utilize questions which would indicate such learner involvement. There are, of course, problems inherent with the use of questionnaires which can produce inaccurate answers. This type of instrumentation should be carefully planned before use. Again it is important that the student not know what is expected of him in determining his success in achieving the stated goal.

4.0 ORGANIZATION AND 5.0 CHARACTERIZATION BY A VALUE COMPLEX

The use of behavioral objectives in these two classifications is not recommended for the majority of behavioral objective writers. The chief reasons are: (1) goals are too general and difficult to break down, (2) accurate evaluation performances with cause and effect relationships are difficult to establish, (3) strategies are almost impossible to develop for the complete concepts involved and too much time is required for this level of change to occur. Sub-category levels and other descriptive information will, however, be presented as guidelines for those who may wish to try. These guidelines are as follows:

Classification Sub-categories	General Definition	Action Words Useful in Planning Evaluation
Conceptualization of a value 4.1 Organization of a value system 4.2	Requires 1.0, 2.0 and 3.0. Initially involves receiving; requires a response and development of values; Must determine interrelationships of values; establishing a hierarchy.	To: criticize, weigh alternatives, relate, form judgments, adopt a course, discuss, choose, abstract, balance, hope, organize, formulate, theorize, compare, define, desire, wish.
Generalized set 5.1 Characterization 5.2	Requires 1.0, 2.0, 3.0 and 4.0. Initially involves receiving, response, valuing and organization of selected values into controlling tendencies with subsequent integration into a total philosophy.	To: face facts and conclusions, revise judgments, develop a conscience, behave according to a system of values, develop a philosophy of life, change, avoid, be rated high, revise, resolve, require, resist, manage, complete.

REFERENCES

1. D. R. Krathwohl, B. S. Bloom and B. B. Masia, *Taxonomy of Educational Objectives,* (Handbook II: Affective Domain), New York; David McKay, Inc., 1968, p. 37.
2. D. R. Krathwohl, B. S. Bloom, and B. B. Masia, *Taxonomy of Educational Objectives.* (Handbook II: Affective Domain) New York, David McKay, Inc., 1968, p. 51.
3. D. R. Krathwohl, B. S. Bloom, and B. B. Masia, *Taxonomy of Educational Objectives,* (Handbook II: Affective Domain) New York, David McKay, Inc., 1968, pp. 125–130.

Chapter 15

CREATING WRITING
FLEXIBILITY

Variety is the very spice of life, that gives it all its
flavor.

Cowper

A place for everything, everything in its place.

Franklin

CHAPTER GOAL

For the reader to be able to conceptualize the solutions to various problems which may occur in the development of performance objectives for specific programs and purposes.

Any process that utilizes models may at times suffer from an acute illness, *modelism*. Possibly the best way to avoid this sickness is to be aware of its existence, so it will not take you by surprise. A model is an illustration, guideline, pattern or plan and, as such, should never be assumed to be either right or wrong: it is right only as long as it is the best plan to follow; and wrong when some other pattern offers better results.

The *outcomes approach* and *goals approach* writing techniques are both models for the writing of performance objectives. Thus, they must each be considered as suspect. Obviously, *goals approach* advocates believe that this technique offers a performance objective user everything that the *outcomes approach* offers, and a great deal more, in most instances. One positive advantage of the *outcomes approach* is that objectives written by that technique are a little shorter. But is this really important?

This chapter does not propose to compare the advantages and disadvantages of the two different writing approaches. The purpose at hand is to emphasize that the true value of performance objectives is their contribution toward (1) defining specific goals or intents, (2)

249

specifying appropriate evaluation measures so that people know when they have successfully achieved their goals, and (3) to provide sufficient communication for users to plan better strategies and procedures for reaching goals.

The assumption may be made that the value of any model for writing objectives must be in its ability to communicate—not only to the writer, but to all potential users and other audiences that may at some time come in contact with the objective.

Questions concerning the diversification and/or flexibility of the goals-approach writing process may arise and may be dealt with without too much difficulty. The most common questions formulated by workshop participants and college students learning to write behavioral objectives by the goals approach for the first time are: (1) Can the process be used for writing behavioral objectives for individuals? (2) What is the procedure for writing for different types of children? (3) How are objectives written for units of instruction rather than for individual skills? (4) How may redundancy be eliminated? (5) How should complex objectives be written which require more than one sentence or one paragraph to state? The purpose of this chapter is to answer these questions and to give necessary illustrations.

RELATING OBJECTIVES TO BOTH INDIVIDUALS AND GROUPS

Any objective that can be stated for an individual can be modified for group purposes or to take care of special types of students. Conversely, behavioral objectives stated for special groups or types of students can be altered to apply to individual students. This is easily accomplished by changing the learner(s) identified in the goal and altering the evaluation component to reflect the change in learner emphasis. An example of the changes required to convert a group objective to an individual objective is:

> Group: To improve the pronunciation and intonation of French I students, with maximum communication and comprehension based on a minimal vocabulary and basic structure, so that given a particular dialogue with which to work and two weeks practice time, 75 per cent of the students will achieve a score of 100 on a teacher-made oral comprehension test.

> Individual: To improve the pronunciation and intonation of Sandra Jane Smith, with maximum communication and comprehension based on a minimal vocabulary and basic structure, so that given a particular dialogue with which to work and two weeks practice

time, she will achieve a score of 85 or above on a teacher-made oral comprehension test.

An interesting feature of any group objective is that the goal statement can serve two purposes and, with slight revision in the evaluation component, both purposes can be evaluated by the same data. In the group objective the learners were identified as French I students and the evaluation component was 75 per cent of the students for teacher expectancy, with a student requirement of a score of 100 per cent. In this objective the teachers and students had a specific intent: to improve the pronunciation and intonation of French I students. Each student would achieve his goal if he scored 100 per cent on a test. It is not likely that all students will score 100, so the teacher set a reasonable standard to determine her own success — 75 per cent of the students will achieve their goals.

In objectives that are stated for individuals the teacher's and student's goals and evaluation components will remain the same; thus, the reference is only to student goal and student requirement. The objective stated previously for the individual, Sandra Jane Smith, based her student requirement upon her own potential, as assessed by the teacher.

In the cognitive domain there are three basic ways to change an objective from one type of student to another, in addition to changing the learner identified in the goal statement. This applies to objectives written for individuals and groups. First, the success level (teacher expectancy and student requirement) specified for the objective may be changed. Second, the objective may be stated at a different level of cognitive understanding. Third, the student requirement may be either raised or lowered. A combination of the three changes would be still another method of making a behavioral objective more appropriate for a particular learner.

In mathematics, average and advanced students might have the same goal, do the same activities concerning common course work, and be evaluated by the same methods. But the percentage used for teacher expectancy and learner requirement will undoubtedly be higher for the advanced student than for the basic or average student. Sometimes the learner requirement will remain the same, but the slower student may be given fewer objectives and/or more time to accomplish them. In some other subject areas it might be expected that the differences between advanced and basic or average students would involve different activities or levels of thinking and a different type of evaluation. Thus, objectives in this area may be stated at a higher cognitive level with or without any change in teacher expectancy or student requirement. The choice is that of the teacher responsible for developing the objective and should represent a careful attempt to meet the needs of all of the pupils both as individuals and as groups.

WRITING COMPLEX OBJECTIVES FOR UNITS OF INSTRUCTION

Two common approaches to writing behavioral objectives for curriculum development are (1) to write for individual skills designated by a skills continuum and (2) to develop objectives for entire units of work. The unit approach involves writing an overall objective which includes many skills. There is one logical rule for choosing the format to follow in writing each type of objective: that is, to write it in the simplest and most concise manner possible with no loss in value of the information being communicated. This means the complete objective, skill, or unit, should retain the information provided in the basic statement of intent and basic statement of evaluation.

The difference between writing for individual skills and units can be seen in the following illustrations:

INDIVIDUAL SKILLS

For male twelfth-grade students to:

(1) increase their upper arm strength as evidenced by their ability to correctly perform 20 standing presses with a sixty pound weighted bar.
(2) increase their upper arm strength as evidenced by their ability to correctly perform 25 shoulder presses with a sixty pound weighted bar.
(3) increase their upper arm strength as evidenced by their ability to correctly perform 15 bench presses with a sixty pound weighted bar.
(4) increase their upper arm strength so that when given a sixty pound weighted bar, they can correctly perform 30 two arm curls.
(5) increase their upper arm strength so that when given a sixty pound weighted bar, they can correctly perform 25 two arm reverse curls.

Note that these objectives have been shortened and some redundancy avoided by stating the learner group separately at the beginning so that the reader will know twelfth-grade students are the learner group for each objective. Each of these objectives has the development of arm strength as its content area skill and is written for the psychomotor domain. Each objective identifies a performance (press or curl with a sixty pound weighted bar) and a success level standard, the number of presses or curls that are necessary in order to achieve success in goal attainment. Stating the learner groups separately reduced the written assignment for these five objectives by twenty words.

UNIT OBJECTIVE NUMBER ONE

For male twelfth-grade students to increase their upper arm strength so that when given a sixty pound weighted bar they can correctly perform each of the following activities:

(1) 20 standing presses
(2) 25 shoulder presses
(3) 15 bench presses
(4) 30 two arm curls
(5) 25 two arm reverse curls

The conversion from individual skill objectives to a unit objective as further reduced the writing assignment by seventy words without changing either the goal or evaluation requirements. The reader should note that this type of unit approach should be used only when the goal or statement of specific intent is the same and/or appropriate for all evaluation performances to be stated. In this illustration we have still retained full communication. In either the individual skill objectives or the unit objective it is possible to identify the correct specific learning task, learner, evaluation performance, and success level standards. Unit objectives can include the statement of two skill performances or over one hundred if the evaluation components are appropriate and the stated goal is specific rather than general.

UNIT OBJECTIVE NUMBER TWO

Individuals writing performance objectives should keep in mind that criterion-referenced measurement is primarily designed for specific content coverage and evaluation activities should provide data that can be used to correct weaknesses that are identified. In an earlier chapter it was pointed out that by use of the systems approach all goals for instructional purposes can be identified down to the individual skill level and their identity retained so that improvements can be made as the need arises. In other words, a teacher may wish to recycle her statement of objectives and instructional strategies if students fail to achieve them.

There are, however, other types of objectives which must be written for situations which are terminal in the sense that there will be no time for recycling or improving the learning behaviors after completion of the evaluation activities. An example could be the use of a consultant for in-service teacher training. In this situation the intent is to establish success standards for the total workshop without particular emphasis upon individual workshop components or skills. Again a unit approach can be used:

For workshop participants to increase their understanding of and technical skills in writing behavioral objectives, so that given a comprehensive written examination and a one-hour time limit, 90 percent of the participants completing the workshop will obtain a score of at least 75 percent. Success in achieving this general goal will be determined by the activities specified on the following examination:

1. Identify in writing the one word that best represents the chief concern in writing objectives in behavioral terms.
2. Correctly write the name of each of the two major component parts of a behavioral objective.
3. Name and correctly summarize in a brief statement of less than seventy-five words each of the two types of performance objectives as defined in the workshop.
4. List, without error, the names of each of the three major criteria that can be used as communication checks of a goal.
5. Describe separately, in correct but brief statements, each of the three distinct behavioral domain areas.
6. Name correctly, as presented in this workshop, each of the three levels for writing objectives and relate each level, without error, to a particular type of objective also defined in this workshop.
7. Explain without error and in less than fifty words the differences between behavioral objectives and procedures.
8. Write and make a critical analysis, without error, of one behavioral objective written at the minimum level.
9. Write and make a critical analysis, without error, of one behavioral objective written at the desired level.
10. Create, without error, from the words stated below, one well organized desired level behavioral objective that is structurally correct with reference to communication checks of the goal and the use of all evaluation components.

In this illustration neither the specific skill goals nor the levels of cognitive understanding would have been the same for the individual activities listed in the evaluation component. All do, however, relate to the basic general workshop goal which in this case becomes the only identified intent. This type of unit presentation and use of evaluation statements is, perhaps, the only truly defensible situation in which specific statements of intent are not used for each evaluation performance statement. Since no recycling or follow-up activities are possible, the unit objective can be considered complete within itself.

Close observation of this unit objective reveals that each of its component performance activities could have been stated separately and become an individual knowledge or skill objective. The workshop leader, however, desired to evaluate both himself and his students and his specific intent was to establish each person's accountability based upon the entire workshop presentation rather than its individual components. Again, the specific intent must be the choice of the person developing the objective. It can readily be determined that this *goals approach* objective is not much longer than an equivalent objective written by the outcomes technique.

PROBLEMS OF REDUNDANCY

The problem of redundancy is more imaginary than real. Any group of goal statements which refers to the same learner or learning group can separate the learner(s) from the rest of the goal and specify only the learning task and evaluation component. Any goals which have identical learning tasks can separate the learning tasks and/or learning tasks and learners from the evaluation components and thus have several objectives identified with just one goal.

All objectives which have unlike learner(s) and/or learning tasks in their goal statements should have complete goal and evaluation component statements. In Chapter 2, several problems were identified which can occur if the goal and evaluation components are not completely identified for either skill level or unit objectives.

Writing objectives by the unit-method approach is one of the best ways to avoid redundancy in the development of goal statements. Sometimes one goal can be appropriate for the development of many skills. When this is the case, it is useless to repeat goal statements by writing each objective individually.

Another way to avoid redundancy and to possibly aid in the clarification of some objectives is to change the manner in which goals are joined to the statements of evaluation. This can be accomplished by either a change in the connecting words or by a separation of some of the evaluation components from the body of the objective. Examples of this technique taken from two proposals developed for Title III funding are as follows:

1. To increase the reading achievement of first-grade students as measured by the total score obtained on the Stanford Reading Achievement test in which students obtain the following:
   (a) 25 per cent decrease in the number of students entering the second grade who are one-half or more years behind grade level than in the previous year.
   (b) an average of 0.2 increase in the grade level achievement of students entering the second grade over the preceding year.
2. To help school personnel to: (1) become more willing to involve themselves socially and professionally in school, (2) perceive administration more positively, and (3) perceive the organizational climate of the school as being more open,

more autonomous, and less controlled, as determined respectively by the following:

(a) the Disengagement, Esprit, Intimacy, and Hindrance scales of the Organizational Climate Description Questionnaire.

(b) the Openness, Autonomy, and Controlled scales of the Organizational Climate Description Questionnaire.

3. To assist students in the: (1) understanding of and skill in dealing with human behavior, (2) perception of the teacher as an individual whose work is helping pupils learn, (3) ability to take initiative in, or responsibility for, trying to work out some of their simpler problems, (4) recognition that data from past studies can be an aid in understanding and appreciating the behavior of others, and (5) application of a causal approach to historical events and to current social problems as evaluated by:

(a) Social Causality Test by Ralph H. Ojemann.

(b) Problems Situation Test by Ralph H. Ojemann.

4. To improve the personal adequacy and instructional efficiency of classroom teachers so that given a fully developed comprehensive in-service training program and one year of program implementation, 85 per cent of the teachers will successfully be performing the following activities:

(a) working in harmonious relationship with other faculty members on problems of common concern.

(b) developing written reports, project activities, and pupil analyses resulting from in-service training.

(c) increased teacher utilization of more innovative materials, equipment, and teaching techniques.

(d) writing more accurate and objective diagnosis procedures to determine individual student needs and progress.

The success of these evaluation activities will be judged by an evaluation team which includes the building principal, county staff supervisors, and visiting teachers.

In these examples only the first and fourth objectives were written at the desired or criterion-referenced level. Objectives two and three specified only performances but no success criterions. Objective number four states a teacher expectancy (85 per cent) which is part of a success criterion, but cannot stand alone without the learner requirements of how successful each of the four activities must be. The activities belong to the performance statement.

CHANGING FORMAT

In this chapter flexibility for writing objectives with the *goals approach* technique has been illustrated by stating them as units, by removing the learner(s) and/or learning tasks from duplicated goal statements, and by changing the manner in which the goal statements are attached to the evaluation components. One additional alternative is offered which, although involving drastic changes in format, still will preserve all necessary communication.

The fact has been emphasized that maximum communication efficiency is desirable and whatever changes are necessary to preserve all needed communication should be made. To re-emphasize, it is good communication that makes performance objectives useful, not the preservation of any particular model for writing them.

Goal setting is the key to the whole process of strategy development and to determining evaluation performances. It is, therefore, preservation of the information contained within goal statements that has created the need for a *goals approach* to writing performance objectives. There appears to be no real reason to separate goal statements from evaluation components but if for some projects or uses of performance objectives this seems appropriate, it should be accomplished without permanent communication loss. This can be done through a complete separation of goal statements and evaluation performances, provided the learning program document being prepared specifically provides for the retention of goal statements of intent and for the evaluation components in a one to one relationship.

Two examples of how this might be accomplished in the development of a learning module such as that outlined in the preceding chapter are:

EXAMPLE NUMBER ONE (VOCABULARY)

GOAL STATEMENT	EVALUATION PERFORMANCES
For primary students to:	
1. comprehend the relationship between names and numerals from 1 to 10.	1. given two lists of five pairs of names and numbers to match, the students will verbally match at least four pairs correctly.
2. be able to associate pictures with words.	2. the students will be able to accurately match pictures and word cards 80 per cent of the time.
3. extend their sight vocabulary.	3. students must be able to correctly read from flash cards 90 per cent of the words on the *220 Dolch Basic Word Test*.
4. develop word meaning skills.	4. students must write sentences illustrating the multiple meanings from a given list of words with 90 per cent accuracy.
5. develop word recognition skills.	5. students must be able to recognize *Dolch 220* sight words with 75 per cent accuracy on a written test.
6. develop skill in recognizing synonyms, antonyms, and homonyms.	6. given a written list of words, students can match pairs according to directions with 85 per cent accuracy.

In this simple illustration, primary students were given six goals or basic statements of intent which were listed under a goal statement column. Then, evaluation performances for each goal statement were listed in another column, in a one to one relationship with the goal statements.

There is little reason to anticipate that objectives will be written in this manner. It would be easier to connect the statements into goals approach objectives. This example does set the stage for another type of goal-evaluation component separation. Using the same goal statements and evaluation performance previously given, but this time placing them under the goal and evaluation parts of a competency module similar to the one developed in Chapter 8, would have the following effect:

    I. Module Identification
   II. Coding
  III. Operational Instructions
  IV. Statements of Modules Mission Objective
   V. Entry Prerequisites
  VI. Diagnostic Preassessment
 VII. Specific Goals
      For primary students to:
      1. comprehend the relationship between number names and numerals from 1 to 10.
      2. be able to associate pictures with words.
      3. extend their sight vocabulary.
      4. develop word meaning skills.
      5. develop word recognition skills.
      6. develop skill in recognizing synonyms, antonyms and homonyms.
 VIII. Learning Strategies and Resources.
  IX. Introduction and Rationale.
   X. Recommended Learning Activities and Experiences.
  XI. Evaluation Performances.
      1. given two lists of five pairs of names and numbers to match, the students will verbally match at least four pairs correctly.
      2. the students will be able to accurately match pictures and word cards 80 per cent of the time.
      3. students must be able to read correctly from flash cards 90 per cent of the words on the *220 Dolch Basic Word List.*
      4. students must write sentences illustrating the multiple meanings from a given list of words with 90 per cent accuracy.
      5. students must be able to recognize Dolch 220 sight words with 75 per cent accuracy on a written test.
      6. given a written list of words, students can match pairs according to directions with 85 per cent accuracy.

In this example, goals were identified after diagnostic preassessment activities in the competency module and evaluation performances were not stated until much later, or after the recommended learning activities and experiences. Again, the identity of the goals and their matching evaluation components was retained by the consecutive stating of both with corresponding numbers.

This format could be used if it better serves the purpose of the developer(s) of performance objectives. This is not likely to be the case. In few instances will anything be gained by the separation of the goal statement from its evaluation component. Experiences of the author and of many colleagues indicate that, in the final analysis, the use of the goals approach technique, which connects the goal and evaluation components, will prove to be the most efficient.

GLOSSARY OF TERMS

Complex Objectives: performance objectives in which either the goal specifies more than one specific intent or the evaluation component consists of multiple outcome performances and criterion or a combination of both.

Modelism: an abnormal state or condition in which a person depends excessively upon a pre-established design, pattern or guideline as an example which he can emulate.

Redundancy: in this chapter, the term redundancy refers to possible superfluous repetition of communication check components or other characteristics required in the writing of a large quantity of performance objectives, especially at the skill level.

Units of Instruction: in this chapter, this term means an instructional unit that consists of many skills and is subject to being broken down into multiple goals, but has been retained as a whole unit.

Chapter 16

WRITING NON-LEARNING ORIENTED GOAL STATEMENTS AND PERFORMANCE OBJECTIVES

> In the works of man as in those of nature, it is the intention which is chiefly worth studying.
>
> *Goethe*

> I had six honest serving men: their names were Where and What and When—and Why and How and Who.
>
> *Rudyard Kipling*

CHAPTER GOALS

For the reader to:

1. develop skill in writing non-learning oriented goals.

2. develop skill in writing non-learning oriented performance objectives.

Teachers (classroom managers) and educational administrators have two great concerns: the joys of success and the burdens of failure, both of which they must be accountable for and share. These two concerns are the sum total of all of an institution's instructional and non-instructional commitments. The major difference between the commitments of a principal and a teacher is that a principal is a status leader who heads up a team of teachers who have a common goal in mind.

Communication has often been referred to as the greatest problem in both teaching and administration. Teachers and administrators must be able to communicate in regard to the total goals of the institution, not just in the isolated segment of the program referred to as instruction. Thus, principals must understand and be able to work with behavioral goals as well as non-instructional (non-learning oriented) goals. Teachers, on the other hand, must be able to understand and write non-instruc-

260

tional (non-learning oriented) objectives if they are to function efficiently in their instructional tasks.

There is little difference between the accountability and problem solving requirements of an instructional and non-instructional program. Thus, there is little difference in the expertise or skills in goal setting and performance objective specification that are required of an educational administrator or a teacher as a classroom manager. There may be a difference in time commitment and emphasis, but not in total program planning. The similarity between an administrator's and a teacher's program requirements can be determined by the following illustration.

TOTAL EDUCATIONAL PROGRAM

INSTRUCTIONAL PROGRAMS	NON-INSTRUCTIONAL PROGRAMS
1. Types: All programs representing curricular offerings designed to change students' cognitive, affective and/or psychomotor behavior.	1. Types: All programs designed to provide services which will support the instructional programs, but are not directly concerned with changing students' cognitive, affective and/or psychomotor behavior.
2. Examples: Teaching English, Mathematics, Science, Social Studies.	2. Examples: School plants, transportation, personnel management by objectives, finance, master planning.
3. *Problem Solving Processes* (a) Needs Assessment (problem identification) (b) Goal Setting (statement of specific intents) (c) Performance Objective Specification (learning oriented behavioral objectives) (d) Strategy Analyses and Selection (to achieve identified goal and objective) (e) Implementation Procedures (f) Evaluation (to determine success) (g) Recycle (for program improvement)	3. *Problem Solving Processes* (a) Needs Assessment (problem identification) (b) Goal Setting (statement of specific intent) (c) Performance Objective Specification (non-learning oriented objectives) (d) Strategy Analysis and Selection (to achieve identified goal and objective) (e) Implementation Procedures (f) Evaluation (to determine success) (g) Recycle (for program improvement)
4. Persons Accountable (a) teachers (b) administrators	4. Persons Accountable (a) administrators (b) teachers

This illustration reveals that the problem solving processes of both instructional (learning oriented) and non-instructional (non-learning oriented) programs are almost identical. Each is a functioning part of the environment that must be accounted for by both a teacher and an administrator. Teachers and administrators need to understand both the learning oriented and non-learning oriented classifications of objectives and to be able to write and use them efficiently.

WRITING NON-LEARNING ORIENTED GOALS

Earlier in this text it was pointed out that there are two types of performance objectives, learning oriented and non-learning oriented. Learning oriented objectives were shown to be concerned with goals in which the intent was to bring about a cognitive, affective, or psychomotor change in a learner. Non-learning oriented objectives are concerned with goals in which the specific intent is anything other than a change in learner behavior. Usually, non-learning oriented objectives will be concerned with determination of status, application of a process, development of a non-learning oriented product, or accomplishment of other observable activities for which someone must be accountable.

Non-learning oriented objectives are used more frequently than learning oriented objectives in evaluation of goals identified by systems analysis procedures in developing systems programs of accountability, financial accounting, non-instructional areas such as school transportation and project development and almost all programs of *Management by Objectives.* According to the definition of a performance objective, an objective must consist of two components: (1) a goal statement; and (2) an evaluation statement. Thus, writing non-learning oriented objectives is similar to writing learning oriented objectives; the essential difference is found in the requirement of the basic statement of intent in the goal.

BASIC STATEMENT OF INTENT

A non-learning oriented goal is selected in much the same manner as are learning oriented goals—usually through the identification of a need or a problem, prescription by authority, or by use of systems analysis procedures. A non-learning oriented goal should represent the specific intent of a course of action that is to be evaluated. Some examples of non-learning oriented basic goal statements are:

1. For each teacher to provide all students with an opportunity to have counseling services during the school year.
2. For the Department of Educational Administration to develop and implement by September, 1972, a performance-based curriculum for the training of persons who intend to hold leadership positions in either public schools or higher education.

3. For the Auburn High School faculty to develop by September, 1973, a systematic plan of processes and organizational structures that will enable administrators to better implement programs based upon individualization of instruction.
4. For the school board to provide by October, 1973, a source of legal information for the staff of each school.
5. For the Director of Personnel to employ certified personnel in all phases of the school program by August, 1972.
6. For the Instructional Division to identify by June, 1975, roles and responsibilities of all personnel in the educational program.
7. For the Superintendent to develop, prior to the next school year, district-wide administrative services which promote greater operational efficiency and financial economy.
8. For the Department of Education Administration to prepare and execute product demonstration agreements with local school systems prior to the 1973–74 school year.
9. For the Director of Transportation to increase within two years the efficiency of the school bus transportation system.
10. For the program director to see that all cooperative training students are placed in appropriate training agencies during the first month of each school year.

Every program, project or function—whether it be in instruction, business administration, or other management concerns—will have some distinct focus or intent which can and should be formalized by a goal statement. It is not possible for one person to be knowledgeable enough in all areas to identify each goal; thus, goal statements may require the cooperation of two or more individuals. At least one person must supply the expertise needed to determine appropriate intents and someone must understand the technique for writing goals and objectives.

The previously stated goals were taken from two sources: numbers 1, 4, 5, 7, and 10 were taken from state accreditation standards; the others were abstracted from funded projects to be sponsored by either federal or state departments of education.

COMMUNICATION CHECK OF BASIC GOAL STATEMENT

The communication check of non-learning oriented goals is relatively simple. These goals require no identification of learner (learner group) or behavioral domains. The specific requirements are that they communicate well (1) a specific program task, (2) who is responsible for the task, and (3) when the task must be accomplished. In other words, the learner and learning task in learning oriented objectives are replaced by a program task and other information in non-learning oriented objectives. Intents must answer questions posed by the words who, what, and when.

Due to the variety of uses that can be made of non-learning oriented objectives, it is hard to state communication checks that can be specifically applied to every objective. There are, however, three checks that can be very worthwhile for non-learning oriented goal statements. These checks are (1) who, (2) what, and (3) when. Answering *who* will do *what* program task and *when* it will be done will help bring specificity to goal statements. This, in turn, will aid in bringing specificity to the evaluation components.

Again using our example goal statements, the technique for critiqueing non-learning oriented goal statements may be illustrated:

1. For each teacher to provide all students with an opportunity to have counseling services during the school year
   Critique:
   A. Basic Statement
      (1) Who — each teacher
      (2) Program task — provide all students with an opportunity to have counseling services during the school year
         (a) What — opportunity to have counseling services
         (b) When — during the school year
      (3) Communication check — all requirements met
2. For the Department of Educational Administration to develop and implement by September, 1972, a performance-based curriculum for the training of persons who intend to hold leadership positions in either public schools or higher education
   Critique:
   A. Basic Statement
      (1) Who — the Department of Educational Administration
      (2) Program task — to develop and implement by September, 1972, a performance-based curriculum for the training of persons who intend to hold leadership positions in either public schools or higher education
         (a) What — to develop and implement a performance-based curriculum
         (b) When — by September, 1972
      (3) Communication check — all requirements met
3. For the Auburn High School faculty to develop by September, 1973, a systematic plan of processes and organizational structure that will enable administrators to better implement programs based upon individualization of instruction
   Critique:
   A. Basic Statement
      (1) Who — the Auburn High School faculty
      (2) Program task — develop by September, 1973, a systematic plan of processes and organizational structures

that will better enable administrators to implement programs based upon individualization of instruction
  (a) What—develop a systematic plan of processes and organizational structures
  (b) When—by September, 1973
(3) Communication check—all requirements met

4. For the school board to provide by October, 1973, a source of legal information for the staff of each school
Critique:
A. Basic Statement
  (1) Who—the school board
  (2) Program task—provide by October, 1973, a source of legal information for the staff of each school
    (a) What—provide a source of legal information
    (b) When—by October, 1973
  (3) Communication check—all requirements met

5. For the Director of Personnel to employ certified personnel in all phases of the school program by August, 1972
Critique:
A. Basic Statement
  (1) Who—the Director of Personnel
  (2) Program task—employ certified personnel in all phases of the school program by August, 1972
    (a) What—employ certified personnel
    (b) When—by August, 1972
  (3) Communication check—all requirements met

6. For the Instructional Division to identify by June, 1975, roles and responsibilities of all personnel in the educational program
Critique:
A. Basic Statement
  (1) Who—the Instructional Division
  (2) Program task—to identify by June, 1975, roles and responsibilities of all personnel in the educational program
    (a) What—identify roles and responsibilities of all personnel
    (b) When—by June, 1975
  (3) Communication check—all requirements met

7. For the Superintendent to develop prior to the next school year, district-wide administrative services which promote greater operational efficiency and financial economy
Critique:
A. Basic Statement
  (1) Who—the Superintendent

(2) Program task—develop prior to the next school year, district-wide administrative services which promote greater operational efficiency and financial economy
    (a) What—develop district-wide administrative services
    (b) When—prior to the next school year
(3) Communication check—all requirements met

8. For the Department of Education Administration to prepare and execute product demonstration agreements with local school systems prior to the 1973–74 school year
Critique:
A. Basic Statement
    (1) Who—the Department of Educational Administration
    (2) Program task—prepare and execute product demonstration agreements with local school systems prior to the 1973–74 school year
        (a) What—prepare and execute product demonstration agreements
        (b) When—prior to the 1973–74 school year
    (3) Communication check—all requirements met

9. For the Director of Transportation to increase within two years the efficiency of the school bus transportation system
Critique:
A. Basic Statement
    (1) Who—the Director of Transportation
    (2) Program task—to increase within two years the efficiency of the school bus transportation system
        (a) What—increase the efficiency of the school bus transportation system
        (b) When—within two years
    (3) Communication check—all requirements met

10. For the program director to see that all cooperative training students are placed in appropriate training agencies during the first month of each school year
Critique:
A. Basic Statement
    (1) Who—the program director
    (2) Program task—to see that all cooperative training students are placed in appropriate training agencies during the first month of each school year
        (a) What—place all cooperative training students in appropriate training agencies
        (b) When—during the first month of each school year
    (3) Communication check—all requirements met

Performance objectives are written to establish program accountability. The communication checks of non-learning oriented objectives establish (1) who is accountable, (2) what they are accountable for, and (3) the period of time they have to accomplish their responsibilities. Objectives are written for proposals, research, curriculum process, accountability purposes, and for many other reasons and may be broad or narrow and are used in so many contextual situations that the examples shown were purposely chosen to illustrate flexibility rather than expertise in use of the three communication checks of who, what, and when. Each goal should however, be examined to determine whether or not the checks are included.

Again the reader will wish to note that critiqueing is a mental exercise performed by the performance objective writer and not written except in training sessions. There is little mystery to writing non-learning oriented goal statements. Any reasonable statement of intent will suffice provided it communicates the proper message in reasonable fashion. The differences between characteristics of performance objective goals, both learning and non-learning oriented, are summarized graphically in Figure 16–1.

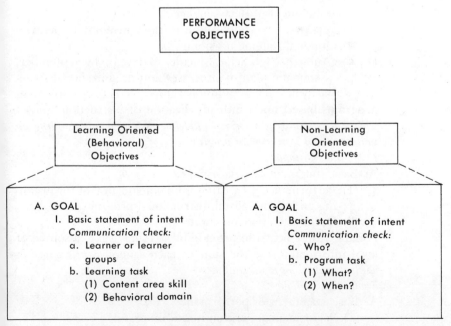

Figure 16–1 Performance objective goal components.

MINIMUM LEVEL NON-LEARNING ORIENTED OBJECTIVES

The non-learning oriented goal statements previously stated will serve as the basis for illustrating the development of non-learning oriented performance objectives. As was the case with behavioral objectives, minimum level objectives are formed simply by adding an evaluation performance statement to each goal:

1. For each teacher to provide all students with an opportunity to have counseling services during the school year *as evidenced by a written log which specifies the dates counseling services are provided.*
   Evaluation Critique:
   A. Basic statement of performance
      (1) Performance—a written log which specifies the dates counseling services are provided
      (2) Optional statement—none
2. For the Department of Educational Administration to develop and implement by September, 1972, a performance-based curriculum for the training of persons who intend to hold leadership positions in either public schools or higher education. *Success in achieving this goal will be determined by the publication of the new performance-based curriculum in the University Bulletin.*
   Evaluation Critique:
   A. Basic statement of performance
      (1) Performance—publication in the University Bulletin
      (2) Optional statement—none
3. For the Auburn High School faculty to develop by September, 1973, a systematic plan of processes and organizational structures that will enable administrators to better implement programs based upon individualization of instruction. *Success will be determined by a written guideline document for installing an individualized instructional program.*
   Evaluation Critique:
   A. Basic statement of performance
      (1) Performance—a written guideline document for installing an individualized instructional program
      (2) Optional statement—none
4. For the school board to provide by October, 1973, a source of legal information for the staff of each school *as determined by written notification to all staff members.*
   Evaluation Critique:
   A. Basic statement of performance
      (1) Performance—written notification
      (2) Optional statement—none

5. For the Director of Personnel to employ certified personnel in all phases of the school program byAugust 1972 *so that when given the established criteria for certification of each position and a list of all school personnel and the position they hold, the names will be visually compared with the proper certification requirements.*
   Evaluation Critique:
   A. Basic statement of performance
      (1) Performance — visual comparison
      (2) Optional statement — so that when given the established criteria for certification of each position and a list of all school personnel and the positions they hold

6. For the Instructional Division to identify by June, 1975, roles and responsibilities of all personnel in the educational program *as evidenced by written job descriptions being published for all personnel.*
   Evaluation Critique:
   A. Basic statement of performance
      (1) Performance — publication of written job descriptions
      (2) Optional statement — none

7. For the Superintendent to develop prior to the next school year, district-wide administrative services which promote greater operational efficiency and financial economy. *Success will be determined by subjective analysis of comparable data obtained both before and after the implementation of new administrative service improvement procedures.*
   Evaluation Critique:
   A. Basic statement of performance
      (1) Performance — subjective analysis of comparable data
      (2) Optional statement — none

8. For the Department of Educational Administration to prepare and execute product demonstration agreements with local school systems prior to the 1973–74 school year. *Proof this goal is attained will be determined by written, signed commitments by both the producer and demonstration school agency.*
   Evaluation Critique:
   A. Basic statement of performance
      (1) Performance — written signed commitments
      (2) Optional statement — none

9. For the Director of Transportation to increase within two years the efficiency of the school bus transportation system *so that when the bus drivers are given new bus transportation routes, including new stopping points, they will drive all scheduled daily routes in less time than they took previously.*

Evaluation Critique:
A. Basic statement of performance
   (1) Performance — drive all selected routes
   (2) Optional statement — so that when the bus drivers are given new bus transportation routes, including new stopping points

10. For the program director to see that all cooperative training students are placed in appropriate training agencies during the first month of each school year *so that when given a list of eligible students and the names of all qualified training agencies, students names can be matched with appropriate training agencies.*
Evaluation Critique:
A. Basic statement of performance
   (1) Performance — matching names with training agencies
   (2) Optional statement — so that when given a list of eligible students and the names of all qualified training agencies

It is obvious that some of the goals from which these minimum level objectives have been developed are still rather abstract or need further breakdown if their evaluation components are to be as specific as desirable. In the real world, however, state departments have often stated rather global or abstract goals and most project proposals state broad goals and objectives rather than the finer intents into which the goals are later developed. Thus, objectives must be stated at the level at which a goal statement has been developed. Broad goal statements require broader evaluation components than do more specific goal statements.

Figure 16–2 compares the characteristics of a non-learning oriented objective with those of a behavioral objective when both are stated at the minimum level.

DESIRED LEVEL NON-LEARNING ORIENTED OBJECTIVES

The desired level non-learning oriented objectives are extensions of the minimum level objectives. This extension, as was the case with behavioral objectives, is designed to add a success level criterion standard when appropriate. Sometimes this will require a rewording or rephrasing of the evaluation component. Generally speaking, objectives should not try to evaluate either more or less than the requirement of its goal. Thus, some of the example objectives should remain as minimum level objectives since success level criterions would not be particularly meaningful or appropriate based upon the goal statement requirements.

1. For each teacher to provide all students with an opportunity to have counseling services during the school year as evidenced by a written log which specifies the dates counseling services are provided.

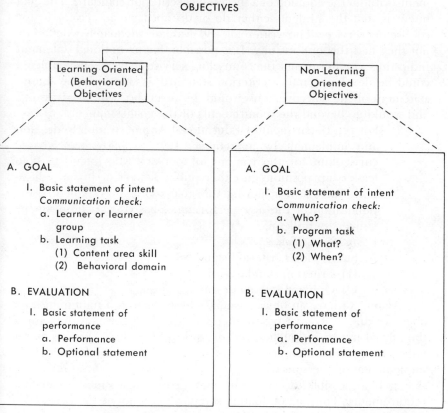

Figure 16-2 Characteristics of minimum level non-learner oriented objectives.

Evaluation Critique:
B. Success level criterion standard
    (1) Criterion standard — none
    (2) Optional statement — none

1a. For each teacher to provide all students with an opportunity to
have counseling services as evidenced by a written log which
specifies the day counseling services are provided and whether
or not they are completed.

Evaluation Critique:
B. Success level criterion standard
    (1) Criterion standard — none
    (2) Optional statement — and whether or not they are
       completed

This is the first example of an objective that meets its goal requirements without the addition of a success level criterion standard. The goal
intent is that the students either do or do not have an *opportunity* for
counseling services. The written log will evaluate adequately whether or
not they had this opportunity. It is possible that an optional statement
indicating whether or not the counseling services have been completed
could be developed into a criterion standard as shown in the second
statement of he objective. This would, however, be "window dressing"
and would go beyond the requirements of the goal statement.

2.   For the Department of Educational Administration to develop
     and implement by September, 1972, a performance-based
     curriculum for the training of persons who intend to hold
     leadership positions in either public schools or higher educa-
     tion. Success in achieving this goal will be determined by the
     publication of the new performance-based curriculum in the
     University Bulletin.
     Evaluation Critique:
     B. Success level criterion standard
         (1) Criterion standard—none
         (2) Optional statement—none

Again, we have an objective that may remain as a minimum level
objective due to its goal requirements. Since the University Bulletin is
the official university publication for approved courses, changes in the
bulletin can be considered as proof of both course development and
implementation. Persons writing performance objectives must recognize
that it is impossible to leave value judgments out of most evaluation
requirements. Thus, all evaluation standards will not be the same, even
for the same goal statements. Evaluation components should, however,
represent a meaningful interpretation of the true intent of each goal.
Since the goal of this objective was to implement as well as develop, a
criterion standard could be developed that would have required students to actually be attending performance-based courses. This however,
could, again, have been "window dressing" since the courses placed in
the bulletin will be the ones which are implemented.

3.   For the Auburn High School faculty to develop by September,
     1973, a systematic plan of processes and organizational struc-
     tures that will better enable administrators to implement pro-
     grams based upon individualization of instruction. Success will
     be determined by a written guideline document *that has been
     approved by the superintendent and school board, after first meeting
     all formative and summative evaluation requirements for installation
     of an individualized instructional program.*
     Evaluation Critique:
     B. Success level criterion standard
         (1) Criterion standard—approved by the superintendent

and school board and meeting all evaluation requirements

(2) Optional statement—none

4. For the school board to provide by October, 1973, a source of legal information for the staff of each school as determined by a written notification of all staff members *that includes the name, address, and phone number of a practicing lawyer who has been employed to provide free legal services.*
Evaluation Critique:
B. Success level criterion standard
(1) Criterion standard—that includes the name, address, and phone number of a practicing lawyer who has been employed to provide free legal services
(2) Optional statement—none

Again, we have a goal that might not require a success level criterion standard. Written notification of the source could be interpreted by some people as adequate evaluation. Whereas, other people might insist that the standard for the written notification must include information such as name, address and phone number. Again we have a situation in which some value judgments must be made.

5. For the Director of Personnel to employ certified personnel in all phases of the school program by August, 1972, so that when given the established criteria for certification of each position and a list of all school personnel, including the position they hold, *one hundred per cent of the employees will be found to meet at least minimum certification requirements* according to a visual comparison of the people and the criteria established for the position they hold.
Evaluation Critique:
B. Success level criterion standard
(1) Criterion standard—one hundred per cent will meet requirements
(2) Optional statement—none

The reader should note that the optional statement or statements attached to evaluation components may appear in either the performance statement or as part of the success level criterion standard statement or both. In the event there is only one optional statement in the evaluation component, and it has already been recognized in the minimum level objectives, such as in the objective just stated, it will not be again listed as part of the criterion standard.

6. For the Instructional Division to identify by June, 1975, roles and responsibilities of all personnel in the educational programs as evidenced by written job descriptions being published for all personnel.

Evaluation Critique:
B. Success level criterion standard
  (1) Criterion standard — none required
  (2) Optional statement — none
This objective points out the crucial role played by persons who perform goal setting functions. For example, a more specifically stated goal could have required additional information in the evaluation component such as the specifics that must be covered in the written job descriptions to be published. The goal did not, however, state this requirement, thus the evaluator decided it was unnecessary to state a criterion standard. Subjective judgment and approval by a higher authority is always implied as a criterion.

  7. For the Superintendent to develop, prior to the next school year, district-wide administrative services which promote greater operational efficiency and financial economy. Success will be determined *by each of three external auditors attesting to the improvement in efficiency and economy* after subjective analyses of comparable data obtained before and after the start of new administrative service improvement procedures.
  Evaluation Critique:
  B. Success level criterion standard
    (1) Criterion standard — each of three attesting (100 per cent)
    (2) Optional statement — none

  8. For the Department of Educational Administration to prepare and execute product demonstration agreements with local school systems prior to the 1973–74 school year. Proof this goal is attained will be determined by written signed commitments by both the producer and the demonstration school agency. *All signed commitments will specify in detail the responsibilities and roles to be assumed by both parties.*
  Evaluation Critique:
  B. Success level criterion standard
    (1) Criterion standard — all signed commitments will specify in detail the responsibilities and roles to be assumed by both parties
    (2) Optional statement — none
This objective points out two important considerations. First, criterion standards need not always refer to how well something or someone will perform, but may refer to something that is necessary or needs to be included or any other information that will place additional requirements upon the performance activity. In addition, the objective has been written in three sentences instead of being limited to just one or two as was the case with those objectives previously stated.

9. For the Director of Transportation to increase within two years the efficiency of the school bus transportation system so that when the bus drivers are given new bus transportation routes, including new stopping points, they will drive all scheduled daily routes in *twenty minutes* less time than previously and *will travel five miles shorter distance.*

Evaluation Critique:

B. Success level criterion standard

(1) Criterion standard — twenty minutes less time and five miles less distance

(2) Optional statement — none

10. For the program director to see that all cooperative training students are placed in appropriate training agencies during the first month of each school year so that when given a list of eligible students and the names of all qualified training agencies, *each student's name* can be matched with a training agency *which accepted his or her services.*

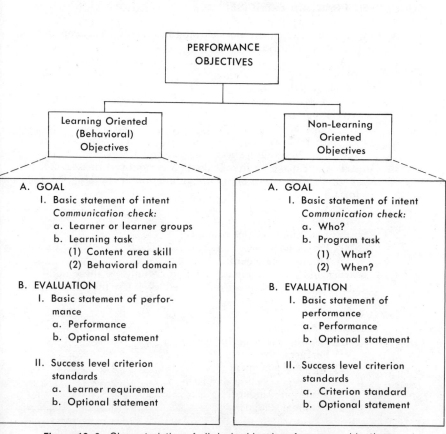

Figure 16–3 Characteristics of all desired level performance objectives.

Evaluation Critique:
B. Success level criterion standard
    (1) Criterion standard—each student's name matched with agency accepting his or her services
    (2) Optional statement—none

It should again be obvious at this point that the writing of performance objectives requires at least two ingredients: first, a knowledge of the writing technique; and, second, a certain amount of subject-matter expertise. This text and the examples utilized for illustration are primarily concerned with the presentation of technique and flexibility. Specialists in any program area should be able to write the best objectives for his own area once he has mastered the technique.

Figure 16–3 illustrates the characteristics of both learning oriented and non-learning oriented objectives stated at the criterion-referenced performance objective or desired level.

SUGGESTED PRACTICE EXERCISES

A. Develop and critique five non-learning oriented goal statements utilizing the following format:
    1. GOAL: _____
    Critique:
    a. Basic statement of intent
        (1) Who — _____
        (2) Program task
            (a) What — _____
            (b) When — _____
        (3) Communication check — _____

B. Construct and make written evaluation critiques of three non-learner oriented objectives written at the minimum level. Use the following format:
    1. Objective: _____
    Evaluation Critique:
    a. Basic statement of performance
        (1) Performance _____
        (2) Optional statement _____

C. Construct and make written evaluation critiques of three non-learner oriented objectives written at the desired level. Use the format outlined below.
    1. Objective: _____
    Evaluation Critique:
    a. Basic statement of performance
        (1) Performance _____
        (2) Optional statement _____
    b. Success level criterion standards
        (1) Criterion standard _____
        (2) Optional statement _____

Chapter 17

MANAGEMENT BY OBJECTIVES: ACCOUNTABILITY THROUGH NON-LEARNING ORIENTED GOAL SETTING

> No matter how lofty you are in your department, the responsibility for what your lowliest assistant is doing is yours.
>
> *Bessie R. Jones and Mary Waterstreet*

CHAPTER GOALS

For the reader to:

1. Develop skill in setting goals for general purposes of educational program accountability.

2. Acquire skill in goal setting for personnel accountability.

3. Acquire skill in setting goals and writing objectives for staff development.

4. Develop skill in using both learning and non-learning oriented goals for the individualization of instruction.

5. Be able to apply his comprehension of the use of performance objectives in the development of educational specifications.

Perhaps the best illustration of the necessity and advantages of goal setting in writing performance objectives lies in the concept "management by objectives" (MBO). It should already be clear to the performance objective writer that the heart of the performance objective development process is goal identification. This truth has been neglected by many contemporary performance objective authors who, in their haste to capitalize upon outcome performances, have failed to give full recognition to the importance of the goal in the educational process.

Some goals are easy to distinguish; other goals can be very obscure and may need to be determined by needs assessment. Traditional goals in grade reporting were clearly defined—sixty-five was a D, seventy-five a C, eighty-five a B, and ninety-five an A. Thus, a goal set to achieve a certain letter grade was easy to spell out and success in achieving the goal was easy to evaluate. This is not the case, however, with most educational endeavors.

A goal is the only reason for the existence of an objective; that is, an objective is formed specifically to identify and evaluate the achievement of a goal. This concept can be extended to include the entire educational enterprise—the reason for the existence of educational institutions is to attain the goals of society. A global goal of educational institutions in America could be that "educational institutions exist for the purpose of promoting the improved living of all of the people through the development of each individual according to his own capacity." The systems approach breaks this goal down into subsystems until the thousands of goals in an educational system are identified and each of these goals becomes a performance objective, establishing how each will be evaluated to determine success. This is what should be done and is what the use of performance objectives and systems is all about.

Looking at the educational enterprise, it is found that, in order to promote the growth of each individual, a school system must be composed of a diversified group of professional and non-professional people. The board must employ a superintendent or executive manager, the superintendent must hire his assistant superintendents and directors as part of his management team. Each school must have a principal or person in charge to provide leadership for system-wide and local programs and then there must be a strong core of professionally trained teachers. Support goals involving such areas as finance, transportation, building and maintenance, custodial, and clerical, must be added to the achievement goals established for each of these people.

Another important concept is that involved people are what make a system (education or any other) effective. Thus, people must work together in any comprehensive system in both goal setting and goal achievement. A system must be composed of compatible elements. There will, in a school system, be community goals, system-wide goals, local school goals, and individual goals for all employees. Thus, the goals established for employees must be compatible with (and within) the framework of the goals of the community, system-wide goals, school goals, and other individual achievement goals—and they must be evaluated if accountability is to be established.

People desire prestige, an adequate salary, job satisfaction and other personal growth variables which must be a point of concern in a total educational system. When all goals, personal and otherwise, have been identified and stated as performance objectives and when strategies for goal achievement and evaluation have been established, an educational system or institution can be said to have an *ideal program of educational accountability*. Therefore, when a total system of educational accountability is established, it will automatically account for both individualization of instruction, and general personnel evaluation.

GOAL SETTING

Goal setting for educational accountability under the MBO concept, should begin with top management and filter down. Thus, educational accountability should start at the top. Too frequently a school system or other educational institution attempts to begin accountability with teachers or the support staff.

Within the framework of the global goal of an educational system or institution major goals for which the top administrator has overall accountability are set. He then joins with his top assistant administrators to establish the nescessary goals for each division to achieve in order to accomplish the system's major goals. Each of the top assistant administrator's chief assistants will help select the goals for which he and his subordinates should become accountable. These chief assistants will be accountable to the top assistant administrators just as they are accountable to the superintendent. The chief assistants meet with their subordinates to set goals for the subordinates to achieve and for which the subordinates will be accountable to the chief assistant administrators.

This process is repeated from the office of the top administrator down through the offices of all levels of subordinate administrators until the process includes all administrators and support personnel. An important concept to remember in this process is that goals are established cooperatively, in so far as possible, by the person who will perform the function and the person to whom he is accountable. Each of the goals set must be evaluated in order to determine success in its achievement which means any goal which is important enough to identify should be stated as a performance objective.

Setting goals in this fashion is often called systems analysis. Systems analysis is performed by professional program planners or by the individual persons involved, as previously described. Systems analysis is simply a procedure for determining *what needs to be done* in order to achieve a desired mission or global goal. This process attempts to identify problems and determine every major function and task needed to solve each problem identified.

Each function and task identified is normally stated as a non-learning oriented goal. These goals are then coded to retain their identification within the system and converted to performance objectives by specifying how success in achieving each goal will be determined. Systems analysis, whether formal or informal, is designed to develop and make use of many non-learning oriented performance objectives.

MANAGEMENT BY OBJECTIVES: UNIVERSITY LEVEL

Every educational institution has a board of control, a chief executive officer with line authority, assistant administrators with both line authority and staff responsibilities, and many levels of administration, supervision, instructional, and other assignments. Goal setting will be important at each level of the total operation of any institution. Most goal setting will begin at the top level and filter down through cooperative administrator-subordinate interaction and planning. Goals at the top level of an organization or institution generally tend to be non-learning oriented; goals intended for students tend to be mostly learning oriented. Employees at each hierarchy level must develop their goals within the framework and under applicable constraints placed on them by the setting of goals at higher levels of authority.

A board may develop a policy that will require the chief executive officer or president of a university to implement, within three years, all of the institution's curricular offerings in the form of competency modules. This then becomes a target, intent, or goal of the president. It may be stated as follows:

> For the president to have developed, by (date), a comprehensive curriculum in which all course work is presented in the form of competency modules.

The president will then meet with his vice-president, deans, and other heads of divisions to determine how they can best implement the program by the required date. From this meeting, and subsequent ones, goals will be established for each of these staff members. One goal for the Vice-President or Dean of Instruction could be:

> For the Dean of Instruction to develop and implement a comprehensive in-service education program to train faculty members in the development of competency modules, with training to be completed by (date).

The Dean of Instruction, in meeting with his department heads, will help them determine goals pertinent to their positions and responsibilities, such as:

> For each Department Head to determine the specific in-service training needs of faculty members of his department by (date).

This procedure can then be repeated for faculty members and other employees who will have to share in the responsibility for developing and implementing the president's new program. Many employees will have several minor goals stemming from the president's goal. The president's goal is rather general, but goals tend to become more specific and less abstract as they proceed down the organizational hierarchy. The final set of goals to be established (those that will represent the content of the competency modules) will be very specific.

As soon as all goals have been specifically identified and stated, the people who will be accountable for achieving these desired intents will need to decide what type of evaluation will be required in order to determine whether or not they are successful in achieving their assigned goals. This evaluation information will then be added to the goal statement to represent the specific performance objectives of the project, program, or person.

Examination of the goals stated for the president, dean of instruction, and the department reveals one very specific point: each of the goals developed to implement this project would be non-learning oriented. However, the goals to be developed later, to implement the in-service training program, will be learning oriented since they are designed for teacher learning tasks. In addition, the goals later used in the development of the competency modules will be learning oriented (behavioral) since they represent learning tasks for students.

MANAGEMENT BY OBJECTIVES: PUBLIC SCHOOL

Another way to see how non-learning oriented goals and objectives can be used would be to take a hypothetical problem involving personnel accountability and individualization of instruction and trace it through several developmental steps of program generation. This will make obvious the procedure by which goals are converted to objectives, and also will illustrate the use of both learning oriented and non-learning oriented goals.

Assume that a board of public instruction has charged the school system superintendent with the responsibility of developing a general program of accountability for the entire system. By using a few simple illustrations of program development it will be possible to show how components of an accountability system can be developed as a model of how an entire accountability system might be formulated, thus the use of goals and objectives for both learning and non-learning oriented activities may be seen.

The superintendent, having overall responsibility for the system, would need first to identify, along with the board, his own goal. This could be the following:

> To develop and implement by a specified date a system-wide program that provides for individualization of instruction and personnel accountability.

As soon as this goal has been officially adopted as a system-wide program focus, the superintendent can call in all of his principal staff assistants which, in this instance, will consist of assistant superintendents for instruction, administration and finance, staff development, and personnel. At this meeting he may pose two major questions or points of discussion.

First, he will identify the goal for which he has become accountable. Second, he will ask, "What do we need to do in order to fully achieve this goal and implement the program two years from now?" Finally, he may pose the question, "How can I evaluate our progress so that the board will know whether or not we have been successful?"

Immediately the superintendent's staff will begin to react by asking questions and making statements concerning how their particular divisions and subordinates may be affected by and fit into the new program. The Assistant Superintendent for Instruction will begin to explore the alternatives which will influence curriculum development. The Assistant Superintendent for Administration and Finance will become concerned with costs and other implications for his division. The Assistant Superintendent for Staff Development might concentrate upon the in-service training responsibilities of such a program. The Assistant Superintendent for Personnel will begin to explore the implications for staffing.

The round table discussion that takes place at this meeting will probably reveal that each division of the school system will be affected by the superintendent's goal. During the course of this meeting and later ones, it will become apparent that each division will begin to identify needs and problem areas which must be resolved if the superintendent's goal is to be achieved.

Thus, from these problems that are identified, each division will create its own specific goals and these goals will become the basis for strategies which are later developed to achieve them. As these goals develop, the superintendent obtains an answer to his first question as to what needs to be done. Eventually the planning proceeds to the point that it becomes quite simple to answer the superintendent's second question on how to evaluate success in achieving his goal. As soon as this becomes known, the superintendent's goal is then converted into a performance objective by adding to it an evaluation component. This performance objective could be:

> To develop and implement by a specified date a system-wide program that provides for individualization of instruction and personnel accountability. Success will be determined by both the implementation of the program and written guideline documents, acceptable to the Board, that fully specify how personnel accountability and individualization are being achieved.

In this instance the superintendent's goal and performance objective were relatively easy to specify. His goal was rather specifically prescribed to him by the Board and success can easily be determined by whether or not the program was developed and implemented.

The next step is to identify each division's goals and convert them into performance objectives through meetings between the division heads and their subordinates. This is accomplished through meetings similar to the ones held by the superintendent and his staff. This process then continues through all levels and classifications of employees until the total program is developed. An important principle to remember as this hypothetical program develops is that the superintendent did not dictate or impose the goals, objectives, and various responsibilities upon his staff. Each staff member had an opportunity to help determine his own goals and how they would later be evaluated.

The same process should be carried out in all goals and objectives developed at all levels and for all classifications of employees. In each instance the person in charge should identify at least mentally, what many of the goals, objectives, and strategies might be for his subordinates. However, they should be changed and/or formally arrived at only after interaction with and questioning of the subordinates in such a manner that most of the goals and objectives are arrived at and chosen by the subordinates as though each goal were fully his original idea. Some of the goals will be the subordinates' original ideas.

Eventually all of the goals will be identified and objectives specified for each component part of the new system-wide program for individualization of instruction and personnel accountability. Someone, either a professional or support employee, will be assigned the responsibility of successfully implementing the strategies designed to achieve each of the goals. Each person will be held accountable for the results obtained by an evaluation performance that is specified in each specific performance objective. This is known as *management by objectives* or *program and personnel management by objectives.*

Neither time, space, nor the purpose of this chapter, would be best served by any attempt to develop the full system-wide program called for in the superintendent's performance objective. The author is primarily concerned with technique and does not presume to be knowledgeable enough in all of the different areas involved to develop goals and objectives for all of the divisions. Two examples will be chosen, however, to illustrate the selection and use of both learner oriented and non-learner oriented objectives that could develop from the superintendent's mission. These examples are as follows:

EXAMPLE I—STAFF DEVELOPMENT: GOAL AND OBJECTIVES

The Assistant Superintendent for Staff Development would be charged with the responsibility for developing an in-service education program which will give all persons to be involved in the new individualized instructional program the required knowledge and skills to function effectively. Thus, he might first develop, along with his staff, a mission goal for the in-service education systems that will be used. The mission goal is:

> To develop within sixty days a system of in-service education for the training of professional employees to write and use performance objectives. The major subsystems must be stated as performance objectives and their subsystem components stated as goals.

This mission goal of the Staff Development Division can become a mission performance objective by simply adding an evaluation component as follows:

> To develop within sixty days a system of in-service education for the training of professional employees to write and use performance objectives. Success in achieving this goal will be determined by a written report that includes an outline of the in-service education system, a list of all subsystem objectives, and a list of all goals established for the subsystem components.

We have now stated a non-learning oriented performance objective. The program task is "to develop a system of in-service education for the training of professional employees to write and use performance objectives." We can now begin to illustrate graphically our system:

Subsystems

In-Service
System

Writing
and using
performance
objectives

1. Conceptualization

2. Goal components

3. Evaluation components

4. Objectives

5. Cognitive taxonomy

6. Selection and use

The subsystems, as seen by the Assistant Superintendent for Staff Development, would involve training the professional staff in six sequential steps in order to achieve the mission objective of the in-service system. The subsystem objectives could be as follows:

For all professional employees to:

1. Be able to conceptualize the task of writing performance objectives as determined by a written examination upon which each employee scores at least eighty percent correct answers.
2. Be able to develop skill in writing performance objective goals as evidenced by their correctly writing one original learning oriented and one non-learning oriented goal without error in communication of the basic statement of intent.
3. Be able to critique evaluation components designed to determine success in the achievement of specific goal statements so that when given ten evaluation components, each employee will correctly critique at least nine.
4. Be able to write and critique performance objectives as determined by their correctly writing and critiqueing without error two unique performance objectives.
5. Be able to write behavioral objectives based upon complex behaviors and skills so that when given a written examination which includes the writing of objectives at skill levels, seventy-five percent of the employees will score seventy-five percent or better correct answers.
6. Develop an understanding of how objectives are selected and used as determined by an oral examination upon which they correctly respond to each of five questions they are asked.

We have now accomplished two things. We have used a non-learning oriented objective as the mission objective and have developed six behavioral objectives for the subsystems. Each type of objective, learning or non-learning oriented, is determined by its goal statement of intent. The next concern is to break the subsystems down into their components.

In-Service System: Writing and Using Performance Objectives

Subsystem	Subsystem Components
1. Conceptualization	1. Definitions
	2. Selective information
	3. Writing approaches
	4. Theory
	5. Problems
	6. Comprehension
2. Goal Components	1. Learner-oriented goals
	2. Non-learner oriented goals
3. Evaluation Components	1. Minimum level B.O. components
	2. Desired level B.O. components
	3. Minimum level non-learner components
	4. Desired level non-learner components
4. Objectives	1. Learner-oriented objectives
	2. Non-learner oriented objectives
5. Cognitive Taxonomy	1. Knowledge level
	2. Skills and ability levels
6. Selection and Use	1. Selection process
	2. Use of systems approach
	3. Individualization
	4. Accountability
	5. Competence based modules

This illustration divides the subsystems into subsystem components as they might be envisioned by the Assistant Superintendent for Staff Development. The goals for these components can be stated as follows:

For all professional employees to:

1. Memorize the definitions for performance objectives written by both the goals and outcomes approach techniques.
2. Be able to recall selective information concerning the two major classifications of performance objectives.
3. Acquire the knowledge of the major difference between objectives written by the goals and outcomes approaches to writing performance objectives.
4. Be able to recall theoretical information which establishes the value of goals as ends and evaluation as means.
5. Know at least six problems which can be affected by the selection of the technique for writing behavior objectives.
6. Be able to comprehend and interpret the differences between learner oriented and non-learner oriented goals.
7. Develop skill in writing behavioral goals.
8. Develop skill in writing non-learner oriented goals.
9. Be able to write and critique unique minimum level behavioral objectives.
10. Develop competency in writing and critiqueing unique desired level behavioral objectives.
11. Be able to write and critique evaluation components of unique non-learner oriented objectives written at the minimum level.
12. Be able to write and critique evaluation components of unique desired level non-learner oriented objectives.
13. Understand the techniques for writing and critiqueing behavioral objectives.
14. Understand the techniques for writing and critiqueing non-learner oriented performance objectives.
15. Develop skill in writing behavioral objectives at the knowledge level.
16. Develop a knowledge of how to write objectives based upon complex behaviors and skills including the definitions of cognitive behavior classifications, the behaviors required in each classification category, and how to critique skill level behavioral objectives.
17. Be able to select specific goals for conversion into performance objectives from various types of input information.
18. Be able to develop specific goals from a broad general global type of goal statement by use of the systems process.
19. Be knowledgeable concerning the use of behavioral obtives for the individualization of instruction.
20. Be able to understand the systems approach to establishing programs of educational accountability.
21. Be able to develop a module for use in a competency based instructional program.

Completion of the subsystem component goal statements provides the evaluation needed to determine the success of the mission objective. A written outline has been developed specifying all subsystem objectives and the subsystem component goals. It must be kept in mind that most systems are open and can be developed into any subsystem and subsystem components which appear to solve the problem at hand and that have all of the characteristics attributable to the system.

The subsystem and subsystem components which have been used to illustrate this in-service education system were partially chosen to reveal two levels of abstraction into which behavioral objectives could be broken down. The subsystem objectives could have been used to train and evaluate the professional employees, but this evaluation would have been broad and general without many of the desired specifics.

The goal statements representing the subsystem components are much more refined and specific than are the goals in the subsystem objectives. The next step in this in-service program would be to add evaluation components to each goal and to use the resulting subsystem component objectives for the development of strategies and evaluation of employee success.

EXAMPLE II—INDIVIDUALIZATION OF INSTRUCTION

Individualized instruction means that each teacher must provide each student with learning experiences suited to his unique characteristics as a learner. To do this the teacher must provide flexibility by continually diagnosing both the strengths and weaknesses of the learner and prescribing flexible learning tasks accordingly. This is accomplished through diagnostic testing and teacher-pupil interaction in face-to-face contact.

Student assessment activities reveal a student's status with respect to learning skills and his ability to use organized knowledge such as library materials and reference books. With this information, a teacher can plan individualized goals and evaluation strategies. These objectives will then determine the learning experiences to be included and arranged in the curriculum. Teaching strategies for individualization will include the use of a wide variety of equipment and materials, individual pupil-teacher interaction, and much self-selection of materials and self-pacing in the use of the materials by each student.

All of the activities and learning experiences which must be provided by the teacher in individualizing instruction become goals or program tasks of the teacher and should be stated as non-learning oriented objectives for which she can be held accountable. For example, the development of a reading curriculum may be used to illustrate this point. In this instance objectives will be stated to illustrate concerns and examples given when necessary.[1]

SAMPLE OBJECTIVES

For all reading teachers to:

1. Secure background information on the methods and theories for teaching reading as evidenced by a written document of at least fifty pages which includes contemporary research on the basal reader, language experience, phonic, linguistic, programmed, I.T.A., and the individualized approaches to teaching reading.
2. Assess each student's reading achievement skills and ability to organize knowledge and use library materials as determined by recorded diagnostic reading achievement scores for each student and a log of the date and outcome of each pupil-teacher interview session.
3. Identify an individualized focus for each student's reading development as determined by a written list of the specific reading goals for each student.
4. Prepare learning activities and teaching strategies for each student as evidenced by a written list of teaching units and/or learning experiences each child will pursue.
5. Develop each teaching unit in complete detail as determined by a written document that includes all essential information needed to complete the following outline:
   a. The *name* or *title* of the unit or learning experience.
   b. *Problems* as *topics* of a specific nature which may be studied by pupils or the unit or learning experience that is being carried on in the classroom.
   c. *Behavioral objectives* which may be acquired by pupils if they solve the problems or study the topics.
   d. *Activities* which may be used by pupils to solve the problems or to study the topics. (For example: specific readings, field trips, interviews with laymen in the community, etc.)
   e. *Materials* and *resources* which are needed to carry on the activities so that problems may be solved and topics may be studied. (Books, pamphlets, films, speakers, etc.)
   f. Specific methods and techniques of *evaluation* which will help the teacher and pupils to ascertain the degree to which pupils have achieved the *behavioral objectives*. (For example: tests, self-evaluation, etc.)

Note that each of these objectives is stated as a non-learning oriented objective since each goal statement requires teachers to perform some program task rather than a learning task. Thus, the performances required in the evaluation components were based upon activities other than tests to determine whether or not teachers have accomplished cognitive, affective, or psychomotor changes in behavior. Under objective five, part c, however, the teachers will be required to develop behavioral objectives for students which will have evaluation components to determine whether or not students receive behavioral changes.

MANAGEMENT BY OBJECTIVES: WRITING EDUCATIONAL PROGRAM SPECIFICATIONS FOR PLANNING. PROGRAMMING, AND BUDGETING EVALUATION SYSTEMS

Educational specifications are helpful in assisting a school system's professional personnel in consolidating and clarifying their: (1) basic philosophy of education; (2) program goals, objectives, strategies, and evaluation techniques; (3) needs for physical facilities designed to adequately house present and future educational programs; and (4) program commitments for data to implement PPBES or cost analysis management information systems. Philosophies may be determined by profession inventories. Program objectives and related components are determined by a needs assessment. Facility specifications are determined by program objectives, instructional strategies and physical activities.

Planning, Programming, Budgeting, Education Systems (PPBES) is a concept designed to help determine the allocation of financial resources to a specific program. PPBES is established by the requirements of a specific program, as outlined in its specific program specifications, to meet its objectives which have been translated into cost or budget expenditures.

Educational specifications are usually written separately from budgeting. There are several components that should be considered in the development of educational specifications. Among these components are the following:

1. An *introduction* to the program for which educational specifications are being written.
2. Development of a *mission statement, goals, and specific performance objectives* that will define the purpose and evaluation requirements of the program.
3. Identification of the *methods or strategies, movement activities and organizational structure* of the program.
4. Determination of *physical facilities, equipment, and furniture requirements.*

PROGRAM INTRODUCTION

Introducing a program involves making a statement, usually one page or less, that identifies a school, department or division according to the specific program about which it is concerned, i.e., The Language Arts Department includes: English, listening, oral language, reading, handwriting, spelling, nonverbal communication, composition, speech and drama, and student publications. Extracurricular or related activities should be included if applicable under the program. Personnel, benefits, purchased services, materials and supplies, and other information that can affect program, facilities or budget may be included.

MISSION STATEMENT, GOALS AND OBJECTIVES

Describe the overall mission or goal of your school, department, program, etc., by a global mission statement. Identify the specific goals or intents of the program. Specify each goal as a separate and specific performance objective.

Example:

A. Mission Statement: The mission of the Language Arts Department will be to provide a model continuous progress Language Arts program designed to improve the academic, social, and economic welfare of disadvantaged children, ages four to twelve.

B. Goals
1. To improve the oral reading skills of all elementary children.
2. To improve the sight reading vocabularies of all elementary children.

C. Objectives
1. To improve the oral reading skills of all elementary children as measured by:
   a. Informal Reading Inventory oral reading paragraphs on which ten per cent more children are reading at grade level when compared to pre-test scores.
   b. Eighty per cent of the children successfully completing eighty-five per cent or more of the items related to oral reading on the county adopted behavioral skill list.
2. To improve the sight reading vocabularies of all elementary children as evidenced by:
   a. The word knowledge subtest battery of the Metropolitan Achievement Test so that fifty per cent of the children within each grade will make a fifteen per cent gain in new score over the preceding year.
   b. Ninety per cent of the children successfully completing eighty per cent or more on items related to vocabulary development on the county adopted behavioral skill list.

METHODS (STRATEGIES), MOVEMENT ACTIVITIES, ORGANIZATIONAL STRUCTURE

A. Methods
Identify and describe the methods that will be used in the program's instructional strategies. Indicate whether or not this is a change from previous methods used for instruction involving the same objectives. Example: A combination of different approaches will be used as the method or approach

to teaching reading. The approaches will be individualized to meet the needs of different students. The methods used will include: (1) the individualized approach; (2) Initial Teaching Alphabet; (3) Programmed reading; (4) the linguistic approach; and (5) phonic methods.

B. Movement Activities

Describe the types of movement activity that will occur within the instructional space occupied by the teacher and students. This may (1) include large and small group activities, (2) individual activities, use of audio-visual materials, calisthenics, simulation games and activities and other performances.

C. Organizational Structure

This can include how students are organized for instruction such as large and small groups, class size, flexible scheduling, individualized instruction, independent study. In addition, organizational structure may refer to administrative organization such as different types of administrative organization, school system organization, organization of schools by grades or any other organization concern that may be pertinent to the educational specifications being developed.

PHYSICAL FACILITIES

A. Equipment and Furniture

Specify all the types of equipment and furniture necessary for carrying out the instruction or program that has been planned. Identify number, size, design of all furniture. Laboratory equipment, racks, bookcases, and all other equipment and furniture should be identified.

B. Space requirements

List all types of spaces that will be needed by the teachers and pupils. Examples are: (1) activity space, storage, teaching space, office space. Identify other departments or instructional areas which may be integrated with your program in such a manner that you may share their space.

An example of the development of written specifications is provided by the following example.[3]

I. The Program

A. Introduction

The guidance department aids in the identification of student abilities, aptitudes, interests, and attitudes. It also assists teachers and students to understand, accept, and utilize these traits. In connection with this purpose the department provides opportunities for learning about areas of occupational and educational endeavors and helps the individual in obtaining experiences which will assist him in the making of free and wise choices. The department is interested in the development of value systems, in helping the individual in developing his optimum potential, and in aiding the individual in becoming more and more self directed.

In this junior high school of 1500 students there are three certificated personnel and one secretary who come under county benefits. There is a guidance suite accessible to students with the following facilities: office space for each counselor; a waiting room. Necessary forms for records and secretarial supplies are available. Educational and occupational information is displayed in order to be used conveniently by students. There is also a small sign-in station which is manned by student aides. Testing materials are received from and returned to the county testing coordinator, so are only in this office on an interim basis.

B. Mission Statement

The mission of the guidance department is shared by all persons who seek to help children. Thus, we are classified as instructional support services. The guidance services seek to add new dimensions through systematic planning, providing additional knowledge and professional skills to strengthen existing programs and offering new services where there is a need. A guidance program's purpose is to make it possible for the teacher to perform more effectively by helping students with their needs and to help teachers with their understanding of student needs. Emphasis is placed upon developmental and preventive aspects rather than upon remedial help.

C. Goals

1. To maintain cumulative records for each student.
2. To assist the pupil in analyzing his interests, capabilities, and aptitudes, and relate these to all his alternatives, aspirations and goals.
3. To aid the teacher in identification of and provision for the individual pupil's intellectual, emotional, social and physical characteristics.
4. To assist parents and faculty with their understanding of the individual pupil's growth and development as it relates to school, career choice and society.
5. To effect a smooth transition from one educational level to another for all pupils.
6. To coordinate the efforts of the school, special services, and community resources in providing for the needs of the pupil.
7. To coordinate the testing program for achievement and aptitude tests.

8. To disseminate academic, vocational, and social-personal information to pupils, parents, and teachers through a planned program.

9. To provide a means for gathering developmental information about students, which will be utilized in the processing of the other goals.

D. Performance Objectives

1. To maintain cumulative records for each student. Success will be determined by an established file which contains for each pupil a cumulative record which is developmental and contains up-to-date personal data, record of academic work, attendance and health records, and standardized test results.

2. To assist the pupil in analyzing his interests, capabilities, and aptitudes, and relate these to all his alternatives, aspirations and goals. Evidence will be a counselor's log which indicates the appointment date, student's name, nature of the session, and a checklist determining if material in the cumulative file is discussed. 90 per cent of initial conferences should utilize the record in relating goals and alternatives to personal assets.

3. To aid the teacher in identification of and provision for the individual pupil's intellectual, emotional, social and physical characteristics. Evidence that this goal is met will be (1) counselor's log which shows teacher conferences, (2) a file of bulletins given teachers for the purpose of helping in identification of and provision for pupil needs and (3) checklist in the records room indicating the usage of the cumulative records.

4. To assist parents and faculty with their understanding of the individual pupil's growth and development as it relates to school, career choice and society. Success will be determined by the counselor's log which indicates, (1) parent conferences, (2) bulletins which indicate information of a developmental nature which have been distributed to faculty and parents, (3) records of oral presentations to faculty and/or parents (example, PTA).

5. To effect a smooth transition from one educational level to another for all pupils. Evidence of completion shall be a written report given to the principal upon completion of orientation session. Included will be copies of handouts given in connection with the sessions.

6. To coordinate the efforts of the school, special services, and community resources in providing for the needs of

the pupil. Evidence that this objective is met will be a follow-up record of the action taken by the school's guidance committee and a record and follow-up of referrals to other agencies in the school system or in the community.

7. To coordinate the testing program for achievement and aptitude tests. Success will be determined by (1) records of testing arrangements, (2) lists of scores for students in the guidance office after completion of the testing and scoring period of time.

8. To disseminate academic, vocational, and social-personal information to pupils, parents, and teachers through a planned program. Evidence shall be records of planned programs including the number of students, parents, and teachers involved. Ninety per cent of the students, 100 per cent of the teachers, and 75 per cent of the parents shall be reached.

9. To provide a means for gathering developmental information about students which will be utilized in the processing of the other goals. Success will be determined by (1) at least three reports and discussions in staff meeting of current happenings in the professional field, (2) attendance of all counselors at professional in-service meetings, and (3) attendance of at least one counselor at state and national meetings.

E. Methods and Organizational Structure

The specific objectives listed in the previous section will be met with these strategies. The numbers of the performance objectives and the listed numbers below correspond.

1. The secretary will process all entries and withdrawals for record purposes. This will include the establishment of new files and the sending from school to school for transferred records. The home room teacher will up-date the records. The counselor will assist the teacher in understanding procedures and will check records to be sure that information is current.

2. Individual and group conferences, by appointment, will be the prime means of attaining performance objective No. 2. The counselor will consult with the records for this purpose.

3. There shall be conferences with teachers, written bulletins containing behavioral characteristics of children needing

help, information on referral procedures given either at faculty meetings or in written form.

4. There will be individual conferences, phone calls, and bulletins in addition to presentations to groups of teachers and parents.

5. Two orientation sessions will be given incoming students. The first orientation will be an introductory assembly at the feeder school followed by explanation in small groups of course offerings and procedures for selection of courses. The second orientation will be on campus. After this orientation student leaders of the incoming school will conduct a tour of the campus. After the school year has begun, new transfer students will be given an individual orientation by the counselor and assistance in finding classes by the student aide.

6. A school guidance committee will be established. This committee will include the dean of boys and dean of girls, the curriculum coordinator, three heads of departments, and five students. This committee will meet at least five times during the school year. Counselors will keep in communication via phone with referral agencies in the community, and will work in connection with them and with other pupil personnel service workers (social workers, work-study programs, etc.) in conferences and in seeking assistance. Services will be coordinated through the school guidance committee.

7. Plan testing calendar in advance with principal and heads of departments. Prepare and distribute to students, teachers and parents a notice giving the purpose of the test, time and place in advance of each test. Orient teachers in test administration. Oversee test administration and see that test results are properly recorded by classroom teachers.

8. Group and individual guidance and counseling groups shall be prime methods of dissemination of this information. Presentations to homeroom classes will give some of this information and will invite students to come to the guidance office for additional information.

9. Counselors will share responsibility for staff professional development by participation in professional activities and sharing new knowledge and insights with other staff members.

F. Movement Activities

The waiting room is equipped with seating for eight. It also contains the secretary's station and a sign-in area maintained by student aides. The conference room will provide for groups up to 25 and usage of audio-visual equipment (on loan from the library). Three counselors' offices provide for small groups (maximum from 5 to 10 according to the office) and individual conferences.

II. Physical Facilities
  A. Equipment and Furniture

1. Counselors' Offices		Total Price
4 Steel Casement Double Pedestal Desks	@ $106.91	$427.64
4 Swivel Arm Chairs	@ 37.95	151.80
8 Upholstered Arm Chairs	@ 26.64	213.12
4 Steel Bookcase Sections	@ 25.90	103.60
4 Combination File & Storage Cabinets	@ 57.25	229.00
2. Waiting Room		
1 Double Pedestal Steel Case Desk	@ 121.91	121.91
1 Posture Chair	@ 27.71	27.71
1 Electric Typewriter- Elite Type	@ 258.50	258.50
1 Two Drawer Letter Size Filing Cabinet with 2 Drawers for 3 × 5 Cards at Top	@ 53.88	53.88
1 Round Table 48″ × 29″ Laminated Plastic Top	@ 56.70	56.70
6 Straight Chairs	@ 4.79	28.74
1 Portable Six Shelf Vocational File	@ 98.50	98.50
2 Settees	@ 66.48	132.96
3. Conference Room		
2 Tables, Laminated Top Natural Oak 30″ × 72″ × 29″	@ 40.48	80.96
10 Straight Chairs	@ 4.79	47.90
4. Records Room		
2 Four Drawer Steel Filing Cabinets, Letter Size	@ 43.50	87.00

1 Library Table 72″ × 30″
× 29″ Laminated
Plastic Top   @   40.80   40.80
1 Portable Two Drawer
Steel Desk File With
Sliding Top, Letter Size @   72.85   72.85
   5. Vocational Kits to be used where needed
     1 Chronical File of
      Occupational Information $ 375.00
     2 Work Occupational Kits @   120.00   240.00
   6. Portable Copy Machine — used where needed
     1 Thermal Processor Copy Machine   249.50
                 Grand Total $3,098.07

  G. Space Requirements

Waiting Room (with space for shelves and occupational information files) 25′ by 22′

2 Counselors' Offices 9′ by 10′

1 Counselor's Office 8′ by 9′

1 Office for social worker 8′ by 7′

Records room 10′ by 7′ with shelving

Conference room 11′ by 20′

A P.P.B.E. system, as the name implies, involves the following five major functions.

1. *Planning* involves the steps listed as one and two in the writing of educational specifications.

2. *Programming* consists of the analysis of strategies that can be utilized to achieve objectives. This is in line with the selection of methods and means presented as steps three and four in writing educational specifications.

3. *Budgeting* is the relating of the expenditure of funds to the strategy and means alternatives which may be selected in programming activities.

4. *Evaluation* refers to the level of success in achieving objectives after a program has been implemented.

5. *System* refers to the master strategy that organizes all of the program elements into one whole plan of operation.

Educational specifications can be converted to a PPBE system by adding costs to the specifications and placing them in an accounting structure to produce cost data for management decision making. This can be accomplished by the adoption of financial code numbers which are used to relate specification to program costs. Coding consists of assigning numbers to identify variables such as schools, departments, grade levels or other functional divisions of a school system that the program may apply to. Additional variables that may involve coding are the fiscal year, facility, instructional or non-instructional organization, fund or account group, function, object, program, special cost center (project) and other information that may need identification in the program being developed.

Budgets represent financial forecasts of expenditures. They include information such as: (1) salaries, (2) benefits, (3) purchased services, (4) materials and supplies, (5) capital outlay and (6) other. The example previously stated to illustrate the writing of educational specifications can be converted into a PPBE system budget as follows:[3]

Coding:

Fiscal Year 1972–73 (FY 1972–73)	*3*
Facility Jefferson Davis Jr. Hi.	*0216*
Instructional Organization—Secondary	*30*
Fund and Account Group—General Operating Fund	*100*

Function
    6000 Instructional Support Services
          6200 Guidance Services
Program
    1000 Regular Education
Object
    100 Salaries
        128 Counselor
        161 Secretary
    200 Employee Benefits
        210 Retirement
        220 Social Security
        230 Group Insurance
    500 Materials and Supplies
        510 Supplies
        590 Other materials and supplies
    600 Capital Outlay
        640 Furniture, fixtures and equipment
    300 Purchased Services
        310 Professional and technical services
        410 Telephone and telegraph
        420 Public Utility Service

Budget

Fiscal Year   Facility

	School	School or Administrative Center	District
3	0216	Jefferson Davis Junior High	Duval

Instructional Organization	Fund or Account Group	Function	Program
30	100	6200	1000

Object	Activity Assignment	Employee No.	Sub Object	Amount
128	School Counselor	267–34–2382	Reg & Supp	$ 12,952.00
128	School Counselor	345–67–2918	Reg & Supp	10,220.00
128	School Counselor	356–87–8765	Reg & Supp	9,675.00
161	Counseling Office	321–74–9845	Reg	5,000.00
			Sub Total	$ 37,847.00
210				$ 1,775.80
220				1,261.64
230				549.84
			Sub Total	$ 3,587.28
310	Scoring Services for NCS Answer Sheets			750.00
410				240.00
420				350.00
			Sub Total	$ 1,340.00
510	Office Supplies			215.00
590	Record Cards, Cumulative Folders, Test, Career Pamphlets			470.00
			Sub Total	$ 685.00
640	See above listing (Section 2A)			3,098.07
			Grand Total	$ 46,557.35

Evaluation of PPBE systems can be related to cost benefits (program achievement relating to its needs, goals and objectives), cost efficiency, or other cost effectiveness factors. Again we find that goal setting and objective specification are the key factors in determining program management and accountability.

The objectives used in PPBE systems can be either learning or non-learning oriented. In this guidance program illustration each of the nine goals and performance objectives were non-learning oriented. Again, it is important to note that this PPBE system was developed by a guidance counselor in a real situation which again attests to the value and usefulness of non-learning oriented performance objectives.

Contemporary writers have placed so much emphasis upon goal setting and behavioral objective writing in teaching-learning situations that the processes, methods, environmental context and other variables necessary to implement a total program have been neglected. It is more desirable that educators be trained for tomorrow's programs rather than limit their training to ones which are currently popular but dated by yesterday's experiences. The programs of the future will undoubtedly require more *accountability* through improved *management by objectives* and increased utilization of *systems analysis in program planning and development*. You, the user of this text, should be well prepared to stand up and be counted when special skills requiring the use of non-learning oriented performance objectives are called for in your school program.

GLOSSARY OF TERMS

Educational Specifications: a detailed presentation of an educationally related plan or proposal, frequently including statements of philosophy, goal and/or objectives, strategies, evaluation technique and facility requirements.

MBO: management by objectives. Normally consists of a goal setting process and an evaluation procedure to determine personnel accountability for achieving the goals for which they are responsible.

PPBES: Planning, Programming, Budgeting, Evaluation System. This involves: (1) statement of objectives, (2) analyses of alternatives that can be used to achieve objectives, (3) relating fund expenditures to the strategy and means alternatives chosen to implement plan to achieve objective, (4) determining the level of success in achieving objectives and (5) relating the entire process together into one master plan of operation.

REFERENCES

1. Adapted from material provided by Dr. Maurice R. Ahrens and Dr. Ruthellen Crews, Professors of Education, University of Florida.
2. This example was contributed by Dr. Mildred N. Koger, Guidance Counselor, Duval County Board of Public Instruction, Jacksonville, Florida, December, 1972.
3. Dr. Mildred N. Koger, previously cited as the contributor of the educational specification, also performed this cost information analysis.

INDEX

Learning task, 58
  behavioral domain of, 58
  content area (skill) of, 58

Mager, R. F., 54
Management by objectives, 16, 277, 284
  at the public school level, 281
  at the university level, 280
  goal setting and educational account-
    ability under, 279
MBO. See *Management by objectives.*
Measurement, criterion-referenced, 11–
  13, 18, 66
Measurement, norm-referenced, 11–12,
  19, 66
Mission goals, establishment of, 80–81
Modelism, 249, 259

No-negative-response model, 196, 200,
  226–229
Non-learning oriented goals, 18, 81, 260,
  262–267, 275
Non-learning oriented objectives, 18,
  25–26, 53, 260, 267
  desired level, 270–275
  minimum level, 268–270, 275
Norm-referenced measurement, 11–13

Organization (of a value system), 177,
  183, 247–248
Outcomes approach, 2–4, 32, 46, 53
  definitional problems in, 26–29
  disadvantages of, 49, 51–52, 89–90
  instructional intent clarification in, 2–3
  instructional strategies in, 4
  learning achievement evaluation in, 4
  modules for, 39, 40–41
  problems of, 84
  teacher-student motivation in, 4

Peer-group-expectancy mean, 192
Peer-group-expectancy model, 191–196,
  201, 222–223
Performance objectives, 19, 21–22, 24, 26,
  29, 66, 260, 275. See also *Behavioral
  objectives.*
  accountability in, 31–32
  approaches to, 26–29
  cognitive, developmental problems of,
    89–92
  components of, 21–23
  criterion-referenced, 52, 66, 67

Performance objectives (*Continued*)
  current status of, 10–11
  definitional problems of, 23–31
  desired level, 52, 67, 270–275
  goal identification in, 80–86
  goal selection for, 54–56
  instructional value of, 16–18.
  learning oriented, 21–22, 24, 26, 29, 53,
    64, 69, 74, 138
    goal statements for, 57–62
  minimum level, 53, 66, 69, 260, 267–
    270
  non-learning oriented, 268–275
  optional statements in, 67
  process levels for, 66–69
  systems analysis in, 79–86
  teacher morale and, 50–51
Pleasure-pain theory, 171–172, 175
Preference (for a value), 177, 182, 241,
  243–245
Psychomotor domain, 59
Psychomotor module, comparative developmental approaches for, 37–38
Psychomotor taxonomy. See *Taxonomy,
  psychomotor.*

Redundancy, 255–256, 259

Satisfaction (in response), 177, 181, 239–
  241
Selected attention. See *Controlled attention.*
Skill goals, 83
Standardized measurement. See *Norm-
  referenced measurement.*
Subsystem goal, 204, 211
  development of, 81–82
System, components of, 79–80
System goal, 204, 211

Taxonomy
  affective, 176–184
    categories in, 177
    characterization level in, 177, 179
    organization level in, 177, 179
    receiving level in, 177–178, 180
    responding level in, 177–179, 235–
      240
    valuing level in, 177, 179, 241–247
    writing of affective goals with, 230–
      234
    writing of affective goals without,
      212–216
    writing of affective objectives with,
      235–247